So you
want to be a
PRODUCER

- *Finding Your Story*
- *Obtaining the Rights*
- *Developing the Script*
- *Hiring Your Cast and Crew*
- *Distributing Your Movie*

LAWRENCE TURMAN

Methuen Drama

First published in the United States of America in 2005 by Three Rivers Press

First published in the UK in 2006 by Methuen Drama

10 9 8 7 6 5 4 3 2 1

Methuen Drama
A & C Black Publishers Limited
38 Soho Square
London W1D 3HD
www.acblack.com

The letters between Lawrence Turman and William Goldman were first
published in *Produced By* magazine (Winter 2001)

ISBN-10: 0 413 77584 4
ISBN-13: 978 0 413 77584 9

A CIP catalogue record for this book is available from the British Library

Printed and bound in Great Britain by Bookmarque Ltd, Croydon, Surrey

This book is produced using paper that is made from wood grown in
managed, sustainable forests. It is natural, renewable and recyclable. The
logging and manufacturing processes conform to the environmental
regulations of the country of origin.

CONTENTS

Preface   vii

Why Be a Producer?   1
Can Producing Be Taught?   7
You Already Are a Producer   18
Looking Back: How I Became a Producer   21
What Does a Producer Do?   51
Where Do You Find a Story?   59
How Do You Control the Story?   70
How Do You Develop the Script?   77
Where Do You Get the Money to Make the Movie?   90
How Do You Actually Produce the Movie?   95
How Do You Get People to See the Movie?   136
What Does Producing Really Take?   143
How Hard Is It?   152
Producing *The Graduate*: A Case Study   193
Appendix 1: *Butch Cassidy and the
    Sundance Kid* Correspondence   221
Appendix 2: Contributor Credits   249
Index   265

PREFACE

I've produced more than forty movies, yet never once thought about my intended audience when starting one, though I probably should have. As I'm starting this book, however, I am thinking about you, my intended audience, as I've been given a mandate as to what to write about: "How To Produce." I've been through all the steps, many times, but each time it seems different. It *is* different. Actually, that's one of the beauties, one of the joys of producing.

I will let you in on a secret: Whenever I get a green light to make a movie, I am elated, of course, but I also become nervous and insecure. How do I do this? What am I supposed to do? What should I do first? Why isn't there (as my old writer friend Herb Gardner said) a grown-up around to tell me? Truly, no kidding. It is such a formidable task to start a film from scratch, to build an entire design and manufacturing team, and to produce a prototype product that you have no idea whether anybody wants, and then, when you're done, to break it all up and disband the whole operation. And, hopefully, get more chances to do it all again. At the beginning, all I can think about is how much there is to be done.

So why am I writing this book? A top New York literary agent and successful author, Betsy Lerner, contacted me out of the blue, asking if I would be interested in writing a book about producing. For years my three adult sons had implored me to write such a book. Once, about ten years ago, I actually did try. I would write for an hour every morning before work, but I didn't have a clear idea of what to write about, and thus did more procrastinating than writing. I quit after a month. Betsy, on the other hand, did know exactly what she wanted, and why she wanted me. She had read a very laudatory *New York Times* story about The Peter Stark Producing Program at USC, which I have headed for fourteen years, and which is arguably the preeminent producing program in the world. The *Times* story centered on the many great successes of my very first graduates and noted my own producing history, including *The Graduate.* Betsy wrote that she had been looking for some time for the right person, and she felt I was the one. "You'd be surprised how well flattery works," Oscar-nominated director Stephen Daldry *(The Hours)* said about his work methods. Right on! I immediately faxed Betsy: "Yes!" Because as much as I love producing and want to motivate, educate, and inspire, it's not exactly brain surgery. So, at the same time, I also want to demystify producing. Pinned on the bulletin board behind my desk is Hitchcock's quote, "Don't panic. It's only a movie."

I do know how to produce, as my filmography at the back of this book will attest. I always know what kind of film I want to make, the people who can help me make it, and all the steps needed to get there. I'm still in the game, in the trenches, after forty-five years. Thus I organize a very practical curriculum for my students in The Peter Stark Producing Program. It's so practical, in fact, that the class content is as much like a trade school as what it is: a two-year Master of Fine Arts degree. Where do you find a story? How do you control it? How do you develop it? Where do you get the money? How do you make the movie? How do you sell it? That's the stuff I teach them, and the stuff I will cover in this book.

The reality is that there is no one right way—not even necessarily a best way—to produce a film. I guarantee you Jerry Bruckheimer's methods and means differ from mine. His work is great for him and for audiences around the world, which is the object of the exercise. My methods have worked for me, too—for a long time and for a lot of movies. The plain fact is that each producer works a little bit differently—sometimes more than a little bit. I've interviewed many of the best of them for this book, and you'll often see their commonalities, and sometimes their differences.

In writing this book I relearned a somewhat surprising but valuable lesson: I've had more defeats than victories. Yes, I had any number of scripts that I fervently believed in, but could not get financing for. I've also produced many films that I believed in, though the finished products did not set the world on fire. Yet I've enjoyed a very successful career, both by absolute and relative measure. As every old pro says, it's about survival. Similarly, I am proud of how I have conducted myself personally—with integrity, dignity, and at least a modicum of good taste. I believe how you choose to live each day is the single most important determinant of any success you have in life.

In this book I'm going to tell you what I've lived through, seen, and learned about producing. I've chosen the title *So You Want to Be a Producer* because "How To" is not the art of it. Rather, I hope that when you finish reading you'll feel this is a "Can Do" book.

A really nice bonus in writing this book were the things I learned during the many interviews with my fellow producers. All were wonderfully candid and forthcoming—indeed, I could not have written this book without them—but above and beyond that, to my surprise and pleasure, they all proved to be instructive and, I'll be damned, inspiring to me. Each made me proud to be his or her colleague. I remember a moment thirty-five years ago, after my success with *The Graduate*, when I was sitting in the Twentieth Century Fox commissary and a voice whispered in my ear, "I'm proud to know you; I'm proud to be in the same business." I turned and saw the great actor Henry Fonda.

Without exception, every single producer I interviewed made me want to emulate him or her. Each had a great attitude—much better than mine—about so many things. Even at this late stage of my life, I'm going to try to adopt their wisdom for myself: Dick Zanuck's physical discipline; Saul Zaentz's acceptance that there's always someone smarter than he; Bill Goldman's and Frank Pierson's outspoken candor; David Brown's comfort in aging; Christine Vachon's fearlessness; Brian Grazer's clarity about himself; Kathleen Kennedy's values and clear overview; and more (for filmographies of the producers interviewed, see the contributor credits section at the end of this book). I rediscovered that one learns by doing, just as in producing.

I do not keep a diary, nor, as a practice, do I make notes after meetings. This book is written from memory. I scrupulously tried to avoid any revisionist history. If my recollection doesn't jibe 100 percent with that of someone mentioned in the book, it is an honest error, and I apologize.

I'd like to say I've had fun writing this, but it proved to be harder work than I'd ever imagined. On every film I produce I am the editor to the writer. Staring at one's own blank page is different. As with producing, I've done my honest best.

WHY BE A PRODUCER?

Why not be a producer? Would you rather sell shoes for a living? Or be an accountant? Both are honorable occupations, but wouldn't you like to wake up eager to go to work, use every part of yourself while at work, and maybe, just maybe, have a tiny impact on the world? That's why I'm doing it.

We all like movies. Heck, that's why you bought this book. We're all critics, too; we know what is a good movie, and we know what isn't. A lot of times we even think we know why. I know I do. Indeed, I felt that way long before I got into the movie business. So, how about a job where you're the one who decides what movie to make, and how it should be made? A producer. That sounded exciting to me a long time ago, and it still does. What's more, producing is that rare profession where you can start at the top—*if* you control a super, terrific, dynamite script.

There are many levels and categories of producing: line producers, executive producers, co-producers, associate producers, assistant producers. Line producers are physical production specialists. Executive producers get their credits for anything from arranging the money, to controlling the property, to being manager of the star or director, to being the studio executive overseeing the film. The associate producer title is a catchall, bestowed upon anyone the producer deems worthy. But the real deal is the producer. He or she runs the show. It's the producer, and only the producer, who accepts the Academy Award for best picture.

I actually feel the same today as I did in 1967, when I was interviewed by a young kid writing for the now-defunct *Cinema* magazine. That young kid was Curtis Hanson, who has since entered the top echelon of writer-directors with an Academy Award best-screenplay win, plus best-director and best-picture nominations, for *L.A. Confidential* (after having directed *The River Wild* for me). When Hanson questioned why I chose to go into filmmaking, I replied: "Nothing could be more rewarding or stimulating. I think everyone in the business feels the same way. If every salary were cut in half, not one person would leave. I chose producing because it would coalesce both my background experience and modicum of ability in business with what I immodestly and laughingly thought of as my good taste and judgment. Boy, what fun to decide whether a picture should be made, to decide or influence a decision that something should be done this way instead of that way, and to see if I can get this artistic quality here within the framework of that kind of budget money there. Each day has new challenges, new battles, new struggles, new frustrations, new satisfactions. Each day as I wake up I figure I'll walk into the office and get hit with a right to the heart and a left to the kidney, but I love it. It's uphill all the way because it's so competitive and ephemeral and frustrating. There are many frustrations within the framework, but the satisfactions are just enormous. Even the complainers love it."

There's hardly a better job around. A producer is the person who decides an idea, a character, or a story is worth telling. I initiate every single film project upon which I work; most of them would not have seen the light of day had I not decided to make them.

I really believe that there are things nobody would see unless I photographed them.

—**Diane Arbus**

That's exactly how I feel about most of the films I've produced. I'm the "starter" and also the "finisher," and am therefore involved in every aspect and most details of production. It may begin with an original idea of mine *(Caveman)*, a book *(The Graduate, The Flim-*

Flam Man), a play *(Mass Appeal, The Best Man)*, reading a play prior to its production *(The Great White Hope, Tribute)*, an original screenplay *(Full Moon on Blue Water, Second Thoughts)*, or an idea or script a writer brings to me *(Running Scared, Short Circuit)*. In all cases, I arrange for the financing, without which a project can't get off the ground. I work closely with the writer structuring and detailing the story. I select the director and, with him or her, select the actors and consult about the look and style of the picture, as well as the actual production of the film, including hiring the crew, editing, selecting the composer, and discussing what kind of music is to be used and where it should be placed in the film. I am also involved in the ad campaign and the overall marketing and distribution strategies. As producer, I am the editor and sounding board for all the other creative talents, hopefully enhancing their work and coalescing all into a unified whole.

As a producer, you use every part of yourself. It's always challenging; you're never bored. It's creative, it's working with interesting, diverse people, exercising your taste, your judgment. You also get to meet and know unusual, accomplished people—in my case, everyone from Wernher von Braun, father of the space program, to Noel Coward, to Henry Kissinger. The job involves travel to unusual places, for me from the Kentucky Derby to the car races in Le Mans. Each movie project becomes a journey of discovery. Each has different types of characters; each is in a different setting or environment; each deals with things you haven't seen or heard before—you're learning and growing all the time. And each movie involves a new, different set of collaborators—all worldly, creative, and stimulating— and many will become lifelong friends.

> *I love making movies . . . so much. I mean, there's plenty of pain and heartache, and every day is a roller coaster. . . . I will never retire. I am a person who wants to discover and learn, and that sort of drives me. . . . The experience of every movie is a different experience of the variables in that equation, and that's not only exciting and dynamic, but it's challenging in that trial and error, hopefully, if you're aware, moves you to a better, more evolved place the next day.*
>
> —Brian Grazer (Academy Award–winning producer of *A Beautiful Mind*)

What could be more gratifying? Very little, I think. And I've just been talking about the icing on the cake. The cake for me is my personal expression. The idea or theme behind each film I choose to do is my conscious or, sometimes, unconscious signature, through which I express my values to my peers and to the world. I like to think—I do think—that I can affect the world, or at least a few people in it. My concerns, my themes, seem to be consistent. *American History X*, a film I executive produced, made audiences confront how destructive hate can be. It's the story of an American racist neo-Nazi skinhead who ultimately rejects that way of life, but whose own brother is murdered as a consequence of his actions. *The Great White Hope*, which I produced thirty years earlier, was also about racism. It was the story of the first African American heavyweight boxing champion, Jack Johnson, who, by merely holding the title of world's best, inflamed not only the white boxing establishment but many people throughout America. When Muhammad Ali visited the set, he told me, "That's my story!"

> *The idea of getting to sit in a room with a cup of coffee and talk about a story for a few hours is really one of the privileges and pleasures. There's nothing more fun than talking about some movie like* Memoirs of a Geisha, *and you sit around with some really smart writer, and you're talking about how some woman might behave in 1920s Kyoto. And then, literally a half-hour later, you're talking about Custer and how he changed American history. I just love a day that takes you from ancient Rome to the Old West.*
>
> —Doug Wick (Academy Award winner for *Gladiator*)

Even the seemingly "guns and giggles" *Running Scared* (Billy Crystal's first screen role), which I co-produced, had a serious underlying theme: two cops (Gregory Hines is the other) who are near retirement decide to play it "safe" and avoid getting hurt by not tempting danger. Except all hell breaks loose and they succeed by reverting to their true natures, by not "running scared." The moral? You've got to try your hardest all the time, whether you're a cop, athlete, or producer.

The Best Man, based on Gore Vidal's play and which I co-produced, is a political movie about compromises, backroom deals, distortions of the truth, the power of the press, and the glare of public life, all of which are as pertinent today—if not more so—than decades ago when we made the film. Those themes are pieces of myself. I'd like the titles of those films, plus others I've produced, engraved on my tombstone. (Well, there are a couple I'd like excised.)

Is there anything more exhilarating than completing a film that began life as an idea in your head and then sitting in a crowded movie theater, hearing the audience laugh, or hold its collective breath, seeing tears flow, and perhaps hearing some applause? For me, no—unless it's seeing my sons grow and flourish. But they also began life as an idea in my head.

Is it a roller-coaster ride? For sure. One reason to be a producer is that it's a damn exciting life. I guarantee you'll never be bored. But you'll also never be relaxed. As the great baseball player Satchel Paige said, "Don't look back. Someone might be gaining on you." It's not that it's a competition with your fellow producers. There are just so few movie slots at each studio, and so many—too damn many—producers chasing them. That's why you have to be creative. And isn't using your creativity in trying to make movies, and then actually making them, the biggest reward? I think so. You're constantly using your imagination, your ingenuity, and your brain power. Each day at work you'll be living to the fullest. So why not play the game, where you decide what movie to try to make, and sometimes get it made? What beats that? Maybe scoring the winning touchdown in the Super Bowl . . . but even that takes less creativity than producing movies.

> **Each movie presents a genuine new challenge. On every movie I feel like you learn something you need to know, that I didn't know. It never gets dull.**
> —**Christine Vachon** *(Far from Heaven, One Hour Photo, Boys Don't Cry, Happiness)*

If your imagination is fired about becoming a producer, I say go for it. Or go for whatever your dream is because if you don't, you'll live to regret it. "I shoulda; I coulda," are words you do not want to even think, much less utter, five or ten years down the road. My favorite line in all of musical literature was written by Oscar Hammerstein, in *Carousel:* "I let my golden chances pass me by." Or, as the poem by Whittier says, "Of all sad words of tongue and pen, the saddest are these, it might have been." However, if someone—family or a friend, perhaps—can talk you out of it, beware . . . you probably won't make it. It is tough and it is competitive. If you're not prepared to give 100 percent, just about all the time—and I mean more than an eight- or nine-hour workday—forget about it. But if you are, if you do, I guarantee it's worth it.

> *Until one is committed, there is hesitancy, the chance to draw back, always ineffectiveness. Concerning all acts of initiative (and creation), there is one elementary truth, the ignorance of which kills countless ideas and splendid plans: that the moment one definitely commits oneself, then providence moves too. All sorts of things occur to help one that would never otherwise have occurred. A whole stream of events issues from the decision, raising in one's favor all manner of unforeseen incidents and meetings and material assistance, which no man could have dreamed would have come his way. Whatever you can do or dream you can, begin it. Boldness has genius, power and magic in it. Begin it now.*
>
> —J. W. von Goethe

CAN PRODUCING BE TAUGHT?

ALL BABIES LEARN TO WALK.

I did ask myself if producing could be taught, and if I could teach it, in 1991 when I was invited to head what was then called The Peter Stark Motion Picture Producing Program. I was still at the top of my game (indeed, among those at the peak of the Hollywood mountain), so I decided to decline the time-consuming job of running an academic program. But then I had an epiphany: I reflected that in my life and career, the few regrets I had were the result of saying "no" to something instead of "yes."

For instance, in 1968–69, right after I produced *The Graduate*, I was flavor of the year, the hottest guy in town. In Hollywood, everyone looks backward (but not too far), not forward—to what and who were "hot" and commercial last night, last week, last month. Thus, I was solicited and offered the prestigious, desirable job of head of production by two different major movie studios. But I liked making individual pictures rather than overseeing a slate of films, and—happily—my percentage of profits from *The Graduate* assured I would have no worries about eating or paying the rent, so I declined both jobs. A mistake!

In retrospect, it was perhaps a large one. Running a studio, giving the "green light," is every kid's Hollywood dream. It would have been a very rich (double *entendre* intended), worthwhile experience, and surely would have given me broad new knowledge and world-wide relationships in financing, distribution, and marketing. I turned it down. What could I have been thinking? It needn't have been forever; the office of studio head is generally a revolving-door job with a golden-parachute producing deal at the end.

At about that same time I was also asked to produce the Academy Awards show. I declined that, too. It's only a show that's seen by a billion people around the world and puts the producer in close contact with all the major players and studios in Hollywood. Where was I when I needed me?

In retrospect and reality (this is after all a book about producing, not psychology . . . except, as in most professions, the two are tied together), I realize I'm basically not a corporate guy. I value my freedom too much. And I'm a tad selfish. I want to worry about, nurse, my personal movie, not a studio slate of other producers' films. Sometimes a seemingly rational decision really isn't. Now, decades later, I frankly think I could have, and would have, done a fine job at both, but we'll never know. Both studios flourished without me, and the Academy Awards show is still going strong. And I continue to make pictures. So, in 1991, with all that floating through my mind, I told USC I would "take a look" at their producing program.

My first day "looking around" got my competitive juices flowing and aroused my need for perfection. Though The Peter Stark Motion Picture Producing Program was well regarded, one look at the curriculum convinced me I could do it better—or, at least differently. Its founder, A. D. Murphy, a reporter for *Variety* who was often quoted in the *New York Times* and the *Wall Street Journal,* had organized the curriculum primarily as a business model, in which a two-year curriculum for an MFA included two courses (of sixteen) on entertainment law and one full semester devoted to labor relations. Ugh. That is not teaching producing. Most producers have their own attorneys and, if attached to a studio, utilize its legal staff. My interest is in the creative and the entrepreneurial. I accepted the chair and immediately got to work. For starters, I got rid of the words *motion picture* in the program description title and introduced television courses to the curriculum. Producing is producing, whether it's in films, TV, music videos, or commercials. The first day on the job I got a wonderful fax from a friend, which read, "Congratulations. What a novel idea, hiring a producer to run a producing program."

HOW I TEACH IT—THE PETER STARK PRODUCING PROGRAM

A fight for love and glory, a case of do or die . . .
> —lyrics by Herman Hupfeld, "As Time
> Goes By" (from *Casablanca*)

Anything that can be learned can be taught: painting, typing, cooking, playing the piano, and, indeed, writing, directing, and producing. So yes, producing can be taught. I teach it with conviction and pride, as Chair/Director of The Peter Stark Producing Program. I began by defining my own, and thus the program's, credo:

> A Producer is the person who causes a film to be made. A good Producer causes it to be made well. The Peter Stark Producing Program believes that a Producer is a creative originator of films, an entrepreneurial self-starter who is often first to recognize ideas that have merit creatively and/or commercially. We believe these criteria also apply to the studio executive, and that together the two must have passion, a sensitive nose for story and audience, plus the organizational ability and practical smarts to put together a project, and guide it to and through the marketplace. The Peter Stark Program's goal is to give our students the practical skills and knowledge by which they can accomplish their personal goals as filmmakers, with integrity to their own values and artistic dreams.

The word *savvy* is my touchstone for designing the curriculum to be as practical as a trade school's while constantly exhorting the students to "aim for the stars." I give equal weight to the business side and the creative side; both are absolutely necessary in making a film. On the business side, in the first semester the students take a course that provides an economic overview of how the movie business works, a course that deals with how every department functions at a major studio, and a course that details the world of independent film.

Along the way, the students learn how to schedule and budget, how to market a film, and the various ways films are financed. The students write, produce, direct, operate the camera, and edit short films throughout the entire first year of the program. They each make an eight-minute film, and then, in the second year, they compete for financing of three films, twenty minutes in length, with professional standards. From the get-go, they're using their creative imagination, while simultaneously learning about the technical side of how movies are made. Throughout the program is the all-important story aspect: script analysis in the first semester, leading to how to develop a script in the second semester, writing a full-length feature script in the third semester, and finally a daunting, important thesis project that is required for graduation.

THE IMPORTANCE OF VALUES AND ETHICS

> *At my dry goods store, a customer gives me $20 to pay for a $3 box of ribbon. Sticking to her $20 bill is another $20 bill that she does not notice. Ethics is, do I tell my partner or not?*
>
> **—Yiddish folk story**

Just kidding!

It may sound pretentious, but what I believe I really teach are values. Film is the conduit, the medium—not the message. I try to imbue my students with a strong desire to search out meaningful themes on pertinent, life-affirming subjects, to be true to and trust their own values, and to harness and hone them within the commercial film and television world; to value their hearts as much as their brains; and to be aware of the larger world, which can only enhance their chosen field and more importantly, their own lives. There can be meaningful work outside of the commercial mainstream. I encourage my students to pursue their dreams and to not be afraid of trying to inspire, to lead, to exalt. I passionately believe in the transforming power and beauty of art. Life is more important but, happily, art and life can be conjoined. How you live your life is more important than what you do in your life.

Although ethics are paramount with me, they really can't be taught. I think morality and values are formed and ingrained early on. But that doesn't stop me from trying to teach them. The very first seminar/lecture the students attend upon entering The Peter Stark Producing Program focuses on ethics. At our recent ethics seminar, the lecturer, the renowned Michael Josephson (founder of the respected Josephson Institute of Ethics and consultant for the NFL and many prominent corporations) posed the following dilemma to my incoming students: Your best friend's life story is fascinating and dramatic. He verbally agrees to give you the motion-picture rights; he even says you can take liberties with it as long as you do not change the ending. Once you get to Hollywood, a studio wants you to produce a film about your friend's life for a large fee, but wants you to change the ending. How many of you would do it?

Of the twenty-five students, half a dozen raised their hands. I was surprised by their willingness to break the trust of their friend, and by their willingness to admit that they would do so. I thought political correctness would override those who, in the deep recesses of their heart, would indeed be willing to sell out their friend. Josephson and I exchanged a look and rolled our eyes, and then he asked, "Why would you do that?" It turns out that everything the students had heard or read about Hollywood and how business is done made them feel they had to lie, cheat, steal, and pillage to get ahead. I was more saddened than shocked. I staunchly believe one can be moral and ethical and still have a very successful career . . . in any field. I jumped in to explain that having integrity is the best business, and the best way to live. Josephson interrupted me, disagreeing: "It may not be the 'best business' every time. You can lose a particular deal or job to someone who behaves unethically, but it will not hinder your long-range career." He was right. I stood corrected. But I still think I was also right.

> **When the great scorer writes against your name, it's not**
> **if you won or lost, but how you played the game.**
> **—Grantland Rice**

Shortly after Jack Lemmon committed to do *Mass Appeal* with me, I received a phone call from Mike Ovitz, the big gun himself. The founder and head of Creative Artists Agency and arguably the most powerful person in Hollywood asked if I would come by his office for a meeting. I said yes with alacrity, not even knowing what he wanted to talk about; this was *the* Mike Ovitz. When we met, he offered me a complete package of his clients for *Mass Appeal:* John

Travolta for the young priest, Charles Durning for the older priest, and hot director Colin Higgins (he'd directed the Chevy Chase-Goldie Hawn success *Foul Play*). Not only was that package appetizing creatively, it would probably be a slam dunk raising the money, especially with Ovitz spearheading. And I had been struggling, unsuccessfully, to obtain financing. I was flattered and grateful, but had verbally committed to Jack Lemmon, so had to reluctantly tell Mike Ovitz "no can do."

That was the end of it until a couple of days later, when I got another call from Mike Ovitz: "Larry, I don't understand you. I know two other producers [he named two of the most prominent in Hollywood] who, if I had made the same offer to them, would have had a case of the best champagne on my desk the next morning. You, however, turned me down." I answered with the truth: "Mike, I would like nothing better than to take you up on your offer of that package, but I solicited Jack Lemmon and told him I would do *Mass Appeal* with him." I know it sounds self-serving, but it's simply who I am. My word is my bond (and yours better be, too).

Having integrity is its own reward, but it can also pay off. I got to make my movie after all, through the largess of Mrs. Joan Kroc of McDonald's, who agreed to personally finance *Mass Appeal* after meeting Jack Lemmon. How did she meet Jack? He was asked to toss out the first baseball of the season for the San Diego Padres team, which Joan Kroc just happened to own! (Should this be in the section on luck, or what?) It was an altogether amazing experience, and I'm proud of the film. And, despite Mike Ovitz's frustration, he had increased respect for me. Ovitz himself, by the way, got hoist on the petard of integrity by assuring the employees of his agency that he was committed to his company, Creative Artists Agency, while secretly negotiating to head a studio. He was found out, and it started a downward career spiral for him, even though he's the very same super-smart guy he's always been. There are no secrets in Hollywood, or in life.

FORMAL SCHOOLING VS. THE SCHOOL OF LIFE

In every field there are great practitioners who did not have formal instruction. The legendary producers Selznick, Zanuck, Spiegel, et. al.

never went to school to study the art of moviemaking, yet produced great films. Nor did Thalberg awardee and three-time Academy Award–winning producer Saul Zaentz have formal training. And neither do you have to. If you're extremely motivated and can get a toehold, you can get on-the-job training and experience, as I did.

I didn't go to film school. I was "taught" by going through the process from beginning to end with someone who had done it before. My first four films were produced in partnership with Stuart Millar, who had grown up in the business. His father was press agent for the great director, William Wyler (and three-time Academy Award winner), and Stuart had been Wyler's assistant. (How do you think that happened?) Stuart was very bright and had already produced one film, *Stage Struck,* for which he had smartly chosen Sidney Lumet to direct. Four years prior, I had broken into the business as an agent, where I learned to evaluate scripts, reading them for my clients. I learned about actors. I learned how to negotiate contracts. So I already had some useful on-the-job practical background before I produced my first film, *The Young Doctors,* with Stuart. United Artists, who financed it, did not have their own studio facilities or personnel, and gave all their producers total latitude and control. I signed every single check to every single person on the film—that was a huge learning experience in and of itself. I learned on the job how to organize a production, as well as a little more about dramatic structure, actors, editing, and marketing—all pieces in the mosaic that make up producing.

> **Doing Cinema *magazine was my film school. It didn't put me with contemporaries headed down the same path I was, but it gave me a unique opportunity to learn by observing and listening to artists I admired.***
> **—Curtis Hanson**

So is there an advantage to being taught producing in a formal academic environment, in film school? You bet, especially in Hollywood and, to a slightly lesser degree, in New York, for the contacts and proximity to the action and players. The prolific Roger Corman, who has produced literally hundreds of films, told me, to my surprise,

"Film school today is mandatory." I do not totally agree, but who am I to argue with a legend? By the way, Roger himself holds an engineering degree from Stanford.

> *I think school helps a great deal. First of all, you know the syntax of films. And you also are networking with a group of people, competing for jobs.*
>> —**David Brown (Thalberg honoree, four-time Academy Award nominee)**

While at USC film school, Suzanne Todd produced a short student film directed by Jay Roach. Was the movie *Austin Powers: International Man of Mystery* an enormous hit? Yes—so much so that it led to two successful sequels. Jay Roach directed all three. The producer of all three was Suzanne Todd (with her sister and partner Jennifer). How do you think that happened?

> *I think going to one of the schools is a good thing because you get the feeling, a smell of what it's about from people who know what they're talking about.*
>> —**David Wolper** *(Roots, L.A. Confidential, The Thorn Birds, Willy Wonka and the Chocolate Factory)*

WHAT CAN'T BE TAUGHT?

You can lead a horse to water, but . . .

>> —**folk saying**

Any skill that can be learned can be taught, from brain surgery to pastry-making. But can one learn to be a leader? Can one learn to defer pleasure for a later payoff? Unfortunately, what can't be taught is the most important thing: character—who a person is, his or her feelings and taste. It can't be taught to a would-be violinist or architect, either. It's what separates people who have all the skills and the technique from those who also have all the heart and imagination. It's what makes Robert De Niro a great actor and someone else merely good or competent. Whether one comes out of the womb a certain way or is irrevocably formed in the first six months to ten years of life informs how each of us sees and reacts to the world, whether passionate or cool, opinionated or unsure, assertive or meek. The ongoing psychological and sociological debate of nature versus nurture is unresolved, but whatever proportions make up a person, there is an innate quality that separates a Scorsese, a Fellini, or a Jerry Bruckheimer from the run of the mill. What can't be taught is one's own innate sense and style. That comes from life experience, and from each person's emotional formation/journey.

Sofia Coppola says of her father, Francis Ford Coppola: "He always was a big champion of personal filmmaking, films as an expression of what you're thinking about."

I was a good friend of Stanley Kubrick's long before he made his wonderfully serious black comedy *Dr. Strangelove.* He would, at my home over dinner, passionately discuss his interest in, and consuming knowledge of, Herman Kahn's book *On Thermonuclear War.* His personal concern about the possibility of the world being blown up led to Kubrick's classic film. Stanley was such a complete, assured filmmaker that his films seemed to go right from his brain directly to the silver screen, without even passing through the technical processes of camera and sound, etc. I'm not a "techie," yet I always felt I could be a director of photography on one of Stanley's films and he'd make me look good.

The smartest person, or one with the highest IQ, generally does not end up heading the biggest corporations; producing, directing, or writing the great artistic masterpieces; or becoming president of our country. A "sense of proportion" is what it takes—when to act, when not to act; when to come on strong, when to be deferential or shut up and listen. When someone doesn't return your phone call, how many times should you try to reach that person? Do you, should you, resort to fax or e-mail? That comes down to personal style. It's like that classic song: "It ain't what you do but the way that you do it, it ain't what you say but the way that you say it." Imagine two young children holding either end of a jump rope and the jumper watching the rope turning, turning, until, just at the right moment, he dashes in to the rhythm of the rope. That can't be taught.

Who a person is, is what I try to assess in the students I select for The Peter Stark Producing Program. I say jokingly (but with a modicum of truth) that I'm like a football coach: If I recruit the quickest, strongest, and best players I'll have a winning season whether I am a good coach or not. So, while I teach producing rigorously, seriously, exhaustively, and in great detail, which student I select to teach is critical. Number one is motivation. You've got to really want to be a filmmaker. An outgoing personality is generally preferred (most of us run on nervous energy), but there are success stories about shy, introverted producers. Assertiveness is helpful; brashness is not. Confidence is good . . . it's contagious, it's persuasive. But only if it's genuine.

> *You have to have a work ethic. You learn this job only by*
> *pounding at every decision.*
>
> **—Doug Wick**

My dear friend Gilman Kraft, who was publisher of *Playbill,* the theater magazine, was the most contemplatively smart person I ever knew. He felt that the ability to make connections between ideas, between things, was the hallmark of true intelligence, of savvy people who succeed in almost everything they try. They have the ability to see that a scene on page thirty of a script connects to and affects a scene on page eighty. A connection I made (and will refer to later) between falling in love with an edgy, dark story about murderers and at the same time seeing the first film from a young director-producer team (a twenty-minute short about teenage skateboarders) led to me connecting the two to make a film I'm proud of, *Pretty Poison.* It's the same kind of connection that producer Lindsay Doran made in choosing the barely known director Ang Lee (who had previously done the small Asian character films *Eat Drink Man Woman* and *The Wedding Banquet*) to direct the sweeping *Sense and Sensibility,* a larger-scale historical film about upper-class Brits. A person's ability to "see" and connect the dots is innate. You can't teach that. Picasso looked at a toy car, saw the head of a simian, and so used it in creating his famous "Baboon and Young." That's what made him Picasso.

What also can't be taught is plain, old-fashioned stick-to-itiveness. In my experience, focus, determination, and a willingness to withstand rejection and "pick yourself up, dust yourself off, and start all over again" count more toward being successful than talent, taste, and imagination. You have to really, really want to get your project made—more than almost anything, and with unwavering clear focus. Think of the films you've liked. Aren't they often about a character who wants something very badly and has to overcome obstacles to achieve it? It's my favorite theme (and one I feel audiences around the world like to see).

Essentially, two things can't be taught: creativity and character. Both happen to be critical in the producing process. Character gets you on the playing field. Creativity is that ineffable thing that enables someone to score a touchdown or hit a home run. When I talk about character, I don't mean it in a moral, ethical sense. I'm talking about personality. Personality is evident in someone who gets knocked down and immediately picks himself up, as opposed to someone who gets a rejection or two and loses confidence in the project he chose in the first place. Maybe I should use the word *backbone* instead of *character.*

Character, who a person is, is formed early on. Creativity is innate, although surely it can be nurtured. The classic Greeks illustrated character by differentiating between the "choleric" and the "sanguine." Two people walking down the road encounter a huge rock blocking their way. The choleric one says, "Son of a bitch!" and kicks the rock. The sanguine one smiles. "Ah, a rock," he says, and walks around it. Producers need a little of each quality.

YOU ALREADY ARE
A PRODUCER

JUST SHOWING UP FOR WORK IS EIGHTY PERCENT
OF IT.

—WOODY ALLEN

Here's the good news: You already are a producer. Yes, really. No, it's not a trick or a gimmicky statement to give you false encouragement, but rather to call to your attention that in your everyday life you already are a "producer." Because producing is simply thinking ahead, planning, and getting a series of things done to accomplish a goal you set for yourself. You have to work backward: Start by figuring out everything you're going to need at a specific time in the future, and then make sure it's ready when you need it to be ready. It's mostly common sense and being organized.

Making a picture is not a difficult task. If you can count from one to ten and have any sensibilities (I'm not talking about artistic sensibilities), you can make a picture.

> —Saul Zaentz, Thalberg Award honoree and three-time Academy Award–winning producer (*One Flew Over the Cuckoo's Nest, Amadeus, The English Patient*)

Whenever you invite your friends to come to your place for dinner, you have to "produce" it. You must plan it and then organize it, so when your friends show up there's food on the table and enough chairs for the number of people you invited. It doesn't matter whether you live in a huge mansion or in a one-room apartment; if you invited one hundred people or just two; if you're serving a six-course dinner with wine or opening a can of beans and a soda—the process is exactly the same. You have to plan ahead so that when people show up, everything is ready. Just as on the first day of filming, whether it be a $75,000 film financed by friends and relatives or a $100 million studio-financed film, you better be ready when the cameras are supposed to turn. Which, again, means planning ahead, which means thinking and working backward. You'll have to figure out if one can of beans is enough, if they are better served on a plate or in a bowl, if they should be served hot, if you have a pot to heat them in, where can you buy the beans, if your market will be open on the day of your dinner, and—most important—which are the best beans.

Or maybe another food would be better. Something you can cook ahead of time or serve cold, so you can hang out with your guests instead of being stuck at the stove. Also, which would go better with your meal: soda, beer, wine? Are your guests nondrinkers? Do you need napkins? Unless you run a nonsmoking apartment, you'll need an ashtray to save your furniture. If it's raining, do you have somewhere to put wet umbrellas? After dinner will you watch TV, play cards or charades, or sit around and talk? If someone needs to use the bathroom, do you have clean towels? If you want to clean up your place before your guests arrive, do you have a dustcloth and a broom? How about some flowers to brighten up the place?

What about the guests (casting), the reason you're doing all this in the first place? Do you want just a couple of people to attend? That would make it very intimate and nice. But which people? Do you invite friends you see all the time, or someone you know less well but find interesting and would like to know better? Why not both, if you have the room? Ah, but would they like each other? Maybe different people would make it a better, more interesting night, or maybe all together would be best of all. But could you afford that out of your weekly paycheck? What is this entire dinner party going to cost? Might your guests be so special that you'd be willing to dip into your savings account, or do without that new pair of shoes you were thinking of buying?

I am a very experienced producer, and I'll bet I forgot to list a dozen other things that you'd likely have to think of. You must measure and weigh what it is you want to do against how much money you have to do it. That's what a movie producer is constantly doing.

How well your little dinner party works out is a function of your taste, the choices you make, and how well prepared you are. If your party flops, did you perhaps not take into account that one of your guests had a fight last month with the person you're having the dinner for? Did you not remember that your friend has hay fever and your strong-smelling flowers brought on a sneezing fit? Was that when you realized you were out of Kleenex? And while you're dealing with all that, you better make sure to not overcook your beans until they're a soggy mess.

I'm being a wise guy, but I could go on because producing a dinner party, like producing a movie, is all about crisis-management. "The best laid plans of mice and men oft go astray," the Scottish poet Robert Burns observed. He was right. No matter how deeply you think, how carefully you plan, you can count on something going wrong. It will, I assure you, and at the worst possible time.

I think you get the idea. It's the same process, and the same things apply, whether the scale is large or small. Producing is all about figuring out what you need to happen on a certain date, then starting early enough, spacing the necessary work so that everything that needs to be done actually gets done, and at the right time. Sounds easy? Well, it is and it isn't. You and I can juggle two balls. Some of us can juggle three or four. Professional jugglers do six or seven or more. But unlike juggling, producing is not a one-person act. As a bus gathers passengers, you gather helpers as you go along. But more of that later, in a chapter on preproduction.

> *When I produced my first film, I really didn't know anything. That sense of fearlessness that you get from absolute ignorance was a real friend to me.*
> **—Christine Vachon**

Producing is working hard; having a goal, common sense, desire, and stick-to-it-iveness; being resourceful, adaptable, and aware of alternatives; not letting surprises, disappointments, even rejection throw you off; enjoying people; accepting challenges; and keeping your eye on the ball and your goal, even when you feel overwhelmed. It's all about loving movies.

LOOKING BACK: HOW I BECAME A PRODUCER

Hollywood is full of wannabes. Half the restaurants in Beverly Hills are staffed with wannabe actors, writers, directors, and, yes, producers. Most, alas, do not achieve their dreams. But some do. I did, and you can. I am writing this book to make producing seem less intimidating and, I hope, a realistic and achievable goal. I was a wannabe myself, fifty years ago. In my case, I was running away from something: boring, dreary work selling fabrics for my father, who had a tiny two-person wholesale textile business. A UCLA liberal arts graduate with a middle-class upbringing, I had no burning desire, no plan (surprising, in retrospect) for any particular kind of job or career. I thus drifted into my father's textile business, a seemingly easy, unthinking, decision. Except you pay for everything in life, one way or another.

Selling fabrics was not my idea of fun. I was interacting with people who had little interest in the things I was interested in. I was mostly cruising on automatic pilot, using only a fraction of myself and what I believed I had to offer. My dad, whom I loved dearly, was a real success on his terms. He had to leave school in the eighth grade to help support his family, something he continued to do his entire life. The business was tiny, but it was his, and he did well enough to take care of his sister and help out his brothers and other relatives when necessary. He also made sure I went to college, which, of course, helped make me not want to spend my life selling fabrics.

I soon realized that I got little satisfaction, and no pleasure, trying to convince some clothing manufacturer to buy periwinkle blue lining from me instead of, say, royal blue from my competitor. Worse, our competitors sold pretty much the same fabrics, in pretty much the same colors, and often at cheaper prices. Even when I was successful with a sale or two, I used hardly any of my brain and surely none of my soul. The thought of doing that kind of work for the rest of my life was scary and depressing. But how to get out? And to what? There's a Jewish homily that says, "You don't throw away dirty water until you have clean."

I stuck it out with him for four years, until I was twenty-seven, an age in old Hollywood days when guys like Irving Thalberg and Pandro Berman were already running MGM and RKO. But twenty-seven wasn't too late for me to get started (and I've accepted students in their thirties into The Peter Stark Producing Program). I was lucky in that I was still living at home and didn't have to worry about paying rent. What I didn't realize at the time was that, although I hated my job, it toughened me up. I learned a few basic things that have served me well as a producer. First and foremost, rejection: It won't kill you. Second, patience: Most worthwhile things in life are not attained as quickly or as easily as one might hope. Last, playing the percentages: If you call on six customers, you might not make a sale; if you call on sixteen you stand a much better chance; if you call on twenty-six, I'll bet you make at least one sale, if not more; if you call on thirty-six, you're ahead of me, and you know the likely result.

Writing this book allows me, or rather forces me, to reexamine my entire career. I realize that, just as I've had more failures than successes, I also had a surprising number of false starts in trying to get into the business before I finally hooked up with the Kurt Frings agency. For instance, I occasionally played golf with Henry Rogers, a burgeoning public-relations honcho. Henry and I liked each other, and he knew of my desires, and offered me a job. His well-known firm represented some prominent actors, so I excitedly accepted his offer.

The first week, I was assigned to work with his partner Warren

Cowan, doing publicity for a small department store in Glendale, a suburb of Los Angeles. Tagging along with Warren, I admired his energy and enthusiasm for what he was doing, but I didn't share it. By my third day I had such anxiety that I wasn't sleeping at night. By the fourth day I was walking around in a funk, depressed. Publicity clearly was not the field for me. On the fifth day, Friday, nervous with trepidation, I walked into Henry Rogers's office and told him I did not want the job, nor would I take a paycheck for the one week I'd worked. Warren, to this day, loves telling that story. Given the career I've had, ditching the PR business proved to not be a mistake. But it might have been. Had I the gumption to stick it out, it could have put me on a zigzag course to producing. Such was the case for Rogers and Cowan alumni John Foreman, producer of *Butch Cassidy and the Sundance Kid*, and Guy McElwaine, who became production head of Columbia Pictures. Arthur Jacobs, the producer of the original *Planet of the Apes* and the original *Doctor Dolittle*, also segued to films from his own public-relations firm. I repeat: There's no straight path. Jerry Bruckheimer was in advertising, Saul Zaentz in the music business, "Etc., etc., etc.," to quote a memorable line often uttered by the king in *The King and I*.

At the time I worked for my father I had one friend in the movie business, Alan Pakula, who was the assistant to a producer at Paramount (Alan later became a successful producer himself, and then a sensitive, excellent director). He loved his work; I hated mine. Alan was so involved, almost consumed by his work, and so damn happy. I was envious. He and I would talk for hours about current movies. We both had strong, passionate opinions. I remember one night we were critiquing *On the Waterfront*. We both loved it, as well we should have (it won Academy Awards for best picture, director, and actors). I recently screened it for my Peter Stark Producing students; it's still great and, like all true art, holds up to the test of time. Seeing it again got me juiced up; I felt my blood flowing and saw why I got into the movie business, why I love it—warts and all—why I feel it's so rewarding, and why I'm proselytizing by writing this book.

When I decided I wanted to be a producer, I found myself in a golf foursome with Jess Oppenheimer, writer/producer of *I Love Lucy*. He seemed to be an easygoing guy, although I was later to learn there are hardly any of that kind in show business. I told him my dream.

"How do I get started? How do I get in?" I asked. He answered, straight-faced, "If you want it badly enough, you'll find your own way in." I felt then as perhaps you do now: pissed and confused. What the hell did he mean? I sure didn't know. But Jess was trying to be helpful. And, in retrospect, he was. He meant desire, which equals tenacity.

Because there isn't an easy way in. You have to use any means possible, every tenuous contact or relationship you have or can create. Your goal is to get a toehold. As director John Badham, a Yale drama school graduate, said about himself: "I was standing across the street from Universal Studios when the thought occurred to me I'd be better off in the mail room *inside* than standing on the street *outside*, looking in." John was able to wrangle a job in that very Universal mail room, which led to his being an assistant casting director, which led to his being a casting director, which in turn led to his directing episodic television, which then led to his directing major feature films like *Saturday Night Fever,* starring John Travolta, and, for me, the hit *Short Circuit.*

I don't know how John got that mail-room job, but I do know a guy in the export business who was living in Hong Kong, and desperately wanted to work in Hollywood. He wrote a hundred cold letters to studios, production companies, and agencies. He received only a single reply. But that one reply, from CAA (Creative Artists Agency), got him into their mail room, from whence he rose to being a successful agent, and more important, a happy one. He's now a player in the game—and a well-paid one.

I myself was single-minded about wanting to become a producer, even though I wasn't quite sure exactly what a producer did. And so I entreated Alan Pakula to help me. Pal that he was, Alan arranged for me to meet the number two executive at the time (early 1950s) in the Paramount creative hierarchy, D. A. Doran. D.A. was a very bright, tasteful, lovely man. The town called him "a tower of jelly" precisely because he was a lovely man in a world of cutthroats. D.A. graciously arranged for me to meet Jerry Wald, the big-time producer thought to be the prototype for Sammy Glick in Budd Schulberg's classic Hollywood novel *What Makes Sammy Run?* Wald officed at Twentieth Century Fox; he had his own bungalow with kitchen, bathroom, all the goodies. Our meeting was brief. He tossed me

William Faulkner's *The Sound and the Fury,* saying, "Read this and tell me if you think it would make a movie." It was a hard read for me because, great as Faulkner is, his style is dense and prolix. But I eagerly plowed through it and then wrote a memo recommending that Wald make it. He, however, chose not to. He also chose not to hire me. Four or five years later, Wald did indeed produce a film of *The Sound and the Fury,* though I don't think it was successful.

Through a friend of a friend, I managed to get an interview with Sam Jaffe, head of his own prominent agency, which numbered Humphrey Bogart among its clients. I was tongue-tied at that interview, and once again didn't get the job. Good guy that he was, D. A. Doran arranged yet another interview for me, with David Lewis, a producer at MGM. I offered to work for him for nothing, just for the chance to hang around and be his assistant. He, too, turned me down. I was batting .000. I knew of no more alleys, even blind ones, to try, so I hied myself to New York, where I had a friend to bunk in with.

In New York I had no contacts, so I tried the CBS mail room. I dutifully filled out their employment form prior to a meeting with the low-level exec in charge. He said there was nothing in my background that showed any interest or experience in movies or TV, so he turned me down. This was for the mail room! Then, this time through a friend of a friend of a friend, I got a one-day, nonpaying job as assistant to Larry White, a successful TV producer who was doing a special variety show. It was exciting and fun. I scurried around and did his and anyone else's bidding, after which I begged him for a regular job. He asked what I could do. I told him I could do anything and everything. How about cameraman? No. How about sound? No. How about props or wardrobe? No. It was a sobering interview. Out of avenues to pursue, I returned to L.A., my tail between my legs.

Fortunately I had a bed at home, and there was food in the refrigerator, so I was okay. But not really. My psyche was at low ebb. I even took some modern dance classes with the then-famous Lester Horton Company, for the discipline of it and to keep my body from getting too slothful. Then I had the bright idea of placing a "job wanted" ad in *Variety.* And I got a response. One. A very minor director, Reginald LeBorg, suggested we meet at his apartment. I couldn't wait. His apartment was dingy, tiny, and in a tawdry neighborhood.

But no matter. It was a job! Or so I thought. His offer? If I would invest tens of thousands of dollars in a film he wanted to direct, then I could be his assistant. Live and learn. It was at that point that I found myself crying the blues to TV writer/director Walter Doniger at a small party at Alan Pakula's apartment. He asked, "Why not be an agent?" Even though I had taken the meeting with Sam Jaffe, I said, "I don't want to be an agent, I want to be a producer." He counseled, "Don't dismiss it so quickly. It's a good way in."

Not a week later, I was reading the trade paper *Variety* when an ad jumped out at me. "Experienced agent wanted. Box 2, *Variety.*" I immediately wrote them a candid letter: "I have no experience, but I'm full of energy and will work very cheaply." The ad had been placed by a small but elite actors' agency, Kurt Frings, which represented Audrey Hepburn. I was interviewed by Frings's number two person (of four agents, two secretaries, and an office manager), Bill Josephy. The interview wasn't going very well, when Kurt Frings himself happened to wander in. After talking to me only briefly, Kurt offered me a job on the spot, for $50 a week. "Son, I'm going to teach you a profession," he said. That sounded like heaven to me, but why and how did I apply for a job as an agent when what I wanted to be was a producer? I had no other choice.

When I showed up for work, they put me in an office with an experienced agent, Bill Robinson, who had previously worked at MCA (the premier agency that segued into owning Universal Studios). Kurt Frings marched in that first morning and handed me *Daily Variety* and *The Hollywood Reporter.* "Here," he said, "read these every day." That's the last thing he ever "taught" me. So much for teaching me a profession! In retrospect, though, he did me a favor. Trial by fire, on-the-job training—call it what you will, I learned by doing. It was scary, but wonderful. Early on, I was talking on the telephone and when I hung up, Bill asked, "Why are you all hunched over like that, facing the wall?" I was so timid, I was obviously trying to hide so I wouldn't be embarrassed by having Bill overhear my conversations.

Bill Robinson is an expansive, confident guy, the opposite of me. Together, we would visit clients on movie sets. Bill would walk in like he owned the place, while I would slink around in the background. I did, however, begin having as much success as he, and that proved to be my first learning experience—that different methods and styles can work equally well. He called everybody by their first names, but I used "Mr. Dozier" to address the head of RKO, or "Mr. Wald," or Mr. Whomever. Different as we were, together we made a great team.

Here's the advice Bill Josephy gave me on how to sign a new client or, rather, to steal one from another agent. You walk up to Actor X on the set where he's filming, knowing he is getting $3,000 a week for the job, and ask, "What are you doing a piece of shit like this for?" That's jab number one to his fragile ego. Then you follow up with the clincher: "They're probably only paying you five thousand dollars a week besides." I could never do it because that's not who I am. I believe in being straight-ahead, honest, and sincere—all the things that sound corny but are, I think, the more satisfying way to live and that ultimately lead to a better kind of success. The end result of Josephy's advice that I couldn't follow was that a year later, Kurt Frings fired him and promoted me to his job.

I was a full-bore, gung-ho agent. I had found my field. My MO as an agent was to be informed, be specific, be brief, and meet everybody. I made sure I saw at least one episode of every TV series on the air so I could be current about the actors, writers, directors, and producers. I went to every studio screening to which I could wrangle an invite, to meet people, and to get to know the films. Setting an actor for a minor role in a secondary TV series for, say, two weeks at $1,500 a week wasn't, I suppose, so very different from selling four hundred yards of lining fabric to a cloakie (coat and suit manufacturer), but it seemed so to me. As much as I hated the former, selling fabrics, was how much I loved the latter, showbiz. As the old joke goes, when the guy at the circus whose job it is to clean up the elephant dung was complaining, his wife asked, "So why don't you quit?" He replied, "What, and leave show business?"

I had some memorable and unusual experiences as an agent. The head of business affairs at MGM at the time was Benny Thaw, about whom it was said, "When he opens up his mouth to laugh, out comes dust." Benny gave me a lesson in patience. I represented fading star Joan Fontaine and suggested her to him for the lead role in an important film. Benny smiled as he said, "It's only nine o'clock at night." Puzzled, I replied, "What do you mean?" Benny answered,

"I'm a single guy. When I'm in a bar at nine o'clock, I'm very picky about who I try to meet and hopefully go home with. By midnight, I'm much less choosy." I began to hit Benny up every week about Joan Fontaine, and after a couple of times, he said, "It's ten o'clock" which, of course, gave me encouragement. I persisted, and pretty soon it was eleven o'clock. Evidently, they couldn't get the several other stars they were angling for because one day he said, "It's midnight," and we closed the deal. I kept Joan informed throughout and, old pro that she was, she stayed calmly amused.

At one meeting with Benny, the MGM resident doctor entered from a side door and Benny, while continuing to talk to me, rose from his chair, dropped his pants, and got a vitamin shot in the ass. The only incident to top that was my first and only meeting with Kirk Douglas. I was led into his private bungalow on the Universal lot, where he was getting a massage. As we chatted, Kirk rolled off the table and stood, stark naked, all the while continuing to talk with me. I made sure to maintain eye contact throughout our meeting.

It was fortuitous that the Frings Agency was small. I had the run of the town, including all the studios and TV networks, unlike at the larger agencies, where they assigned agents to cover specific studios and specific clients. I feel I crammed a dozen years' worth of experience into the four years I worked as an agent. I knew I was doing well because I began to get job offers from other agencies, some for a lot more money. But I didn't want to jump ship, as I was still aiming to be a producer—not that I had a specific plan for how to achieve that goal. I figured if I failed as a producer, those other agencies would be my fallback, which was naïve of me: Job offers are rarely open-ended. But at the time it was heady because when you turn down a job, they seem to want you more, and up the ante. Even the king of agents (and beyond; see the Connie Bruck biography *When Hollywood Had a King*), Lew Wasserman of MCA, solicited me. That was a big compliment. The only better compliment I got also came from Lew. After the industry screening of my first film, *The Young Doctors*, a voice behind me whispered, "I see now why you turned me down. You were right to do so." It was Lew.

Lew's largess remained consistent. Three decades later, my partner David Foster and I were making *The River Wild* at Universal when, one day, I found the studio lunch commissary completely full. Lew Wasserman had his own special table overlooking everything and everybody. That day, as he was leaving, he stopped to say hello and asked why I was waiting. I said there were no tables available. He turned to the maître d' and said, "Please give Larry my table." From that day on, whenever I lunched at the commissary, the maitre d' and his staff did everything but genuflect before me.

I loved being an agent. I was no longer trying to sell a thousand yards of black satin for thirty-six cents a yard, competing against someone selling the same thing for a penny less. Now my product was Christopher Plummer, a brilliant, classically trained actor with a mellifluous voice, an individual and unique choice for certain roles (e.g., *The Sound of Music*). I admired his talent and personally found him engaging.

In those days, agents made the rounds of the studios. I'd walk the halls of MGM and Paramount to familiarize myself with the players, and think up reasons to meet producers, directors, and executives. That's where I first learned the value of doing my homework—which director was doing which film, how I could get a copy of the script or at least knowledge of the story, who had already been cast and which roles were still open. I signed on to represent a few directors of photography, which gave me a reason to meet producers and directors earlier in the process, before casting. Every studio commissary had a writers' table, to which I gravitated. I developed relationships with writers, which fed my producer's soul. They were all far more interesting than the cloak and suit manufacturers I used to deal with. I was in pig heaven, so much so that even though my motivation was to become a producer, I flirted with the idea of making agenting my career.

I tried, unsuccessfully, to engineer a merger between Kurt Frings, who was strong in feature films, and the Ashley-Steiner Agency, the primary strength of which was in television. That Ashley was Ted, who later ran Warner Bros. Studios and asked me to be production chief, which—in a grievous error of judgment—I turned down. Ted subsequently chose John Calley, who did a remarkable job until he left the business for a decade, only to return to greater success, resurrecting United Artists and going on to head Sony Pictures.

I tried yet again to engineer another merger, this time with the classy writer-director agency Ziegler, Hellman, Ross: Evart Ziegler was a top lit agent who I later hooked up with Bill Goldman, only to be repaid by Ziggy shutting me out of the *Butch Cassidy*/Twentieth Century Fox deal in favor of his complaining, high-commission TV client Paul Monash (of *Peyton Place* on network three times a week, thank you very much); Jerry Hellman was later to become a selective producer himself; and Hal Ross was a TV agent who later became an important William Morris agent. But that amalgamation also failed to gel. My boss, Kurt Frings, had the usual Hollywood ego and couldn't see giving up his sole name on the door to be one of four or to take on a fictitious company name. So my two merger ideas never got off the ground.

I even thought of starting my own agency with the best young talent agent in Hollywood, Dick Clayton, who worked for the prominent Famous Artists Agency (where the renowned producer Ray Stark began his career, which led to him founding/funding The Peter Stark Producing Program, named for his deceased son). Dick represented James Dean and many other up-and-coming actors. I suggested he and I start an agency together, but he was happy and well-compensated working for the debonair Charlie Feldman at Famous Artists, and thus turned me down. Ironically, Ted Ashley's intermediate stepping-stone to running Warner Bros. was a takeover of Famous Artists.

From my agent days, I began to see "who you know" is important. My new client, producer Stuart Millar, was close with the author Jessamyn West, having met her when he was William Wyler's assistant during the filming of Jessamyn's novel *Friendly Persuasion*. Through Stuart, I became Jessamyn's agent, and sold her novel *South of the Angels* to MGM, to the producer John Houseman. Alas, it was never made into a film, although Jessamyn was very happy with the $100,000 I negotiated for her, as was my boss Kurt Frings. That was an early case of me thinking to myself that I knew how to develop her book into a screenplay better than the producer to whom I sold it. My cockiness was surely unjustified; John Houseman was one of the most literate, classy producers around, having produced *The Bad and the Beautiful, Julius Caesar,* and *Executive Suite,* after a stint with Orson Welles's Mercury Theatre.

Here is a story about how much of an eager beaver I was, just as I'm saying you have to be. I had a date with a drop-dead-gorgeous female executive who worked at United Artists. She had a perfect Miss Universe figure to boot and, to top it off, was among the brightest young women I ever met. We ended the evening at my apartment. I was excited, but shortly after we closed the door, my telephone rang. It was my pal, ace writer Ernie Lehman, who was firmly entrenched in the Hollywood hierarchy. He had a problem, and wanted my opinion. I stayed on the phone with Ernie for at least forty-five minutes, maybe an hour, after which the glorious young lady, who had been cooling her heels, would have nothing to do with me. The evening ended with a whimper, not my anticipated bang.

I was never able to get a date with her again. Later, a composer friend of mine told me he had the most wonderful, passionate, exciting affair of his life with her. He shared details with me, as he was sure I had had the same experience. Alas, no banana for me, I hadn't even come close, and told him so. But hey, Ernie was my conduit to later selling Hitchcock five actors for *North by Northwest*. Was it worth the trade-off? It sure seemed like it then. Now, I wonder. But the point of this particular story is that you're going to be competing against guys like me.

As an agent I even got an education from my clients. I represented the old-time comic Ed Wynn, who had once been king of the hill in vaudeville, Broadway, and early television. My associate Bill Robinson and I got him a showy role in Rod Serling's legendary live-TV *Playhouse 90, Requiem for a Heavyweight*. It was a high-visibility success, and I was thus subsequently able to "sell" Ed to director George Stevens for *The Diary of Anne Frank*. Stevens was one of the all-time great directors, and the *Diary* was a prestigious book of worldwide importance and a hit play on Broadway. Ed wanted $50,000, and I wanted it for him; he deserved it. But the Fox brass didn't want to pay him that much. I thought the exposure was so great for Ed I didn't want to risk losing it, so I broached the idea of lowering his fee. Ed enlightened me: "I've been up and I've been down. When you're down they don't want you and they kick you around. So when you're up, don't let them push you around. Stand firm." So I did; I enlisted George Stevens as an ally, and with his muscle, his firm insistence on Ed, got Fox to pay the $50,000. Even the swiftest ball carrier needs blockers.

While I was an agent, I figured out and began to use the self-serving quasi-legal letter. My client Alan Pakula was a master of charm and seduction. He had a knack for seeming intimacy, revealing enough of himself to make another person feel secure, to open up and bond with Alan. Plus, he was very smart and tasteful. Alan obtained a free verbal option on an adventure book, *Flight from Ashiya*, about an air-rescue organization. I was able to set it up with Harold Hecht of the then-powerful independent company Hecht-Hill-Lancaster (as in Burt), with Alan set to produce. Harold Hecht was not at the top of anyone's integrity list, so after closing the deal I wrote him a letter in the guise of a "thank you," but in reality confirming in writing the terms of our deal: "Dear Harold, thank you for being so forthcoming and helpful during our negotiation for Alan Pakula to produce *Flight from Ashiya* for Hecht-Hill-Lancaster at X thousands of dollars, etc. Your company's creativity, support, and financial wherewithal make it an ideal match for Alan and this exciting property. Good luck to us all."

Hecht called me a few weeks later to say his company decided they did not want to go forward with Alan's deal for *Flight from Ashiya*. I checked with the lawyer the Frings Agency had on retainer, and he confirmed that my letter, although not 100 percent legally binding, was a very strong weapon, especially as Hecht had never refuted it verbally or in writing. So I re-sent a copy of the letter to Hecht with a note saying, "Sorry, we have a closed deal," and it worked. Hecht-Hill-Lancaster honored the deal I had made for Alan and, though the film was never made, Alan got his fee for developing the script, plus an important press release in *Variety* verifying that he was a bona fide producer. The author of the novel (not a client of mine), for whom I had gotten a lot of money, sent me an autographed thank-you in the flyleaf of his book,

By giving me a job, Kurt Frings changed my life. I was a sponge; I soaked up everything. I learned who's who and how Hollywood works. I met everybody I could, which ended up being helpful in ways I didn't imagine at the time. I have relationships and access I could never have anticipated.

In the same way as I was asked to write this book, I was asked to be a producer. Is that luck, or is it working as hard as you can, the best you know how, so you just might stand out from the crowd? The icing on the cake in co-producing my first film was that I had un-

knowingly negotiated my own deal before I ever knew I was to become the film's producer. The film, *The Young Doctors,* was the first
of the multicharacter popular fiction works of Canadian Arthur Hailey
(he later wrote *Hotel,* which became a hit TV series). It had been produced as a two-hour TV movie starring the future *Star Trek* hero
William Shatner and set up as a feature at United Artists by then MCA
agent Elliott Kastner. It was a joint venture for his producer client
Stan Shpetner and the Dick Clark Company. Dick Clark himself was
to make his movie debut playing the Shatner role. It seemed a shrewd
commercial idea because in 1959 his show *American Bandstand* enjoyed enormous popularity throughout the country.

Although Kastner was more sophisticated about money and deals
than I (he, with his then partner Jerry Gershwin, reportedly made a
$400,000 override for themselves in setting Bill Goldman's *Harper*
script for production, right up there among my major mistakes), he
nonetheless asked my opinion about the deal he was formulating for
Shpetner to produce. *The Young Doctors* was planned to be an inexpensive picture, maybe half a million dollars or so. Kastner was
thinking of asking for a flat $25,000, which would be the standard
5 percent fee for producers. I suggested he ask instead for 5 percent of the final approved budget, but with a floor, a minimum fee,
of $25,000. That's what he did.

Soon after, however, Shpetner seized an opportunity to produce a
more important picture, *Two Rode Together,* starring James Stewart
and directed by the one and only John Ford (four-time Academy
Award winner). I was then able to insinuate my client Stuart Millar
as producer, who, in turn, invited me to leave the Kurt Frings Agency
and be his producing partner. Even though I had been pointing
toward being a producer, I was so enjoying my life and success as an
agent that I didn't have the same impetus to leave agenting as I'd
had four years before to leave the textile business. It did seem, and
was, a natural evolution, though, so I quickly said "yes." My goal,
my dream, of being a producer had just fallen into my lap. As Shpetner leapt at his opportunity, I leapt at mine.

Why did Stuart Millar ask me to be his partner? After having early
success producing *Stage Struck* (directed by Sidney Lumet, his first
feature), Stuart was stalled and struggling in his producing career.
He is very bright and had a steep learning curve working as Willy

Wyler's assistant, but he didn't suffer fools gladly and had alienated some people. I had conviction about his skills and worked very hard on his behalf. As his career began moving forward again, Stuart attributed at least some of that to me, which is why he asked me to be his partner. We were also pals.

So I became a producer by invitation. How often does that happen? Rarely. But it does reaffirm what I've said elsewhere: There's no straight path to being a producer. Since my partner Stuart Millar had been through the producing/production process before, he was, in effect, my teacher on *The Young Doctors.* Yet, since every film is different, Stuart learned almost as much as I did in the process. United Artists, the financing/distribution company, did not have a studio facility, so once they approved the budget and cast, we producers were on our own to set up offices and form the production unit from scratch. That was a big-time learning curve. Stuart had the experience, but I also had opinions, and we would bat things around before arriving at our decisions. Experience is always valuable, and sometimes vital, but it doesn't always trump a clear-eyed, fresh approach.

We got a rude awakening about how the game is played just before we were to start filming. Arthur Krim, the former lawyer who, along with his law partner Bob Benjamin, acquired and ran United Artists, called Stuart and me into his office. Our budget had crept higher (now a million dollars) than UA had expected, and they told us they wouldn't go forward with the picture unless Stuart and I guaranteed completion. That meant that if the budget was exceeded by a contingency amount (customarily, 10 percent), any money spent thereafter would come from Stuart and me personally, not United Artists. That's right, the two of us personally. We agreed instantly. Why so eagerly? Because we were straining at the leash to make our first film as partners, and our secret weapon was we didn't have the money to put up anyway, even if we were actually called upon. Besides, what could UA possibly do to us? "You can't get blood from a turnip," is a saying that came about for a reason. Fortunately, we didn't have to test that maxim, as we finished right on budget.

Our 5 percent producers' fee of that million-dollar budget meant Stuart and I *each* got $25,000 (thank you very much, Elliot Kastner, for asking for my help in the deal). I carefully calculated that $25,000 would carry me for one year. Additionally, our living expenses, while prepping and filming on location in New York for six months, were (as customary) part of the budget. So, going forward, I was buying myself an eighteen-month window to make it as a producer.

The script that Stu and I developed with writer Joseph Hayes turned out to be stronger dramatically than we felt Dick Clark, an untrained actor, could handle. The United Artists brass concurred, and even Dick himself, deep down, likely had some doubt, so we were able to convince him to take a more minor role. We then lured Ben Gazzara, a strong actor and rising Broadway star, for the lead. The big-name star, however, was Fredric March, then near the end of an illustrious career, which included two best-actor Oscars, for *Dr. Jekyll and Mr. Hyde* (1931) and *The Best Years of Our Lives* (1946).

Midwinter Poughkeepsie for *The Young Doctors* was a tough shoot. And we were shooting in working hospitals, which proved to be delicate and time-consuming. At the halfway mark in the filming, we found ourselves going over budget. Even though we didn't have the money to live up to our completion guarantee, we nonetheless felt responsible (appropriately so) to the budget. Our director, Phil Karlson, was a very capable, experienced, mostly B-picture director from the old Hollywood studio system. He was used to taking orders. Stu and I sat him down and told him that the ice-skating sequence at nearby Grossingers Inn, which we had scheduled for night with a hundred extras, would now be a less-expensive daytime scene with only twenty-five extras. The old pro put the camera up high and shot down and tight. The integrity of the story was not compromised, and we regained schedule and budget. If I'd known then what I know now, I would have handled that situation differently. We should have presented our problem to the director, had a discussion, offered our suggestions, heard the director's alternatives, if any, and maneuvered him toward the solution that we had imperiously imposed on him. Veteran that Karlson was, he might have had better time-saving ideas.

On *The Young Doctors,* I learned how much can be done in editing to improve a film. We had a disjointed, bumpy section: Two romantic boy-girl scenes in a parked car, separated only by a brief drive, were repetitious and boring. We were stymied trying to fix it because there was important story content in each of the two scenes. We couldn't eliminate either one. It then occurred to me that we could meld the two scenes and, with some excisions, combine them seamlessly into a single, shorter scene. It worked like a charm and gave me great creative satisfaction, and not a little ego boost. It didn't hurt that we had one of the most skilled editors in the business, Robert Swink, who had cut many films for Willy Wyler and George Stevens. It also showed the value of a partnership because I didn't know Bob Swink from a hole in the wall, but my partner Stuart Millar had met him when working on Wyler's *Friendly Persuasion.* We also chose Elmer Bernstein, very early in his memorable career, to do the music—a prescient choice. For fun-and-games ego, Stu and I had prominently placed ourselves as the only extras in one scene, only to excise the scene—and ourselves—in editing. As F. Scott Fitzgerald once said, "Murder your darlings."

I should be embarrassed to admit this, but here goes: For the print ad, my partner and I decided to put in quotes, but without attribution, "A great film." That must be the definition of chutzpah. We would not, nor would anyone, dare do that today. I know I make it sound like it was the nineteenth century, but *The Young Doctors* was released in 1960.

I'll never forget the excitement of our first preview, and, afterward, sitting in a coffee shop and going over the comment cards. Indeed, everything about that first movie experience is burned into my memory—you can only be a virgin once. We actually tipped the projectionist twenty bucks beforehand to make sure he wouldn't miss any reel changeovers.

Dick Clark himself learned a lesson on *The Young Doctors.* As partners, his production company, Drexel, received an above-the-title credit (shared with us): "A Drexel/Millar-Turman Production." Who and what was Drexel? It was Dick Clark, of course, but nobody knew that. Today his company is called Dick Clark Productions.

The Young Doctors was enough of a success that our partnership got off the ground. We had produced it efficiently and well. We were responsible to the budget, and the picture garnered good reviews. United Artists welcomed us into their family and became the home for our next three films. The great director William Wyler told me, "A successful picture will carry you for four years." He was right then, and what he said still holds true today.

The Judy Garland film *I Could Go On Singing* was the first time I had occasion to work alone with a writer. I liked it. If my partner Stuart had an especially good idea when the two of us were working together with a writer, I of course always appreciated it, and was thankful (just as he was with my ideas), but somehow that third person in the room complicated the creative equation for me. I prefer a situation where I have to convince or persuade only the writer, not my partner as well. It's odd because I've been in partnerships much more than I've worked by myself. But, at least subsequent to Stuart Millar, I tended to work alone on the projects I initiated, and I worked on my partner's initiated projects only when asked. And I wasn't very good at extending an invitation for my partner to participate. Mind you, I always paid close attention to all his script notes on any, and every, completed draft.

Stuart Millar was very big on "momentum." Strike while the iron is hot. (Aside: in later life I had a therapist who counseled me to "Strike while the iron is cold," meaning that I should make decisions dispassionately.) So, at Stuart's urging, we accepted an opportunity to produce, in partnership with the big-time Mirisch Company, a re-make of the classic Bette Davis–starrer *Dark Victory*, but I came down with hepatitis. That prevented me from working on the *Dark Victory* remake, aside from a bit of script work with the gifted novel-ist Jessamyn West and a meeting with the very beautiful star Susan Hayward. That's not a cop-out regarding the non-success of our ver-sion of *Dark Victory* because I did go with the flow. But it planted the seeds of doubt in me about the philosophy of "momentum." It made me reflect on what kind of producer I wanted to be, and helped me decide to be selective and only work on those projects I truly cared about and identified with.

To that end, President John F. Kennedy had just formed the Peace Corps under the supervision of his brother-in-law Sargent Shriver, and Stuart and I volunteered to produce, without pay, a film about the organization. Our idea was to do a three-or-four segment film about individual volunteers in different countries. We enlisted the support of director Arthur Penn and a couple of good writers, then flew to Washington for meetings with Shriver and his staff. Even as gung-ho as we were, and with seeming interest from Shriver et al., we couldn't get this labor of love off the ground. Although UA agreed to distribute it under their auspices, nobody wanted to foot the bill for the actual production costs.

As producing partners, Stuart and I ended up having a nice run. Unfortunately, but perhaps not surprisingly, our partnership foundered. Rightly or not, I didn't quite feel that I was an equal partner. I felt I had to make more compromises, do more "giving in," than I wanted in order to maintain our partnership. That probably says more about me than Stuart, as I talk in this book about my desire for control. Whether I was too timid (or insecure?) and deferential, or he too commanding and overbearing, I became increasingly uncomfortable in our working relationship, even though we continued to be good friends. We shared a passion for good food, and he had a robust appetite for life. When I came to the reluctant conclusion that I needed to fly alone, it was a difficult decision to confront, and even more difficult to enact. I agonized over it and, frankly, felt insecure about breaking up what was a successful partnership with a superbright guy. I shared my fear with my good friend Ernie Lehman. Forty years later, I still remember my surprise and guilty pleasure at hearing Ernie say, "You might prove to be a better producer on your own than you think."

As reassuring as that was, it didn't dissipate my apprehension. But it did help propel me to do the deed. I was only thinking of myself, of course, but Stuart proved to be a better producer on his own, too. He did the fine *Little Big Man*, directed by Arthur Penn and starring Dustin Hoffman, and a serious, worthwhile smaller film, *When the Legends Die* (which Stuart also directed). His career trailed off much earlier than his taste and intelligence warranted.

Our last film as partners was *The Best Man*. We went out in a blaze of glory. The film was ecstatically reviewed, and was the darling of the Cannes Film Festival and the behind-the-iron-curtain Karlovy Vary International Film Festival. Although American critics loved the film, it fared only modestly at the box office. (My rationale to myself: Political stories have traditionally not been big successes.) On the other hand, Bill Goldman, in a letter to me, said, "*The Best Man* got you me." I think that was a deserved compliment to himself, as well as to me.

My twenty-year partnership with my next partner, David Foster, was unusual and yet, upon reflection, that may have been a strength, a reason we were successful. We were complementary, not supplementary. He gravitated toward action and size—*Running Scared* and the remake of *The Getaway*—while I've always been attracted to more intimate, emotional stories like *Mass Appeal* or *Tribute*. I felt that my strength was in script and editing (similar process: storytelling), whereas his was in marketing and relationships. Indeed, it was David's cultivation of relationships with and romancing of studio executives that helped facilitate many of our overhead deals, wherein a studio would give us offices and pay for our secretary, assistants, telephones, messengers, and sometimes a creative development person in exchange for getting a "first look" at all our projects. His ability to arrange those overhead deals was eased by our good track record and our reputation as responsible, tasteful producers.

Our partnership started auspiciously with *The Drowning Pool,* starring Paul Newman. Bill Goldman suggested the Ross Macdonald book to me, but did not want to do the screenplay, having recently done *Harper* from the same author. I was so pissed at myself for having foolishly missed out on *Harper* that I jumped at *The Drowning Pool.* Paul Newman had just formed First Artists (along with Barbra Streisand, Steve McQueen, and Sidney Poitier), was looking for a kick-off project, and liked ours. Plus, Paul's Academy Award–winning wife, Joanne Woodward, wanted to costar. She was from or had gone to school in Louisiana, our story's locale. Paul wanted Stu Rosenberg to direct. That was an easy decision for us; we loved their work together on *Cool Hand Luke.* We prevailed upon Rosenberg to use the amazing Gordy Willis as cameraman, and cast the teenage Melanie Griffith. Through friendship, timing, and a little bit of luck, our partnership had a nice beginning, and flourished for twenty years.

Unlike the breakup of my partnership with Stuart Millar, which I initiated, my partnership with David ended when I accepted the directorship of The Peter Stark Producing Program at USC, as it cut into the time I could devote to producing. David's concern about my time, energy, and commitment going forward had some legitimacy, so I suppose I bear the responsibility for that breakup, too. As it turned out, I've fortunately been able to both teach and produce:

I've recently completed my fourteenth year as chair of The Peter Stark Producing Program and have set a deal with United Artists to do a new version of Gore Vidal's *The Best Man,* and also have seemingly secured financing for a long-gestating, quirky script, which is to be filmed for $2 million. My cameraman son asked me, "Can you make a film for two million dollars?" I told him, "I hope I have the chance to find out." David's career has continued to flourish as well. I guess that's the reason we had such a successful partnership—we both pulled our weight.

By now you know I firmly believe this: Identify what it is you want, and then go after it without hurting anybody else. And I'm talking about life as well as the film business. That's the same advice I tried to give my three sons.

I have to laugh at myself because I am constantly counseling you to be who you are, as if you actually had a choice in the matter. The fact is, by the time we are adults, our character is well-formed and is as inexorable as a glacier in its direction and movement. I realized that about myself shortly after I had done *The Graduate, Pretty Poison,* and *The Great White Hope* back-to-back. Working on the board of a charity (those kinds of solicitations come with success), I became friendly with a rich industrialist who gave me $150,000 (this was the early seventies; that amount is probably the equivalent of a million dollars today) to acquire and develop stories at my discretion. He was to share only the profits, if there were any, and nothing else.

Every producer's dream is to have a discretionary development fund, and one fell into my lap. I could have spent the entire $150,000 on one project, or $15,000 each on ten projects. I chose the latter course, which, had I been paying attention to myself, would have been a warning sign of what was to follow. I struck out on the first two projects; either I chose the wrong subjects or didn't develop them well enough, but the first two died aborning. I was so bothered and concerned about losing $30,000 of my investor's money that I returned the remaining $120,000 to him. This was a guy who had just sold his company for $50 million, but my sense of responsibility—some would call it guilt—overwhelmed me.

Was I foolish? Did I lack entrepreneurial guts? Was I shaken by my first two attempts having failed? Or was I just scrupulously conscientious about someone else's money, which had been entrusted to me? Probably all of the above. Thankfully, my career continued to flourish, so I didn't have to beat myself up about making a mistake in forgoing no-strings-attached development money.

HOW I WORK

Warren Buffett, one of the smartest, richest guys on the planet, is known to work out of a modest office with a small staff. I haven't had the same results as he, but I work much the same way, except he's always been in the same office in Omaha, and I'm a nomad, moving my office film to film or deal to deal. The goal is to have someone else pay my rent, telephone bill, and staff (at least one assistant). If you're doing a movie, all of that is part of the budget and is generally covered for at least a year.

Studio overhead deals (wherein the studio paying your rent, etc., gets first crack at any movie you want to do, at a prearranged fee) are the best because they generally include an assistant or two, and so-called development people, who chase scripts, books, and new writers. Those deals, if not commonplace today, were once available for most top-level producers. However, there has been a slow but steady diminution, as producers as a class have been devalued. The proliferation of producer credits is both a cause and a result. During much of my career, I alone, or with my partner, held the producing credit, whereas today, most films have anywhere from four to fourteen credited producers. Just as inflation makes money less valuable, so multiple producer credits on a film diminishes the value of each individual producer. Gresham's law of economics obtains, "Cheap money drives out dear."

The top-of-the-heap producers today actually have many more bodies working for them than did producers in days of old. Brian Grazer has a good-sized organization; Kathleen Kennedy and her partner/husband Frank Marshall have their own building, which includes a children's nursery; Jerry Bruckheimer, too, has his own place, which is near where he lives, on the west side of L.A., rather than at his home studio, Disney, far away in the Valley. Each oversees a very busy organization involved in many projects and active in television.

Absent a specific film, I've had first-look overhead deals at United Artists, Twentieth Century Fox, Universal, and Columbia, and I have worked on individual projects at and for each of the other studios. Once I accepted the job of running The Peter Stark Producing Program at USC, I began doing my movie work out of my academic office there. All a producer really needs is his brain and a telephone.

IT'S WHAT YOU KNOW, NOT WHO YOU KNOW

You can only sleep your way to the middle.
—former Hollywood starlet

I hear ad nauseam that careers, especially in the movie business, are made by whom you know. Well, that's wrong, even though I've already discussed the value of getting out there and meeting people, something I myself have done from day one. Who you know is good for a one-shot, a single opportunity. But I'm talking career, staying power—having taste and tenacity and working your tail off. It's about what project you have and control. Is your story fresh enough to get a really good writer and director interested? Is it strong enough so that an excellent screenplay will emerge? Are the characters unique and colorful, so that marketable actors will want to act them? Barry Diller has been quoted as saying, "Any really good project will see the light of day." So, if your taste is on the money, and not on who you know, you will indeed see the money.

But a producer *does* need access. You have to find a way to get your foot in the door. Who you know is important, and can surely facilitate the process. The more people you manage to meet and know, the easier it will be. Every press release or *Variety* story about a new studio hire or producer deal trumpets the many strong relationships that person has in the creative community. Hollywood is a club, as every industry is, and it sure helps to belong, to be an insider.

The gifted Paddy Chayefsky, in an interview for a book about screenwriters, said, "It's okay, even valuable, for a young writer to be social and get out and meet people early in his career." And that's for a writer, whose work, whose talent, can be read and judged—unlike a producer, who can only be assessed (and not so accurately) by the finished film. That's one of the reasons producers (most of whom are classic Type A's), but also agents and junior studio executives, hustle to make sure their names are on the industry-screening invitation lists. Meet and greet. See and be seen.

Even the very successful "old-timers" continue to care about who they know and who they don't. I had worked for Kurt Frings only a year when he threw a big party for Audrey Hepburn and, to my surprise, asked me to invite the up-and-coming young talents I knew, but that he and his wife Ketti, themselves a "power couple," did not. Do you invite people you don't know to your parties? I don't, either. But it's done in Hollywood. The good news is that I got to dance with Audrey Hepburn that night.

Hang out with your contemporaries at film school or when you get your toehold job; you'll wake up five or ten years later, look around, and see that the group you started out with are now in positions of power. And they're your buddies. It won't exactly hurt your career opportunities as they move up or from company to company.

My own career has been eased many times by the musical-chairs aspect of the movie and television business. David Picker was studio exec at United Artists on the first film I produced, *The Young Doctors.* Later, he was at Paramount and was very helpful when I did *First Love.* Years after that, he was working with Robert Halmi, and facilitated that company taking financial responsibility and distribution on my TV movie *The Long Way Home,* starring Jack Lemmon.

Frank Pierson was working on the TV series *Have Gun—Will Travel* when I first met him in the late 1950s. He went on to win the Academy Award for his screenplay for *Dog Day Afternoon.* Frank and I developed, and he committed to direct, a film about Walt Disney for HBO (although that company, as an exec there told me, was ultimately too frightened to make the film because of anticipated pressure from the Disney company). Frank is now president of the Academy of Motion Picture Arts and Sciences, where I am on the board of the producers branch. I got Frank to be the USC School of Cinema-Television's commencement speaker, a producer coup. He was brilliant. I asked if his producer's experience helps him as president of the Academy, and he answered, "Yes, because I'm presiding over an organization. Basically I'm free to just have good ideas. I give my best judgment about how to go forward. It's a matter of getting the right people in the room."

While I was an agent, I met Loring Mandel at *Playhouse 90* (CBS), who later developed *Countdown* with me (which was, alas, fated to be made by another producer, not me, with Robert Altman directing his first feature) and the aforementioned Walt Disney script. I also met Mayo Simon, who wrote the script for *I Could Go On Singing*. *Playhouse 90* was a lively, fertile breeding ground for up-and-coming talent and enabled me to meet and have lifelong relationships with ace directors Franklin Schaffner, John Frankenheimer, Arthur Penn, Bob Mulligan, Sidney Lumet, George Roy Hill, my excellent fellow producer Martin Manulis, and casting maven Ethel Winant.

Barry Diller was in charge of TV movies of the week for ABC when I made several of them in association with David Wolper. Later, Barry was head of Paramount when I produced *First Love* there. Barry, no question, is one of the smartest, toughest-minded execs I've ever met.

When I produced *First Love,* Barry Diller's left hand (Michael Eisner was his right) at Paramount was Jeffrey Katzenberg. He went with Eisner to reinvigorate Disney, then later formed DreamWorks SKG with Steven Spielberg and David Geffen. My early relationship with him has eventuated in his staunch support in providing summer internships for my Peter Stark producing students. He's smart, of course, and a good guy, but much of his success comes from a prodigious work ethic. He's been known to schedule two early breakfast meetings back-to-back, and even though it's apocryphal, it is psychologically correct that he is rumored to have told his staff, "If you can't show up on time for our Saturday studio meeting, don't even bother to come in on Sunday!" FYI, dear reader, not only did Jeff Katzenberg not go to film school, I don't think he even went to college. But he has, as Tom Wolfe might say, "the right stuff."

You have to get yourself out there, not only to be known and to know people, but to know what's going on. Never turn off your radar, as a producer or as a person. Keep scanning at all times. When the Russian Tearoom in New York was the showbiz lunch hangout, I made it a point on every single trip to New York to have lunch there my very first day in town. I made sure I was friendly enough with the maître d' that I was seated at the front and could check out everybody coming and going, all the movers-and-shakers. I saved myself half a dozen phone calls in doing so. The back of the restaurant or, worse yet, upstairs, was Siberia.

Who you know is also an example of six degrees of separation in the movie-producing business. Kurt Frings's wife, Ketti, wrote a play based on Thomas Wolfe's *Look Homeward, Angel,* and wanted Anthony Perkins for the lead, not only for his talent, but for his burgeoning stardom (having just been in William Wyler's *Friendly Persuasion*). She didn't know Tony, but I did. He was in my client Alan Pakula's movie *Fear Strikes Out* (yes, I hung around the set and made sure I got to know Tony). Ketti thought Tony's agents wouldn't like having him tied up on Broadway for a year, at very low pay compared to what they could get for him doing several films. She was right. So she asked me to slip her play directly to Tony, bypassing his agents. I did; Tony loved it and committed to do it. It won the Pulitzer Prize for Ketti. It also made it that much easier later for me later to get Tony for the lead in *Pretty Poison.* But no good deed goes unpunished. Kurt Frings didn't even invite me to the big-time New York premiere for his wife's play until I brought up the subject. He then acted like the magnanimous guy he wasn't, and paid for my trip. You have to speak up for yourself. Most producers aren't timid.

I wasn't timid when I wanted Albert Finney for a project, but did not know him. He was appearing in a play on Broadway, so I sent a telegram (that's how we did it in those days!) to the theater saying who I was and that I wanted to talk to him about a particular script, and would show up at his dressing room after his performance the next night. I suppose it was more of an assault than an approach, but sure enough, he let me in when I arrived, and we talked. Unfortunately, I did not have the right ammunition, and he declined my project. But I had bearded the lion in his den, as I'm encouraging you to find ways to do. Be sure, though, to do your homework first.

> *I would do my homework so that if I ever had the chance encounter or create that opportunity, I really did know what Larry Turman or Mel Brooks did. So when I got that minute with whomever, they were impressed with me because I knew something about them. I had an understanding beyond just "You're a power player, I need you." I was very, very persistent. I learned to, with dignity, sublimate myself to assistants, to do whatever it took to get to the artist.*
>
> —Brian Grazer

If top producers are going to have a meeting with a writer or director, they bone up on what that person has done. If they're interviewing a writer for an assignment, they will have read some of his previous work. Actors do homework, too, long before filming starts. I witnessed one instance of this when the German actor Curt Jurgens arranged a dinner with space pioneer Wernher von Braun before portraying him in a film. The dinner was fun but a creative disaster. Jurgens tried to steer the conversation to how von Braun operated in the space-rocket world. But Von Braun was only interested in how Jurgens operated with his leading ladies and starlets. But Jurgens did observe and glom on to von Braun's personality and mannerisms.

In the middle of one of my many sessions with Bill Goldman in developing the *Butch Cassidy* script, we were working in Bill's hotel room in L.A. when his phone rang. I heard Bill's end of the conversation: "You don't have to meet me. I don't wanna meet. Just send me the book. If I like it we'll talk. If I don't like it, what's the point in meeting?" Bill always gets right down to it, pragmatically and quickly. The producer entreating Bill had done his detective work and found out Bill was in L.A. and which hotel he was at, and was able to speak to him personally about his project. Bill's hard-nosed response notwithstanding, the producer was smart and aggressive in managing to get access. You can only ask for your day in court, and that producer got it.

I still, even late in my career, sometimes make it a point to see and be seen. Unlike many people in showbiz, who book lunch dates for every day and far in advance, I eat alone about three days a week. I live so much on the telephone that I'm happy to have a quiet hour, which I often use to read. But I do like to eat well, so I hie myself to a good restaurant, often a showbiz hangout like, in L.A., Toscana, The Grill, or Barney Greengrass. All those "in" places have counters right at the front, which is where I sit. You'd be surprised at the tidbits of information I pick up from industry people who stop and talk to me, or whom I stop. I'm also not timid about subtly dropping the news about a project I'm working on. Director Mark Rydell told me (with a smile, but accurately) that directing a picture buys him a year and a half of being able to say, for the first six months, "I'm going to be doing picture X"; then, while shooting, "I'm filming Picture X"; and then, for the many months of post-production, "I've just completed Picture X." As jocular as that sounds, it's emotionally accurate for most of us. I make sure my face is out there: Don't forget Larry Turman, he's front and center in the club. In fairness, I used to be on top of the mountain, whereas now I'm hanging over the edge and they're stamping on my fingers. But even that's not a bad place to be. And surely you think so if you're reading this book.

One of the bonuses of my academic life, running The Peter Stark Producing Program, is my visibility. I constantly interact with movie and TV executives and creative people in my search for teachers and internships for my students, and for my mentoring program. Those continuing, and sometimes new, relationships give me the ongoing access of the kind I'm encouraging you to be on the lookout for and to cultivate. You *do* need to be able show your wares to those who are buying, to show what it is you do know.

Oddly, in this chapter, where I'm selling "It's what you know," I've talked a lot about "who you know." Do I contradict myself? As poet Walt Whitman said, "Very well then I contradict myself. I am large, I contain multitudes."

The greater the number of people you know, the wider you can cast your net, and the better your odds. Just as if you develop a single movie project, it becomes do or die, whereas if you work on half a dozen, maybe even a dozen, the odds go up that you will actually produce one of them.

I thought that what you did was you went to a room with a writer for a year and then you came out, you took the script, and you made it. When my friend would tell me to work on a few things, I'd say I'm not one of those jerks who throws a bunch of stuff on the wall to see what sticks. I got my pomposity shoved down my throat and I gagged on it. What I came to understand is that you have to have a few shots to survive.

—Doug Wick

LUCK

Luck is putting out buckets so if it rains you catch water.
—attributed to Vince Lombardi

The old saw is true: Luck favors the well-prepared. In plain language, "The harder you work, the luckier you get." In my experience, most smart, hardworking people modestly attribute their success to luck. On the other hand, those who have been blessed with more luck than talent are the very ones who volunteer to everybody within earshot how smart they are. You can't count on luck, you can't plan for luck, but none of us are immune from it, good and bad. Since you cannot completely control your destiny, what matters is your attitude toward it. I keep in the front of my mind what Dick Zanuck told me right after his own father fired him as head of production at Twentieth Century Fox in order to save his own skin (which he did not): "When things are bad, they're not quite as bad as you think they are. And when things are good, they're also not quite as good as you think they are."

Things were bad for a European émigré when he arrived in America and was unable to gain entrance into the cameraman's union. Discouraged, he took a job in the shorts department of MGM, which led him to directing some shorts, and ultimately directing some classics of cinema: *High Noon, From Here to Eternity, A Man for All Seasons, The Nun's Story*. That story was told to me about himself by Fred Zinnemann.

I was lucky my first boss, Kurt Frings, happened to walk by the open door where his prime lieutenant was interviewing me for the job Kurt had advertised. My interview was going poorly; there was no way I was going to get the job. But then Kurt wandered in and liked me. If it were not for that lucky start, I surely would have had a very different trajectory in the movie business. If Dick Clayton, who represented the hottest young actors, hadn't turned me down when I suggested he and I form an agency, I might have ended up an agent instead of a producer.

It was luck that got me that first picture to produce, and it was luck that I got the surprising phone call to advise and improve what turned out to be my own deal on that film. I clearly had some luck on my path to becoming a producer. And what happened to the original producer of *The Young Doctors,* to whom I owed my good fortune? His bad luck was that he got buried beneath the high visibility of Jimmy Stewart and John Ford and, although his producing career continued for a while, it never truly flourished. Frank Pierson tells the luckiest story about luck that I ever heard:

David Ward was a starving writer driving an old wreck on Sunset Boulevard in the rain, when a car in front stopped suddenly and he ran right into the back of this Mercedes. The guy jumps out, furious, and after arguing a bit, the guy asks for David's insurance. David says "I'm sorry, I don't have insurance." The guy asked him how he was going to pay. David said, "I guess I'm not." The guy asked if he had anything to give. David went to the trunk of his car, got out a screenplay—the only one he'd written, *Steelyard Blues*—and handed it to the guy. The guy turned out to be an agent, who read it that night, and sold it the next day to producers Tony Bill, Michael and Julia Phillips. Not only did they produce it, but they produced his next, the Academy Award–winning *The Sting*. Everybody I know has had some kind of break like that. But that's the classic one.

My personal favorite about my own luck is one I dine out on. Some of the smartest top-of-the-heap guys I knew wanted to start a professional volleyball league. The group included the now legendary Barry Diller (then head of ABC movies of the week, which he created), Berry Gordy, Jr. (founder and chief of Motown Records), David Wolper, basketball legend Wilt Chamberlain, and a few others. *The Graduate* was just beginning to become a phenomenon, so I was invited to join the group. I was elated. However, although my ship had come in, it hadn't yet docked, meaning I had not yet received any profit checks from *The Graduate*, so when it came time for each of us to pony up the seed money to form the league, I had to bow out. I simply didn't have the money. I was crestfallen. That volleyball league had a brief, unsuccessful run, and quietly folded after a couple of years, losing everyone's entire investment. Thereafter, whenever I would see Berry Gordy, the smart, rich Berry Gordy (also a super guy), he would point a finger at me and loudly proclaim, "That Larry Turman is the smartest guy I know. He knew better than all of us not to go into the volleyball business." Who was I to refute his compliment?

Luck can be in the eye of the beholder. Years ago, I went to the Broadway opening of *The Subject Was Roses*, a play written by the talented Frank Gilroy (his son Tony is now a successful screenwriter—the apple doesn't fall far from the tree). The producer was Edgar

Lansbury (son of the famous Angela), from whom I bought the very first home I ever owned. He greeted me warmly as I entered the theater. The play had a superb cast: the veteran Jack Albertson, whom I later cast in *The Flim-Flam Man;* and, playing his son, a very young Martin Sheen, whom I had the good fortune to later work with on the TV movie *News at Eleven.* I was obsessing about business worries, and was so self-involved and preoccupied that the play simply couldn't get through to me. I was bored stiff and left at intermission, relieved that I managed to sneak out without my friend Edgar Lansbury noticing. The play was not only a hit, but went on to win the Pulitzer Prize. A year later, *The Subject Was Roses* played in Los Angeles. I thought I should take another look. As I entered the theater, my friend Edgar Lansbury spotted me and rushed up, beaming. "Larry, my good luck charm," he said.

WHAT DOES A PRODUCER DO?

HARD WORK GUARANTEES YOU NOTHING, BUT WITHOUT
IT YOU DON'T STAND A CHANCE.

—PAT RILEY, NBA COACH

Hardly anyone can define what a producer does. You can stop someone in the street and ask what a director, a writer, or an actor does, and get an intelligent, accurate answer. But ask what a producer does and you'll get a fumbling attempt at a definition or a blank look. Some people would likely say a producer raises the money. Well, yes, a producer does do that, but also a heck of a lot more. A good producer does many different things, and must have both creative and business skills. Mainly, producers want to tell stories. But so do writers. So do directors. So do some studio executives. The difference is that it's the stories a producer wants to tell that usually reach the screen.

> *The producer is a generalist. He really has to know less about the specifics of filmmaking than any of the other crafts, less than a director, less than a script supervisor, less than an art director, a grip. A producer, if he can afford it, can just dream about a movie and go about those long months of getting it on.*
>
> **—David Brown**

Other producers know what a producer does, but surprisingly—or maybe not so surprisingly—a lot of people in the movie business do not know. If you have ever been on the set of a movie, you have seen that everyone has a specific job—that is, everyone except the producer. The camera crew is planning the next shot; the electricians are setting the lights; makeup, hair, and wardrobe people are grooming the actors; props and set dressing are doing their final touch-ups; the director is working with the script supervisor. But the producer? He's probably just standing around, or maybe sitting in the chair provided for him, or perhaps back in his trailer office. Even some on the crew think to themselves, "What a racket. He makes the big bucks and just hangs around, sometimes talking to the director." Always remember, the picture wouldn't be happening, and none of the others would be working, were it not for the producer. The film being shot began life as an idea in the producer's head. It was given reel life by the producer's skillful, relentless nurturing, most likely over several years. It sometimes feels as if you're pushing a peanut uphill with your nose.

Here's what the Producers Guild of America says a producer does: A producer is responsible for overseeing all phases of motion-picture or television production, from the conception of the story to the delivery of the final product. The Producers Guild defines a producer as an individual who has exercised decision-making authority over a majority of the following duties:

- Conceiving of the underlying concept of the story, or selecting and securing the rights to the material on which the story is based
- Selecting the writer(s)
- Supervising the development of the script
- Securing initial financing and serving as the point of contact with the financial entity/studio/network
- Preparing (or supervising the preparation of) the preliminary budget
- Selecting the director and other key technical personnel (e.g., production designer, cinematographer, editor, unit production number)
- Selecting the principal cast
- Approving the shooting schedule
- Providing in-person, on-set consultation with the director, cast, and department heads
- Supervising the day-to-day operations of the shooting company, both on location and in the studio

- Viewing dailies and providing in-person consultation on them
- Consulting with the editor and director on initial cut(s)
- Selecting the composer and supervising scoring and recording sessions
- Supervising all titles, opticals, and visual effects
- Delivering answer print or edited master to distributor
- Consulting with distributor/studio/network on marketing and publicity plans

Obviously, a producer is dependent on writers, directors, actors, and studios, but it is he who starts the ball rolling, keeps the ball rolling, and makes sure it stays on the rolling path he has in mind. Do I sound a bit self-serving and prejudiced? Well, I plead guilty. Because that's how I've worked, and so have all the great producers. That takes nothing away from the talented, creative others I've had to convince, implore, cajole, and seduce to climb aboard the train I'm steering. Railroad tracks are a good metaphor for producing; they always head toward a specific, defined destination.

> *A producer is a man with a dream. I say, "I don't write, I don't direct, I don't act, I don't compose music, I don't design costumes. What do I do? I make things happen." A producer is like a chef. You get all the right ingredients together and make a tasty stew. You put the wrong ingredients together, it'll taste bad.*
>
> —David Wolper

MAKING THINGS HAPPEN

What a producer does is generate things. Each day a producer has to get up, create, and engender activity. You have to be a self-starter, initiating every phone call, soliciting every meeting—as many as it takes to get the answer you want or the results you need. So, if that's not in your nature or personality, forget it. If I get to the office and just sit there, nothing will happen. I have to make it happen. I call agents. I call writers. I call publishers. I want to know if they have a particular story they love (and maybe can't sell) or represent a new writer they are particularly keen about (but can't get started). Each call usually leads to more calls.

I scour newspapers and magazines. I read a story recently about a young Israeli boy and his Palestinian counterpart who together painted a mural. To me, that sounds like a possible springboard for a TV movie. Unless I am active and have lunch or breakfast with this agent or that writer or a studio exec, little will come my way. And I won't be savvy about what's going on or who the up-and-coming talents are. A producer ought to (and they all do) see a lot of movies, to know who's doing what kind of work and to hone his own taste. I pay close attention to not only the "above-the-line" elements (writer, director, actors), but also to who does the music, the wardrobe, the camerawork, the editing. And I extend that to plays, literature, even opera. You need to be exposed to life.

A very successful literary agent, Evart Ziegler, told me he could never be a producer because he couldn't initiate all those calls. Ziggy, representing top talent, had producers, studios, and writers calling him, which was just how he liked it. When the American Film Institute first started, its founder/head, George Stevens, Jr., asked me to serve on the advisory board. I did, and took an intern who spent two months following me around. I took that intern to every single meeting I had, and let him sit in on every single phone call I made. At the end of his two months, he reported back to George Stevens and the AFI that there was no way he would ever want to be a producer. The AFI considered it an invaluable learning experience, and rightly so. That young man was Basil Poledouris, who is now a very successful film composer.

To be a producer is to be an entrepreneur, starting a business from scratch each time you initiate a project. I enjoy it and always find it stimulating. You'll be scurrying about, searching for new sources of financing. You may be lucky enough to work with a few of the same people more than once, but it is often a new collaboration. In the course of making a film, your relationship with the director, the writer, and perhaps the studio executive will be as intense and close as most marriages are. Mike Nichols and I, after not having seen each other for several years post-*Graduate*, fell into one another's arms upon meeting again. I feel the same kinship to director Ronald Neame, who shared with me the nightmare experience of working with Judy Garland. Making a film is intense. A producer's basic MO is to explode out of the starting blocks and keep pumping, with focus. If you do not thrive on that and on competition, producing is not for you.

There are days I don't have the energy for it, so I'll goof off and check out the new bells and whistles on my cell phone. That's okay, too if it only happens once in a while. But oftentimes I get so energized I have to tell myself (for a brief respite), "Don't just do something, stand there."

One time a picture just fell into my lap. Before the flamboyant Don Simpson teamed with Jerry Bruckheimer to produce, he was an executive at Paramount. He and a fellow exec, Richard Sylbert (in a brief hiatus from his production-designer career), invited me to produce a movie from a short story the studio owned, "First Love and Other Sorrows" by Harold Brodkey, which itself drew inspiration from a Turgenev short story. Getting invited to produce a movie is a rare, lucky occurrence; fortunately, I liked the story. I developed a script with David Freeman, who has since become an inside-Hollywood fiction and nonfiction writer. His script was slight, like the book, but I liked it. However, Simpson and Sylbert didn't have the muscle at Paramount to get a soft picture off the ground.

David Picker was higher up on the food chain at Paramount than they. His first film as an executive was my first as producer, *The Young Doctors*, at UA, where his father and uncle were important execs. Everybody likes David, as well they should; he's an affable straight shooter. At the time, he was married to Nessa Hyams, who had been a movie exec herself and was, I knew from personal experience, a strong feminist. So, to make my picture "happen," I made a gambling calculation. I enticed a new female director, Joan Darling, to the project. Joan had some heat, having directed a couple of Norman Lear–produced TV shows. I'll never know for sure if pillow talk between David and Nessa helped get *First Love* made, but I did indeed operate and succeed on that calculation.

Joan proved to be anything but a darling. She was, like me, strong-willed and highly opinionated. Directing a strong sex scene, she actually told me, "Every woman secretly wants to be raped." I bet that's news to any woman, let alone every. Ultimately, I had to take over the editing, which of course Joan didn't take lying down. She tried to involve her friend Steven Spielberg, showing him her edit, relaying to me and others at the studio how much Steven loved it. I don't know how true all that was, but I wrote Steven a note to defend myself. And I had Paramount's support. What a heavyweight group! Barry Diller, Michael Eisner, Jeffrey Katzenberg, and Don Simpson, each of whom subsequently ran his own shop. And how! Marketing exec Frank Mancuso (later head of MGM) agreed with my editing changes, as each successive preview of my subsequent three received increasingly positive audience reaction. We never did overcome the softness, or the lack of plot (which I should have caught in the script stage), but there are some lovely, fresh scenes and performances.

There are so many different things that must coalesce to take a film from idea to finished product. It's the producer's job to find people to do what he himself can't do, or indeed may not know how to do. Even Armani, dazzling designer that he is, needs someone to run the factory, and people to cut, sew, fit, pack, and ship his label.

> *There are all kinds of producers. When I think of real producers, my model is David Selznick. They have an idea how a picture can be made, go and get the best writers, get the best screenplay, get the right director, get the right casting, and supervise all the way through editing and distribution. That's real, honest-to-God producing. That is all consuming. A producer may be on a project three, four, five, even ten years, getting something from the original idea to the screen.*
>
> —Frank Pierson (Academy of Motion Picture Arts and Sciences president, Academy Award–winning writer of *Dog Day Afternoon*)

(Selznick was famous for approving absolutely everything in every frame, from editing to wigs and clothes. Someone once asked him, "David, if you're going to approve absolutely everything, every decision, why don't you direct it yourself?" He said, "Because I have more important things to do.")

Your job, as a producer, is to get made what you want to get made, the best way you can, and to see that it gets out there in the world in the best way, that it gets attention with a good ad campaign, and a comprehensive marketing plan, and that you try your damndest to get the people to come. It's a responsibility that someone gave you; either a company or private investors have given you money to make a movie, so it's incumbent upon you to do what you can, to help them not lose money—to *make* money—hopefully without bastardizing your own artistic dream for it. This was perfectly expressed by the talented director Alexander Payne (*Sideways, About Schmidt, Election, Citizen Ruth*): "My own philosophy is I never care if my films are hits, but I do want them to make at least one dollar profit, so I can keep making them."

I tell my nonshowbiz friends a producer does everything a real-estate developer does, except at the end he has a movie instead of a shopping center. They both start with an idea, pick the property (a script or book), acquire it legally, select the architect (writer), give creative input balanced against the financial limitations, hire a construction supervisor (director), oversee the entire project from beginning to end, and finally have to market (sell) the shopping center—or movie.

Every producer has two jobs: One job is hustling all the time and the other, a whole separate job, is looking for that one great story. Baseball legend Ted Williams said, "My first rule of hitting is to get a good ball to hit." I do not know a producer who has time to read during the working day. So, most weekends, and often at night, there is a never-ending stack of scripts and books to cover. For years, I owned a weekend retreat home on the beach at Malibu. Each Saturday or Sunday morning I would take a stroll up the beach. My neighbor was always on his porch taking in the sun. At the next house, the owners were playing Frisbee on the beach, and the family at the house after that was barbecuing. But at the house after that, a man was sitting on his deck, reading a script. Every third or fourth house was owned by a movie person. You could always tell—they were doing their reading homework instead of playing and relaxing. The good news, of course, was that they could all afford those expensive getaway homes. Even for those producers who have readers and development people, the producer is nevertheless the one who says "yea" or "nay." It's like panning for gold—hopefully you'll find a couple of nuggets amid the dross. Warren Buffett, the financial wizard, concurs: "You only have to get one good idea every year or so."

I work on things that interest me. My energy and motivation to do something are completely driven by that passion. When I'm really heavily involved in something that I care about, it folds into my life in a way that it becomes part and parcel with who I am and what I do on a daily basis.

> —Kathleen Kennedy (current president of the Producers Guild of America, Academy Award nominee for *Seabiscuit, The Sixth Sense, The Color Purple, E.T.*)

Your gold may be someone else's dross, and vice versa. Film history is filled with stories of producers who loved a particular story, script, or book when nobody else did, and fought the good fight and persisted against all odds to get their film made, only to be vindicated in the end by having it be a big success. There is no greater satisfaction than that. Indeed, it happened with *Shakespeare in Love, The Pianist, The Graduate,* and even *Star Wars,* which was let go by more than one studio before being picked up by Twentieth Century Fox.

WHERE DO YOU
FIND A STORY?

As in real estate, first and foremost is choosing the right property—a story that you can put your heart and soul into. It's critical. If the land isn't flat and firm, the building will end up looking like the Leaning Tower of Pisa. A friend of mine, Broadway producer Stuart Ostrow (*Pippin*) couldn't make his little old Jewish mother understand what it was that he, a producer, did. In exasperation, he figured it out: "Ma, a producer is a fella who knows a writer." His mother now knows what the rest of us know: The story is the lifeblood, the be-all and end-all (unless Tom Cruise happens to be your very loving brother).

Choosing what material to start with, which story or idea, is all about who you are as a person—*your* character, *your* taste, *your* judgment. I could no more pick a story for you than I could pick what you want for dinner, select your clothes, or decide whom you should marry. For my Peter Stark Producing students I constantly invoke Joseph Campbell's credo: "Follow your bliss." Actually, what other choice do you have? To guess what subject director Bob Zemeckis is looking for? Or what kind of story Tom Hanks wants to do next? Good luck . . . get in line.

My attitude is "Am I interested, entertained, involved, moved?" My assumption is that if I'm reacting that way,

then other people will too. How many other people?
Who knows?

—Curtis Hanson

In *The Lonely Crowd*, renowned sociologist David Riesman differentiated between other-directed people, who want to own a Mercedes because their friends or neighbors do, and inner-directed people, who buy one because that's the car *they* want for reliability, or whatever. No one can tell you what it is *you* like, or should like. And if they try, don't listen. I hope my simple mantra is loud and clear: Know thyself (Socrates), and to thine own self be true (Shakespeare). Be inner directed. The great filmmaker Federico Fellini said it best: "You must be true to yourself. Even if you have a demon inside of you, you must be true to that demon." (That, alas, sometimes describes me.) No one likes falling on his face, but for me—and I'll bet for you—it's a far worse feeling if you fall on your face because you followed another person's advice or taste, rather than your own. That doesn't mean you shouldn't seek out information, get input from others, or wet your proverbial finger and hold it up to the wind. The head of Gold Circle Films, Paul Brooks, who green-lit the huge success *My Big Fat Greek Wedding*, said, "There's no formula. It's about backing one's instincts. Then you just cross your fingers and hope because the audience will tell you either way."

Where do you find a story? Where do you find a girlfriend or boyfriend? At a bar or a club where you know singles hang out? Your church or synagogue? Hobby groups or classes, such as skiing, bird-watching, photography, painting? The answer, of course, is that you have to want to find someone worthwhile to date, and if you really want to, you'll figure out what works best for you. When I was single, I would go to either an upscale market or a museum. I like to cook and eat, and I like art, so I already had a common interest with whomever I struck up a conversation with. And I was unafraid to talk to strangers as my first real-world job (which I hated) had been as a door-to-door textile salesman. Thank you, fabric business, for giving me that confidence.

If you want to be a producer you need to recognize a
story. It's always been that way. There's no secret

**about it. You can get something out of a drugstore
library.**

—David Brown

You can find stories anywhere and everywhere: essentially from
your heart and your brain, and hopefully from deep in your soul.
Finding the stories you want to tell defines who you are as a producer, and as a person. Only you know what food you like, what
kind of clothes you like to wear, or to whom you are attracted. Joel
Silver seems to be drawn to big, rock 'em sock 'em, physical, action stories. He is a super producer, and has had huge success till-
ing his particular field—the popular media and comic books—with
films such as the *Lethal Weapon* series and *The Matrix* trilogy. Ismail Merchant, on the other hand, clearly likes stories that are 180-
degrees opposite of those that attract Joel Silver. Classic literary
novels are his main source of inspiration. He has produced *A Room
with a View, Howards End, The Golden Bowl,* and *The Remains of
the Day.*

HITTING THE BOOKS: INSPIRATION FROM NOVELS

Novels have always been a mainstay source, from *Gone With the
Wind* (1939) to *Midnight Cowboy* (1968) to *The Silence of the Lambs*
(1991) to *The English Patient* (1996) to *The Lord of the Rings* (2001).
I myself was always an avid, voracious reader, even as a kid. Some of
my favorite books have made wonderful films: *Of Human Bondage*
by M. Somerset Maugham; *Robin Hood,* filmed again and again, including the Mel Brooks spoof *Men in Tights;* and Theodore Dreiser's
An American Tragedy, made into the Elizabeth Taylor-Montgomery
Clift classic *A Place in the Sun,* brilliantly directed by George
Stevens. My fifth-grade teacher, Ruth J. Swanholme, read to us every
day from *Ghosts of the Scarlet Fleet.* God knows if I could even track
it down lo these many years later, but the title alone makes it sound
perfect for today's world of high-adventure movies. Think of a book
you read as a kid that you loved so much it stayed in your mind; that
could be your first movie property.

Novels were always my metier. My films *The Graduate, The Flim-
Flam Man,* and *Pretty Poison* all began life as books. I met novelist
William Goldman before he had ever written a screenplay through

reading his novel *Boys and Girls Together*, even though I decided I was not interested in it as a film. Good places to start looking are your local newspaper and the nearest library or bookstore. They list the current bestsellers every week. My dear, departed friend Alan Pakula drew his greatest producing success from Harper Lee's novel *To Kill a Mockingbird*. Alan told me he wasn't even in love with the book. He had just suffered a failure in his first and only foray into producing for Broadway, but instead of licking his wounds, Alan got busy looking for a new project. He noticed that *To Kill a Mockingbird* hung on the bestseller list month after month. So he went after it, got it, made it, and the rest is movie history—Academy Awards, commercial success, a film for the ages, and the real launch of Alan's great career success.

Okay, anybody can check out the bestsellers. As Civil War general Nathan Bedford Forrest famously said, "You've got to get there firstest with the mostest." And that means the studios or big-time, long-established producers with deeper pockets are going to get there ahead of you. But what about asking your local librarian or favorite bookstore clerk what his or her favorite book is, past as well as present? What about polling your friends? Surely some of them read. I know a producer who was turned on to a book by a member of his wife's monthly book club; it became his most successful movie. You can go to any bookstore, and the book jackets will give you summaries of the stories and characters—enough information for you to decide if you want to read the entire book. You can very quickly leaf through many books that way until you find the story that grabs you.

First novels are my special inspirational source. I especially have an affinity for obscure, little-known ones. I think the writer's guts are on each page of a first novel, and that's something I respond to strongly. *The Graduate*, *The Flim-Flam Man*, and *Pretty Poison* (changed from the book title *She Let Him Continue*) were all first novels. *The Graduate* was a little-known, poorly selling book before the film was released. After, in paperback, it sold millions of copies.

KNOW YOUR HISTORY: INSPIRATION FROM THE PAST

History has been a fount of inspiration, from the first *Ben Hur* to the recent *Gladiator*. And how many films have you seen about World

War II? A ton. Biographies of the famous (*Patton* and *Lawrence of Arabia*, both films Academy Award winners) and not-so-famous (John Nash of *A Beautiful Mind*) provide a rich vein to be mined. There have been films and TV movies ad nauseum about Lincoln, Hitler, FDR, the Kennedys. Sports fans know of many athletes who have lived colorful, heroic lives—Muhammad Ali, Lou Gehrig. I'm expecting a Lance Armstrong film. One I produced, which combined biography, history, and sports, is *The Great White Hope*. It is about the first black heavyweight boxing champion, who incited a wave of anti-black sentiment in post-WWI America.

USE YOUR IMAGINATION: HARVESTING YOUR OWN IDEAS

You can dream up an idea, as I did with *Caveman*. I was watching Johnny Carson's *The Tonight Show* one evening and the late Buddy Hackett was being interviewed. He was a comic, short and fat, but sweet and adorable with an odd, funny way of speaking. I said to myself, "If he were wearing a loincloth, that alone would make me smile." From that wisp of an idea, two years later I was making the movie. Buddy Hackett wasn't even in it. We tested John Lithgow but weren't smart enough to see his talent. But no harm done: We picked Michael Keaton, before his star ascended. Except he turned us down. So we "settled" for Dennis Quaid, who was wonderful and whose career has gone straight up since. Ringo Starr played the lead. At our kickoff party I introduced Starr to the beautiful Barbara Bach, who was also in the film. They've been married ever since. Although *Caveman* was a campy comedy, I guided the script to make sure the story reflected my values: Being smart is better than being strong, and being good is better than being beautiful. (I know . . . why not be both? I agree.)

FRIENDS AND FAMILY: INSPIRATION FROM FAMILY LIFE

You'd be surprised at what some of your friends have lived through and have stories about. One of mine had an anorexic daughter who, sadly, had to be institutionalized. Her older sister, on a visit, discovered she was smoking dope as well, and had the horrible dilemma of whether to keep that secret out of loyalty to her sister or reveal it to the institutional authorities and perhaps help her sister's recovery. I was so struck by that situation that I sold CBS a similar idea for a TV movie, but changed the characters to two brothers. *Between Two Brothers* is the story of a criminal whose brother learns that fact and has to make the wrenching decision of whether or not to inform on his own brother. *Between Two Brothers* gave me enormous satisfaction; it grew out of my heart and head soon after I heard the real-life story of my friend's daughter.

READ THE HEADLINES: INSPIRATION FROM THE NEWS

You can stumble across a story. The newspapers are full of them, although these are generally better suited to TV. Feature films are reaching for, and getting, a global audience today, thus looking for big event films, full of expensive-to-shoot physical action and special effects. Years ago, I was struck by a newspaper story about a teenage boy who got his girlfriend pregnant and wanted to adopt the baby himself rather than allow her to go through with her planned abortion. I produced a very worthwhile TV movie, *Unwed Father,* about that for ABC, but did not need to acquire any specific rights because we created a fictitious story about fictitious characters. I seem to be fascinated by that moral dilemma; years later, I got financing from a British company, EMI, to direct as well as produce a feature film, *Second Thoughts,* on the same subject. To my dismay, I was not clear enough about injecting my own values into that story; the guy in *Second Thoughts* kidnaps the girl and plans to hold her captive until it becomes too late for her to have an abortion. Fortunately, in the film he does not succeed; nonetheless, I was not tuned-in enough to see how unsympathetic his actions were. And I'm pro-choice.

ON STAGE: INSPIRATION FROM THE THEATER

Whenever I'm in New York I see a play almost every night. I adore going to the theater. I've produced four films based on plays: *The Best Man, The Great White Hope, Tribute,* and *Mass Appeal.* Two of them I didn't even see until after I had acquired the movie rights. I first read *The Great White Hope* and *Tribute* (two favorites among my films) long before I saw them performed. What's on and off Broadway is listed every day in the *New York Times,* and if you can't get to see the show, you can usually get a reading copy by tracking down the producer or the playwright's agent.

Just for pleasure, I saw *Mass Appeal* at a tiny theater prior to its move to Broadway. It's the story of an older priest who has lost his faith through his relationship with a fiery young priest and regains it. I'm a sucker for father-son stories, which this in essence also was. I was so moved by the play that afterward I left a note backstage asking the playwright, Bill C. Davis, to please call me. He did so the next day. I told him I'm an irreligious Jew but I so loved his Catholic play that I had to turn it into a film. I went through a lot of ups, such as getting Jack Lemmon to say "yes" in the most charming way: "Larry, who else have you sent the script to?" "No one," I replied. "Good," he said, "because if you had, I'd kill you." I also went through a lot of downs (no studio wanted to finance a talky religious film with no female characters) before a lucky accident got me the money to produce the film. Similarly, *The Best Man,* among my most prestigious successes, also began life as a play with a theme that strongly attracted me; the title, *The Best Man,* is ironic; America rarely nominates the very best man for the presidency, but rather a compromise choice (who, however, often rises to the responsibility).

FILM SCRIPTS: SORTING THROUGH THE SLUSH

There are countless people writing film scripts that you can chase down, including working writers and aspiring writers. That's a labor-intensive task, but there are good stories to be found, if you roll up your sleeves and dig in the slush pile or go through writers' agents or film schools that have strong screenwriting programs. It's sort of like kissing a lot of frogs before you come across a prince or princess.

With the right story and the right writer for your story you'll get the script you want, and you'll be home free. Well, not quite. The business is too competitive for anyone to ever be home free. It's always a fight, but with a strong unusual property it's a fight you can win, and end up making your movie. Barry Diller says a truly good story will always see the light of day. So how does one recognize and choose a good story? I wish I knew . . . I'd have produced only wonderful, successful movies every time out. Unfortunately, no bell rings when you come across a great yarn—nor rings to signal a lousy one.

> *At the core of producing is something my father [the legendary Darryl Zanuck] drilled in my head: a sense of story. Because you can know all the mechanical parts of how to make it happen and put it together, but you gotta have the story. It all begins and ends with that.*
>
> —Richard Zanuck (Thalberg honoree,
> Academy Award–winning producer
> for *Driving Miss Daisy,* nominee
> for *The Verdict, Jaws*)

WHAT ATTRACTS ME TO A STORY

What I do know—indeed all I know—are the stories that attract me. And my attraction, my choices, are always emotional, subconscious. They're usually about someone who wants something very badly and has to overcome obstacles to get it, after which, and because of which, he finds his true self, his inner core, and is changed for the better. I am drawn to characters that are like me psychologically. I'm the AWOL kid on the lam (Michael Sarrazin) in *The Flim-Flam Man;* I'm the weird-seemingly crazo (Anthony Perkins) in *Pretty Poison;* and yes, even though I'm white and Jewish, I'm the black world heavyweight boxing champion Jack Johnson (James Earl Jones) in *The Great White Hope,* as well as the old priest (Jack Lemmon) in *Mass Appeal.*

There's a wonderful story about Tennessee Williams who, after a reading of his play *A Streetcar Named Desire* at a literary salon, was confronted by a woman gushing, "Oh, that character Blanche DuBois. I feel her. I am Blanche DuBois." "Madam," said Tennessee Williams, hand to heart, "*I* am Blanche DuBois!" During the filming of *The Graduate,* a *Life* magazine reporter asked me to describe the leading (fictional) character Benjamin Braddock. In a wise-guy mood, but nonetheless honest, I smiled and said, "That's me." The reporter looked startled, and said, "I'll be damned! When I interviewed Mike

Nichols he said the same thing!" Talk about a producer and director being on the same wavelength! No wonder making the film was such a memorable experience (and would have been even had it not turned out to be as successful as it was).

On the other hand, director Sydney Pollack *(Sabrina, The Firm, Tootsie,* and winner of Academy Awards as producer and director for *Out of Africa)* told me he chooses characters far afield from himself and then, in the development process, kneads the dough of their character toward who and what he himself is. Nichols and Pollack march to their own drummers, as do all the greats, and as you must. Listen to and trust yourself.

> *I would say, in picking a movie, it still gets back to what's in my gut and if I like it. . . . You're sort of saying to the audience inside you, "This is what I'd want to see."*
>
> **—Doug Wick**

The theme of finding one's center attracts me over and over again. I was passionately drawn to *Mass Appeal* because the story is about anyone who has caved in and accepted living without passionate involvement or belief, in this case a Catholic priest giving his congregation pap, corny homilies, until he reclaims himself and begins to deal with his parishioners as real people with real issues. In both *The Flim-Flam Man* and *Pretty Poison* the lead young man, for moral and ethical reasons, voluntarily goes to jail rather than continue with the feckless life he's been leading. These stories appealed to my goody-two-shoes moral code.

CONSIDERING YOUR AUDIENCE

In my introduction I said I don't think about the audience when choosing a story, but most producers do, and you probably should. Even the same Doug Wick who says he follows his gut admits that "If you're being a producer, you have to find out why you're making the film, who you're making it for."

My taste in story selection is not even close to the mainstream. But then that's never been my motivating criteria, although there's sure nothing wrong if it is for you. Truth be told, the more mainstream your taste, the greater chances for success—yours and your films'. When we sent director John Badham *(Saturday Night Fever, War Games, Stakeout)* the script for *Short Circuit,* his opening comment was, "This is a $100 million grosser," and in box-office terms he was pretty darn close. It is very, very warming to sit in a theater and hear an audience palpably embrace your film. *Your* film. Mind you, you have small but critical audiences to please before you can even make your film—agents, writers, directors, actors, financiers, and lawyers.

> *What is it about this story that people are supposed to want to see? Because we're all in the business of giving pleasure.*
>
> —Bill Goldman

Screenwriter William Rose's favorite line was "Aw, that Shakespeare, all he wanted to do is please the folks."

BEING PASSIONATE ABOUT YOUR STORY

> *Without passion, all the skill in the world won't lift you above your craft.*
>
> —Twyla Tharp, *The Creative Habit*

The word *passion* is smeared like mustard on a hot dog by nearly everybody working in the movie business. Producers, executives, directors, writers, even agents often sound like they're on automatic pilot when they talk about how passionate they are for this story or that piece of talent. It seems like every project is "a labor of love." So why are there so few wonderful films?

> *Never mind an Academy Award, they should give an award just for getting a picture made.*
>
> —Billy Wilder (Thalberg honoree; Academy Award–winning director, writer, and producer)

It's very hard to even get a film made, let alone to have it turn out to be wonderful. Many stories, many decisions get watered down or bastardized by groupthink. That's to say nothing of the compromises that you as producer may feel you have to make to get your film on. The key, in pilot's jargon, is to never go "past the point of no return" in compromising the basic, fundamental integrity of your intention.

Many producers can be smitten as easily with the wrong subject as by the wrong mate. But, as with the right mate, passion can grow. The French have a phrase: *"L'appetit vient en mangeant"*: The appetite comes with the eating. I myself have experienced that, when I produced *The Best Man* and *The Flim-Flam Man* back-to-back. In each case, when I started I was more "in like" than I was "in love." *The Best Man,* although it had a great theme and colorful characters, was very talky. *The Flim-Flam Man* was corn-pone rural, and I'm a city boy. But I fell deeper in love with film as I worked on the script and casting. By the time we were editing, each was "my baby." Both films were embraced by the critics and received reviews as good as those I later got for *The Graduate.* But, unlike *The Graduate,* both were commercially tepid. Neither *The Best Man* nor *The Flim-Flam Man* was a personal mistake; I'm inordinately proud of both. But United Artists and Fox, respectively, might have made a commercial mistake in deciding to finance those pictures.

Then again, possibly not. David Picker, when he was production head at United Artists, quotably said, "If I had made the twelve pictures I turned down instead of the twelve I green-lit, I probably would have had the same success/failure ratio." It's far easier to think up something clever like that to say than to pick a box-office winner, which is why I counsel you throughout this book to pick what and who you like. And if your passion is genuine, you'll know. As Shakespeare said, "Who ever loved that did not love at first sight?"

HOW DO YOU CONTROL THE STORY?

YOU CATCH MORE FLIES WITH HONEY THAN VINEGAR.

—PROVERB

TAKING AN OPTION

There's no magic to taking an option. Generally, you pay money. Buying an option on a book or a script is no different than buying an option on a car or anything else. There are only three salient issues involved: How much are you paying to have exclusive rights to control the project, for how long a time, and how much do you have to ultimately pay to own it outright? Of course the negotiation can be complex, but you've likely been negotiating your whole life, whether it's which movie to see with your boyfriend or girlfriend, or trying to buy something for less than the stated price. Be sure to put every deal in writing, no matter how much you trust the other person. They could be struck by lightning that very night, and you'd have no proof that you legally control your desired object.

The deal memo can be a single page and often is, especially if you negotiate and write it up yourself. Or it can be as thick as a book, as some entertainment lawyers are wont to do, trying to cover every imaginable contingency. You may think you only want the movie rights, but the deal better cover videocassettes, DVDs, television, paid and free TV, and more, in every country in the world. Just to be safe, lawyers now put in language to cover any means of transmitting images that have not yet been invented, and beaming to planets not yet inhabited.

Most decent-sized libraries will have a book on contracts that you can resource. Whenever possible, I do my own negotiating because I'm experienced and I like to judge the situation moment by moment, if need be. That's only for the main points. The bundle of other rights and protections (e.g., for advertising and publicity) I know less about, and surely not the requisite language, so I leave that for the attorneys—mine or the studio's. I've successfully concluded deals in one phone call or one meeting, and I've had others drag on for months and months. There's no rule of thumb. Old-time comedy novelist Max Schulman said it charmingly in one of his early books: "How long should a man's legs be, Mr. Lincoln?" To which Lincoln replied, "Long enough to reach the ground, son."

The way it's usually done is to take an "option" on the motion-picture rights for a certain length of time, rather than trying to acquire the story outright. That will give you control, and control is the name of the producer game. Control is what you want and need. Control means having a legal piece of paper that says you own something, whether it be a condo or motion-picture rights to a story. That is, irrefutable proof that you are the owner, even if you owe a large mortgage on your home, or a large payment is due upon the exercise of your option on a book or script.

No one gives anything away for free. You'll have to pay some money up front, customarily 10 percent of the ultimate purchase price, but you can surely try for less. You want to make sure the option includes all motion-picture and television rights, and for as long a time period as possible. The owner almost always keeps print publication and live performances on stage and radio for himself. The option payment is applied against the purchase price, if you choose to pick up the option and make your movie. If you don't pick up your option, the owner keeps the option money, and you have no hold on the property. It's smart also to negotiate for additional extension time.

Ultimately, you will have to pay the big money. But you won't have to pay it; the studio will. If you have a good nose for story and trust your instincts, you may want to buy a story that nobody else seems to want. In that case, you may be able to option it for virtually nothing, especially if you're persuasive. As George Burns once said, "The main thing is sincerity. If you can fake that, you got it made."

The development process can take a long time. You want to give yourself enough time to have a screenplay written and find someone—a studio—to put up the money to make the movie. Sometimes that happens early on, but nearly always to an established producer with a track record and who has studio relationships. You should try to get an option for a couple of years, but at the least for one year, renewable for a second year. As an inducement to get a free or inexpensive option, you can be generous about the actual purchase price. You want the seller to feel that there will be a pot of gold at the end of his rainbow. I feel it doesn't much matter if your film's budget is $3,025,000 instead of $3,000,000 or $27,100,000 as opposed to $27,000,000, if the extra $25,000 or $100,000 you offer the writer gets paid *only* when the film is made, it enables you to tie up control of the story you love.

> ***Owning is critical. You must own something, even if it's just the ether of an idea. . . . You can try to create your own ideas or find something that you can be part of . . . an idea, book, or piece of material that you can own in a way that you, too, are giving birth to it.***
>
> **—Brian Grazer**

Even if you envision a minuscule budget of, say, under a million dollars, it doesn't matter much whether the author gets paid $5,000, $10,000, or even more for an option. A flexible rule of thumb is that you should spend 5 percent of the total budget for the story rights and screenwriter combined. Common sense says you can always raise your offer, so start low enough to give yourself room to maneuver and raise if necessary to close the deal. As they say in golf, "Never up, never down." In putting, you must stroke the ball strongly enough to reach the hole. Each deal will be different. Carefully assess the players involved and any potential competition and be cautious about out-negotiating yourself by making an offer so low as to be insulting, causing the author or his agent to walk away from the deal. There are even rare occasions on which you should overpay. William Goldberg, a famous trader in rare diamonds, summed it up best: "Anybody can try to buy a ten-thousand-dollar stone for ninety-six hundred dollars. The real feat is to pay ten thousand five hundred dollars if you know you'll later regret not having bought it."

If the story gets your blood racing, you want to control it. That's what makes a producer like Scott Rudin the genuine article. He'll mortgage his home to capture a story he's passionate about. Often, and usually, a prelude to making the offer is to sell yourself. For me, it's based on my track record. For you, it's your enthusiastic passion, your energy, your desire, maybe your creative approach. Years ago, I read an aphorism: "In every relationship, there's one who loves and one who lets himself be loved." You're the lover, and if your love is genuine, the other person (the author, the agent) will recognize it and be impressed by it. I know, I know, I'm full of these analogies, and some are even corny, but I've lived by them and succeeded with them, and that's why I'm sharing them with you.

OBTAINING THE RIGHTS

There's no point in developing a script based on a story you don't own. It's like having a car parked in front of your house, which you polish and buff to within an inch of its life, only to have your neighbor jump in it and drive off. Here's where producing starts to require your detective skills. The author owns the motion-picture rights to his own book, but who is the agent who represents those rights? Try the publisher, the library, the Author's League, or the Internet. If you can contact the author directly, great. Get him or her on your side, as ultimately that's whose decision it is. Convince the author of your appreciation for his talent, and maybe lay out your plan to get it made (if you have one). If the author feels your enthusiasm, you'll end up negotiating with his agent or his publisher.

As I've said, you want the longest possible option. Nothing happens as quickly as you'd like—at least it hasn't for me. Obviously, you want to try for the cheapest possible price without blowing the deal, especially if it's out of your own pocket. In any negotiation, you can always raise your offer, if need be. Even if you walk away from the deal as a negotiating tactic, there's nothing to stop you from acceding to their demands a few days later. Maybe the book you want is so old that no one has ever expressed an interest in the movie rights, and you can get a freebie. Convince the author's representative and the author that your enthusiasm and energy might get this otherwise fallow book made into a movie, and a good one at that. You might even choose to make the author your partner and share any future monies earned on some percentage basis, rather than having to lay out money of your own.

MAKING IT ON YOUR OWN

The only time I put up my own money for an option was for *The Graduate*. Even though the novel had already been published, to little recognition and poor sales, I could not convince the publisher (David Brown at New American Library before he became David Brown, studio executive and renowned producer) to give me a free option, so I put up $1,000 of my own money. And believe me, at that point in my life, I felt a tightening in my throat doing it. But that novel spoke to me. I wanted, needed to control it—and it proved to be a better-than-okay investment.

If you can think up an idea, it's yours for free and forever. It nonetheless pays to protect yourself by registering the idea with the Writers Guild, or at least writing it down and sending it in a registered letter to yourself, never unsealing it unless you have to prove legally that someone has stolen your idea.

> *For me, the idea is the employer of everything—everything and everybody. When I really had nothing, when I exhausted every option, my uncle said, "Look, you've got nothing, kid! You don't own anything. You've got no money. You can't buy anything. The only choice you've got is to write something that you can hold in your hand." So I wrote several stories that became movies. Sometimes I just got the "story by" credit.*
>
> **—Brian Grazer**

Owning gives you power. Sylvester Stallone has been a movie star for almost thirty years because he wrote, and thus controlled, the original *Rocky* script. He refused to sell it many times, and for a lot of money, until and unless whomever bought it agreed to let him star as Rocky. Stallone's courage, gambler's instinct, and control got him where he wanted to go.

PITCHING THE IDEA WITHOUT AN OPTION

Once you're an established producer (not necessarily easy to do so; that's why you're reading this book), you can try to sell something you don't own if it's "a free ball," meaning no one else owns it yet. That's what I did when I solicited Twentieth Century Fox to buy *The Great White Hope.* Although the play got some critical attention at the small Arena Theater in Washington, D.C., very few movie people had a chance to see it during its brief run. I myself had only read it. But I got Twentieth Century Fox to shell out $1 million on my behalf. That was just to acquire the rights; they spent another $8 million to make the film. (So much for the 5 percent rule of thumb.)

Conversely, on a trip to London, very early in its run, I saw the play *Amadeus* and fell in love with it. Immediately upon my return to Los Angeles, I went to every studio and raved about the play and what a great film it would make. But I struck out everywhere. Guys in powdered wigs and silk pants, and serious classical music? No way. I was at the top of my game with attendant cachet at that time, but there were no takers. So I gave up—not a good thing to do if your passion is genuine—and mine was. Later, Saul Zaentz, a very selective and classy producer, pulled together the financing and made a fabulous movie, with the brilliant aid of two-time Academy Award–winning director Milos Forman. Frankly, their movie turned out better than the one I had in my head, so I salute them. I consoled myself with the fact that Saul Zaentz couldn't get conventional studio money, either, and had to piece together the financing. But he did it, like the skillful producer he is.

Without owning the projects you submit, however, you are vulnerable. When David Begelman was running Columbia, I submitted a story to him that he smoothly turned down. A short time later, he made a deal for the very same story with another producer, a good and successful one but, more importantly, a friend of David's. Begelman was a charmer, but he was also an unctuous scoundrel; I should have known better than to trust him after my dealings with him for Judy Garland, which I discuss in a later chapter. Most people in life earn their reputations.

There are, of course, stories that are in the public domain, available to all. Copyrights are finite and do run out. And if you're interested in, say, doing a movie on the life of Christ or Moses, you needn't acquire any rights at all—as Mel Gibson well knows, several hundred million dollars later.

NEGOTIATING

Generally, I always prefer negotiating deals myself, whether for my services or to acquire the rights to a book or script. The perceived wisdom is that that's a mistake. And I don't disagree. It's just that I always like to see the whites of their eyes; it enables me to better judge the tenor of the other person's position, and thus allows me to decide my own flexibility, rather than relying on relayed information. Again, I don't necessarily advise it, but it is how I like to work. I do not want to lose a deal because of how an intermediary presented my offer, or because information was relayed inaccurately.

There's another reason I like making deals myself: I never seek the very top dollar or very best deal for my services, and sometimes a lawyer's or agent's own ego or need to win or set a precedent takes over and can blow a deal. Producers are well paid, if and when they make a movie. When the prevailing top fee for producers was, say, half a million dollars, I was never unhappy if I got "only" $450,000. I made my movie (the object of the exercise), and where I come from, $450,000 is still a lot of moolah. I never try to get the negotiating edge on anyone; on the other hand, I sure don't want anyone to get the edge on me, so I am reasonably wary and do my homework to get all the necessary facts of the situation. When I was new, still an agent, I heard that a top MCA agent, Berle Adams, was an ace negotiator. I solicited a meeting with him and asked what his secret was. He laughed. "Either I want them more or they want me more," he said. And that's usually the case.

HOW DO YOU DEVELOP
THE SCRIPT?

A CAMEL IS A HORSE DESIGNED BY COMMITTEE.

—SHOWBIZ SAYING

SCREENWRITERS

Okay, so you have the rights, but who is going to write it? Do your homework. What movies have you seen where the writing struck you as being particularly good, or in some way apt or congruent for what you have in mind for your movie? Contact agents who represent writers and read samples so as to become savvy about whose work you like. Bill Goldman says, "Talent jumps off the page." Since you're a newcomer, you'll have to sell yourself to the literary agents, too. You probably don't have the money to hire a writer. Where can you get it? From the studios, of course, unless you have some unsophisticated friends you can hit up. But the studio execs don't know you, so how do you get to them? Most likely, by getting to someone whom they do know, such as an already established producer. But you don't know those people, either, so what to do? I can't tell you, but successful, entrepreneurial, would-be producers, myself included, do it every day—through enterprise, imagination, and hustle. I am very big on direct frontal approach, a brief, catchy fax or e-mail. (So is my agent. That's how this book came about.)

I see my job working with a screenwriter as helping the writer realize his intention. Mind you, I have my own intention, so hopefully I will have chosen a writer who shares it. Developing the script with the writer is, for me, one of the best and most satisfying parts of producing.

> **About sixty percent of my job is development. There's nothing more fun.**
>
> —**Doug Wick**

Nor is there anything more difficult. And too many times, it seems to take forever to get it right. Most producers, including me, think they're pretty good at developing. Mike Ovitz, at the peak of his CAA power, told me "Larry, you're a good developer; that's why you'll always make pictures." Hey, we all have an ego; I liked hearing that from someone as powerful and successful as he, even if he was only buttering me up. But he proved to be correct. If you choose wisely in the first place, and know how to develop a screenplay, you'll have the most powerful magnet to attract everything else needed to make a film—director, stars, and financing.

> **I respond most to a producer who has some kind of honesty, where he'll say, "Listen, I have to have a star for this. I know it's not a star project. We have to build up the star. I can't get it made without a star." Whatever it is, I want to know the producer's needs.**
>
> —**Bill Goldman**

There are as many ways of working with a writer as there are food choices at your local deli. Your goal, obviously, is to get the best possible work that the writer is capable of. I always choose someone based on their best work, even if I've read other scripts of theirs (or seen films, in the case of a director) that I don't like. Why? Because I have confidence that I will be able to get their very best work out of them. Chutzpah? Perhaps, but a producer's got to have at least a little. There's a famous story about Samuel Goldwyn telling a writer who had just delivered a draft of his script that it wasn't good enough. The writer rewrote, and turned it in again, only to have Goldwyn complain yet again that it wasn't good enough. So the writer did a third rewrite. When Goldwyn said that also wasn't good enough, the writer exploded: "Dammit, I've worked my tail off;

that's the absolute best I can do!" "Good," said Goldwyn, "that's what I wanted in the first place."

Otto Preminger, a journeyman director but a great producer (*The Man with the Golden Arm,* etc.), felt he should always accommodate himself to the writer's way of working. That's an enlightened method, but, right or wrong, I'm more controlling than that. After picking a writer I think sees the material the same way I do, I ask for an outline. It can be just a couple of pages, but I want to know who is doing what to whom, and why. Most people in Hollywood talk about a script in terms of the classic three-act play structure:

(1) Trouble/dilemma
(2) Complications
(3) Solution/resolution

Solution/resolution is nearly always a new beginning (tomorrow is the first day of the rest of your life), as in *Midnight Cowboy* or *The Graduate.* Or, the resolution can have finality, as in *Easy Rider* or *Butch Cassidy and the Sundance Kid.* Occasionally, but rarely, the resolution will be ambiguous, as in *Rashomon* or *The 400 Blows.* Sometimes an ending can have it both ways, with the finality of death but also a new beginning—for instance, if the protagonist's spirit lives on by passing the torch of his ethos, as in *Braveheart* or *One Flew Over the Cuckoo's Nest.* The writer's outline tells me, I hope, that the writer and I see the story the same way. However, I don't want the writer to feel that he or she must slavishly follow the outline.

Once the writer starts the script, if the characters and the writer's imagination take the story in some new, surprising direction, that's okay with me. I want to encourage, not stifle, the writer's creativity. But I do like to see each act as the writer finishes, so any possible new script direction doesn't go too far down a road I don't want to travel. After all, I started the project; it's my baby. And we do have our outline to fall back on. How I tell them, how I interact with a writer, goes back to "whatever works." Obviously, a gentle nudge is better than a sledgehammer.

We writers are very insecure. It depends on the way the producer deals with me. If he lets me know he loves me, if

he lets me know that he really likes part of the script . . .
he might hate the whole thing, but if he says, "Hey, this
part over here, I wish we could make it really better" . . .
you want to kill for him.

—Bill Goldman

You have to accommodate the writer. Each writer has his or her own pace, rhythm, and method for solving problems. I produced *The Flim-Flam Man* and *Pretty Poison* almost back-to-back. William Rose, a penetrating, thoughtful writer, took one year to deliver the script for *The Flim-Flam Man.* Lorenzo Semple knocked out a superb draft of *Pretty Poison* in six weeks. Both were book adaptations. *Pretty Poison* was voted the best screenplay of 1968 by the New York Film Critics, and *The Flim-Flam Man* got reviews as good as, if not better than, those for *The Graduate.* Some producers push for delivery of a script; the way I see it, though, whichever writer first said, "Do you want it fast or do you want it good?" said it best. In William Rose's case, I hired him because he had such perceptive clarity about what the story needed. *"The Flim-Flam Man,"* he told me, "is the story of a charming old con man who takes up with a young neophyte and teaches him the tricks of the trade. What the script needs is for the audience to see that this kid learns everything there is to learn about con from the old man, but turns his back on that kind of life even though he admires, respects, and even loves the old flim-flam man." I replied, "Wow. You got the job." It took him one year to solve that problem, and solve it he did, brilliantly.

I like to sail into the eye of the hurricane whenever a screenwriter and I encounter a problem. Rather than try to sweep some unwieldy or untoward situation under the rug, I try to make sure we deal with it and at least acknowledge it in dialogue. I learned the technique from the multitalented Joe Mankiewicz, Academy Award–winning producer-writer-director *(All About Eve),* who worked under the strict Hays Office moral code, yet managed to insert strong sexual content in his films. He succeeded in doing so by having another character say, "It's wrong what you're doing. Don't you know that it's wrong!"

What you never want to do is what a so-called creative executive at Sony-Columbia did in a first story meeting: Before the writer uttered a word, the executive began telling him what, where, when, and how to tell the story. I immediately jumped in, saying, "Hey, let's hear from the writer. We're buying his talent and ideas; there is always time to say if we don't like a particular idea or approach and offer one of our own." It'd be a juicier story if I gave the name of the exec, but to what purpose? Suffice it to say, that exec was let go from the studio within a year. But this is Hollywood; he moved on to head a major star's production company. They call that "failing up."

When you can work with good people, you can never just tell them to turn right or turn left; you have to argue your case.

—Doug Wick

NARRATIVE DRIVE

I like strong narrative drive, even though some of my very favorite films are more internal and meandering, like *The 400 Blows, Terms of Endearment, 8 1/2, Wild Strawberries,* or *Lost in Translation.* One of the greatest filmmakers to never win an Academy Award, Alfred Hitchcock, felt that making a movie was "like telling a story to your seven-year-old niece, sitting on your knee. If at any point in the telling you stop, you want her to eagerly ask, 'And then what happened?' "

Arthur Miller, one of America's greatest playwrights *(Death of a Salesman, All My Sons),* in his preface to his collected plays, likens a writer to a district attorney trying to convict someone for murder. His jury is the writer's audience. The DA only introduces questions that will help his chances of conviction; he does not ask if the suspect was a good husband, a good father, a charitable person in the community. Like all aspects of moviemaking, it's about choice, it's about selectivity.

So, how do you develop a script? Very carefully. There's a reason most, if not all, scripts go through draft after draft. It was Ernest Hemingway who said, "Writing is rewriting." (I relearned that one writing this book!) Similarly, Hugh Jackman, a smash Tony Award–winning success on Broadway singing Peter Allen's songs, self-effacingly but accurately said, "I don't think I'm so talented I can transcend the material. If the music's not good, it doesn't matter who's out there singing it."

If you're going to tell me a story about your first date, your first job, your first sexual encounter, you want it to be clear, compelling, and entertaining, and to have me, the listener, satisfied at the end. That satisfaction doesn't have to mean happy; the classic movie *A Man for All Seasons* ends with the leading character, Sir Thomas More, being executed. But it's an execution he chose rather than desert his personal beliefs of truth and justice. I, the audience, felt ennobled and enriched living through his experience.

There have been many books written about screenwriting, but some of the best and most successful writers have neither read them nor formally studied dramatic construction. The craft, of course, can be learned, but not the skill, the art. The great Ernest Lehman began writing for New York press agents, and then moved on to short stories, one of which he sold to Hollywood, starting his movie career; the classic *North by Northwest* was his original. He gave me an important touchstone about script development: "Each scene should be an arrow into the next scene."

Think about that, and then think about it some more, and it will make great sense. Here's the best example I know of: Three friends are having a heated discussion, which leads to an argument, during which one pulls a knife, stabs another, and then flees. That's pretty damn dramatic, right? Wrong. It's theatrical. But what would make the scene a dramatic arrow into the next scene would be for the remaining person, after the stabbing, to say, "I'm going to get that son of a bitch if it's the last thing I do." Now people are leaning forward in their seats, saying, "Whoa. What's he going to do? How's he going to get him? What's going to happen next?"

A long-ago Paramount exec, D. A. Doran (father of producer Lindsay Doran . . . the apple doesn't fall far . . .), explained development to me: "Act one, you get somebody up a tree, act two you throw rocks at him, and act three you bring him down from the tree." Mind you, that's pretty classic, standard stuff—Drama 101 structure. It's used often because it works. That simplistic but basic formula allows for very different twists and turns, which, again, cannot be taught. Only you—the producer—and/or the writer and director, can conjure up and decide what kind of tree to put your character in; what kind of rocks to toss at him, what size, and in what order; how to get him down from the tree; what change your character goes through; and what it is, if anything, he—and hopefully your audience—has learned in the process.

You should see some movies. They're part of the literature; they're part of our culture. And there are things to be learned. I studied the Clark Gable/Spencer Tracy/Myrna Loy classic *Test Pilot* while developing the *Butch Cassidy and the Sundance Kid* script with Bill Goldman. Its theme of two guys in a dangerous profession, both in love with the same girl, was applicable to us thirty years later. I once overheard a well-known director say, "Let's run *The Hustler* again and see what we can steal [from writer/director Robert Rossen]." But do remember what one wag admonished: "If you're gonna steal, make sure you only steal from the best." The World War II classic *Thirty Seconds Over Tokyo* (1944) and the Western epic *Red River* (1948) both had—I'll be damned—the exact same scene. Before the training mission to prepare for the climactic bombing raid in *Thirty Seconds Over Tokyo*, Spencer Tracy's dialogue was, "Men, this is the roughest, toughest thing you're ever going to have to do in your life. If anyone wants to drop out, do it now." In *Red River*, John Wayne's dialogue was, "Men, this is the roughest, toughest cattle drive anyone's ever undertaken. If you're not up to it, drop out now." Both worked equally well, as each was right for the drama. There are probably parents who have advised a son or daughter, "The film business is the roughest business in the world. If you can't stand the gaff, you ought to drop out now."

ADAPTATION

Even though it can be easier to adapt a novel into a screenplay than to start from scratch, it ain't necessarily so. The more solid and strong the book, the easier the adaptation, unless the book is so massive that whittling it down becomes a problem. A novel should, and often does, give you some semblance of a story line and, hopefully, rich characters. But there's still the problem of selection and compression in trying to figure out what will work for a movie. Ernie Lehman, who brilliantly adapted the musical plays *The King and I*, *The Sound of Music*, and *West Side Story*, as well as the novels *Executive Suite* and *Somebody Up There Likes Me*, said, "Sometimes the best adaptation is changing nothing. Other times the best is changing everything." Really helpful, huh?

So where's the bell that chimes to tell you what to do? There ain't none. Ninety percent of the screenplay for *The Graduate* came verbatim from the book, but that in no way diminishes Buck Henry's screenplay (Calder Willingham also got writing credit). The tone of the movie, through casting and through directorial emphasis, became completely different than the tone of the book. In the novel, Benjamin Braddock's character was a whiny pain in the ass; I wanted to spank him. In the movie, he may have been feckless, but he was vulnerable and sympathetic.

Conversely, the novel *The Flim-Flam Man* gave us a relationship and some incidents, but it took the inventive construction of writer William Rose *(It's a Mad Mad Mad Mad World, Guess Who's Coming to Dinner, The Ladykillers)* to turn out a script that was a cohesive whole building to a dramatic, satisfying climax. Likewise, on Broadway *The Best Man* was a lightweight comedy, albeit about a pertinent political issue, but on film it became a trenchant drama.

A novelist has two big advantages over a screenwriter. The first is that he can write what a character is thinking, whereas a screenwriter has to be explicitly clear in dialogue and action (but subtly and artfully) to accomplish the same thing. I remember in the screenplay for my first film, *The Young Doctors*, Joseph Hayes wrote the stage direction, "As the tension mounts," but he didn't have dialogue or action that showed tension mounting in that particular scene. This is the same Joe Hayes whose novel *The Desperate Hours* became a huge Broadway stage success and an excellent and successful film starring Humphrey Bogart and Fredric March, under the direction of William Wyler. Which just goes to show that even the best sometimes screw up. It's the producer's job to keep those screwups to a minimum. The second advantage a novelist has over a screenwriter is length, the sheer number of pages. Most screenplays are roughly 120 pages, with a lot of white space. When's the last time you read a novel that short?

Often a producer will hire the writer of a novel to do the screenplay adaptation. After all, who knows the material better than he? Sometimes, you can make a better deal that way. But I subscribe to what novelist Calder Willingham once told me: "Doing an adaptation of your own novel is like performing an appendectomy on yourself." I prefer a fresh sensibility, a new look at the material. I assume the novelist has given us his very best shot, and now I want to look for ways to improve upon it, if possible.

ENGAGING THE AUDIENCE

A writing device I love is dramatic irony. That's when the audience
knows something a character on screen doesn't, and it pulls the audience into the story. Rent the classic old comedy *The Lady Eve*, by
Preston Sturges. It utilizes dramatic irony at least half a dozen times
to funny, involving advantage. That old master storyteller Hitchcock
said, "Suspense is nearly always better than surprise." In fairness,
suspense was the genre he owned. The best example of the difference between suspense and surprise is this: A guy is running along,
and slips on a banana peel and takes a fall—a funny surprise. But if
that same man is running along, then we show the audience the banana peel, cut back to the man running, getting closer, then back to
the banana peel, then back to the man, who slips and falls, that's
suspense. It involves the audience in a more direct way, and for a
longer time. It's also an illustration of dramatic irony. We the audience know about the banana peel, while the character doesn't. In
that case, you get two for the price of one.

At the end of Charlie Chaplin's great *City Lights*, we the audience
know that the blind flower girl he befriended can now see thanks to
the operation he lovingly, but unbeknownst to her, has paid for. Having been blind, she doesn't know what Chaplin looks like, so when
she now sees him, she of course does not recognize him as her bene-
factor. Then they touch and she realizes that it was he who earlier
befriended her. But until they touch, I—and I'll bet the whole audience (my students)—was leaning forward, using body language,
silently shouting, "He's the guy! He saved you! He loves you!" It's
heartbreaking and wonderful even though they do not get together at
the end. As I write this, my blood is racing, just thinking and talking
about such a terrific movie. That's why I wanted to make movies—
the art, the pleasure, the excitement—and that's why I feel so very
fortunate, having been able to do just that my whole life.

I'm afraid I can't tell you how to develop a script any more than I
can tell you how to dress for a party. You know the difference between a dress-up affair and a casual one. But my dress-up attire is
different from yours. I don't like jewelry, so I never wear cuff links, a
tie clip, or a ring. Some of you would wear all that, plus chains
around your neck. Similarly, my idea of funny probably differs from

yours. I like humor that is subtle and basically real, not wild, zany farce. I never liked the Marx Brothers, but I really get Billy Wilder's humor, or James Thurber's.

Having said that, and meaning it, I will nonetheless give you some advice on script development.

CLARITY

My main axiom is clarity. Make sure the stories you want to tell, the points you want to make, are crystal clear. A newspaper reporter's rules are ones I swear by: Who, what, where, when, why? I don't care if you're working with the best screenwriter on the planet, if you don't understand something in the script, there's a good chance others won't, either. I often ask who is doing what to whom, and why? Although it's nice if you have a good—perhaps better—idea/suggestion to offer, it's not mandatory. You can simply say to the writer, "I don't get this."

Once in a while, if the writer is thin-skinned, you might arouse his wrath, but as they say in sports, "No harm, no foul." If you do have an idea or suggestion, offer it gently, as a question, a possibility. The writer's rejection of your brilliant idea doesn't mean you can't revisit it a week or a month later. That's what I do because I've learned, the hard way, that if I don't like a scene on the page, I won't like it when it's filmed, I'll be bothered by it when I see it in the dailies, then again in the rough cut, and if it's still in the final version of the film, I'll be annoyed as hell that we weren't smart enough to cut it or I wasn't dogged and persistent enough in cajoling and persuading the writer and director to improve it.

The current vogue and blockbuster success of the special-effects-laden, science-fiction superhero films notwithstanding, movies are pretty much a realistic medium. The mere act of photographing something makes it real to the eye. Even the zaniest, most farcical comedies should have their own internal reality and logic. Neil Simon, arguably the most successful playwright who ever lived (I'm not saying he's better than Shakespeare!), always asks himself whether his characters are doing what people do, and saying what people say.

CONFLICT

If the book—the story—you've optioned doesn't have much conflict, look for ways to insert some into your script. Conflict is what drives most drama. A classic acting exercise is two people in a room, and after a disagreement one gets up to leave, but the other doesn't want him to go. Does he jump in front of the door and bar the exit? Does he apologize and try to sweet-talk him into staying? Does that person forcibly grab the other? The point of the exercise is that two people who want opposite things always make for an interesting situation. That's why, in my opinion, professional football and basketball are the two biggest forms of show business in America. Every single play, every moment, contains conflict and great suspense. Both teams want to win, but there can be only one winner, and the game often isn't decided until the final minutes.

You should carry that philosophy into your script. Your leading character is the home team, the one the audience is rooting for. They want him to win whatever it is he's going after. Or, if he loses, they'll accept it if it is for a noble, understandable reason (e.g., Montgomery Clift's death at the end of *From Here to Eternity*). Try to create colorful detail for your leading character. The same things that made Michael Jordan a star will make your character stand out from the run of the mill, and attract the actors you want and need. Make sure your main character wants something very much, and has a goal. He or she should face problems, obstacles, and conflict to achieve that. And after achieving it, or failing, the character is changed, or the direction of his or her life is changed, or both. For nearly all endings are new beginnings—the first day of the rest of your life. Even Donald Duck and Woody Woodpecker run off to a new future at the end. And, I repeat, make all of that clear to your audience, but without bludgeoning them. Clarity with subtlety, with artistry, is the ideal combination. Unfortunately, I can't tell you how to merge those qualities, any more than I can tell you how to be charming and interesting on a date.

STORY AND PLOT

I differentiate between story and plot, although sometimes they are one and the same. For me, story is nearly always about character and character change, whereas plot comprises the events to illustrate, dramatize, and serve the story. Before we started filming *The Graduate*, Mike Nichols said to me, "*The Graduate* is the story of a boy who saves himself through madness." Think about that: The character of Benjamin Braddock is naïve, full of lassitude, drowning in shallow materialism until he's struck by true love and must go "mad" to win and rescue the girl he loves, who happens to hate him for sleeping with her mother.

POINT OF VIEW

A pet device of mine to both attack and examine story structure is to have the writer do a paragraph on what the story is from the point of view of each main character. It's an excellent way to see if and how those separate stories intersect to make a unified, cohesive whole. For example, *The Graduate*:

1. This is the story of bored, restless Mrs. Robinson, who seduces a boy young enough to be her son, only to learn to her horror that he's in love with her daughter. She, of course, thinks him unworthy and tries to prevent the consummation of that relationship.

2. This is the story of a young girl charmed by and attracted to a young family friend, only to learn to her horror that he had an affair with her mother. She is repelled, and on the rebound and with encouragement from her mother, agrees to marry a seemingly ideal, preppy young man, only to be swooped up and saved at her wedding ceremony by her true love.

3. This is the story of Benjamin Braddock, who, at loose ends after graduating college, allows himself to be seduced by the wife of his father's business partner, only to be forced into dating her daughter, with whom he surprisingly falls in love. Undeterred that the daughter is revolted to learn that he slept with her mother, he chases her, woos her, and rescues her from an ill-advised marriage. Thus, he "saves himself through madness."

Those three points of view surely intersect and make a cohesive whole. That's easy to say after that film's success, but I have worked on scripts where examining the story from various points of view showed that they did not connect or add up to a unified story. This exercise is also excellent for making sure you and the writer are on the same page.

Another exercise that is sometimes useful is to outline a script after it's been written. In shorthand form, you can more readily assess if "who is doing what to whom, and why" makes sense, and adds up to the story you wanted to tell in the first place.

Manipulation is a word I simply don't understand, when it is applied to a film. So many people in the business, and out of it, use the word *manipulation* to describe a movie they didn't like. I always hear it used pejoratively: So-and-so filmmaker goes for the cheap thrill, the sentimental tear, or the easy laugh. Easy laugh?! There is a famous utterance: "Dying is easy. Comedy is hard." The plain fact is that every single movie tries to manipulate; some just do it more subtly, more successfully than others. Every filmmaker, myself included, wants you to feel the emotion he has in mind at any given point in the story and, surely, at the end. Whether you are to feel happy or sad, nervous or relieved, is designed first in the script, then in the making, and ultimately in the editing and music. Even the advertising is designed to make you anticipate and be more amenable to being manipulated. So, far from being pejorative, manipulation is merely the marshaling of all the talent and resources of the filmmakers to make you feel (hopefully) exactly the way they—we—want you to feel. The best producers, the best directors, the best writers, are the best manipulators.

WHERE DO YOU GET THE MONEY TO MAKE THE MOVIE?

AYE, THERE'S THE RUB.

—WILLIAM SHAKESPEARE

I've already said that story/script is the most important thing, so how can I now say that money is the most important? But I do say it because without money you don't make the movie. Without it, you most often don't even get up to bat, to develop a script.

I find it exceedingly difficult to get, first of all, set up, to get the development money.

—Kathleen Kennedy

In filmmaking as in politics, money is mother's milk (so said Jesse Unruh, former California congressman). But I don't know how to tell you how to get it for your hoped-for projects. If I did know, I would have made movies of all, and not just some, of the stories I fell in love with. I still have scripts sitting on my shelf that I continue to love, but I can't find people with money to share my enthusiasm about them. That's the plight of every producer, including those at the pinnacle of the producing pyramid.

I still have enough problems getting enough money for the next picture.

—Saul Zaentz

Obviously, some producers have more juice than others, and when you're hot everything gets easier—not easy, but easier. Just like every NBA team wants Shaquille O'Neal, but only a few want the guy off the bench. When *The Graduate* was at the peak of its success in theaters, I ran into a studio head who had turned it down . . . twice. "Larry," he said, "why didn't you make me make *The Graduate*?" I'm smiling to myself as I write this; he was one of the smartest, best studio executives. I said, "I happen to have a new script I love as much as I loved *The Graduate*. Can I make you make this one?" He did read it, and quickly, but he turned me down . . . again. So what else is new?

STAR POWER

Whoever claims to know how to raise money, that's the book I want to read. I know the route to money, of course. And I do know, and have already stated, the kind of cheese you have to put in the trap to catch the money mouse: an actor of sufficient marketing stature for the amount of money your budget requires. Everybody, including you, dear reader, knows who the mega-budget stars are because their names and faces top the largest ads in your newspaper: Jack Nicholson, Julia Roberts, Mike Myers, Nicole Kidman, Will Smith, Denzel Washington. Like the adage "Horses for courses," lesser names are needed for lesser budgets: Jeff Bridges, Dennis Quaid, LL Cool J. Films with budgets under $1 million and direct-to-video movies want names you've probably never heard of but have recognizability to sell (and rent) enough videos and DVDs to cover the cost of production and then some.

Directors also qualify as cheese for the money trap because it is they, along with the story, who attract star actors. Those actors whose salaries are in the stratosphere—$20 million and up for three months' work—want to protect their rarefied place in the heavens, and they feel the best way to do so is with a top director. They're probably right. A handful of novelists are also big-time money cheese: Michael Crichton, John Grisham. It's really quite simple: All you need is an ace director, a genuine movie star, and a marketable story with a great acting role to attract that star and director. Simple? Yes. Easy? No.

STUDIOS

I've always gone for one-stop shopping, generally sticking with the major studios who, when they green light a picture, pay for everything. In today's world, with some films costing upward of $100 million, studios often like to limit their risk, and thus will jointly finance with another studio, as with *Titanic*, with one taking on domestic distribution, the other foreign. Those deals are nearly always done between the studios themselves, but some big-time filmmakers do originate or facilitate those deals. Many smaller independent companies do this as well. Both sometimes do a so-called negative pickup, wherein you have an agreement that the studio/distributor will pay a fixed amount upon delivery of your film. This means, though, that if you're over budget, it comes out of your (or your investors') pocket.

In *A Moveable Feast,* Hemingway quotes F. Scott Fitzgerald: "The rich are very different than you and me." Hemingway replied, "Yes, they have more money." So it is for independent films versus studio fare. The studios have more money, more resources, more marketing clout, more worldwide reach, yet, for a producer, every movie has the same needs. Meaning, do you have a story worth telling? Are you telling it clearly? Are you telling it entertainingly? Do you have good actors? Is the audience going to feel satisfied at the end? Indeed, I tell my students, with conviction, that making their eight- and twenty-minute films is no different than making a $60 million movie for Paramount. The same kind of problems are going to crop up with the tiniest films and the largest; it's a question of degree, not of kind. Whether you have a director of photography at $25,000 a week with every lens that Panavision has in stock or a digital camera with a neophyte operating it, whether you're shooting in Morocco or on a street in your hometown, the question is the same: Are you able to deliver a finished product that is close to your initial vision?

I know I make it sound simple, yet most of the time it really isn't. The best producers and directors have steel in their backbones. I don't care how charming and seductive they may seem to be, and indeed are, in the crunch; when they want something, they generally are steadfast. And I mean *steadfast,* unmovable. Alan Pakula, who I could not have known more intimately, always seemed gentle, sensitive, almost soft, and he was—unless there was something he needed for his film, in which case he dug in his heels and made sure he got it.

In my experience, studios are tight-fisted with everyone except those at the top of the heap. The very day Warner Bros. asked my partner and me to share a secretary, rather than each have one, I visited Robert Redford on the set of *All the President's Men*, where, in my presence, he received a phone call from a studio mucky-muck urging him to please, please take the Warner Bros. jet to Sundance for the weekend.

Studios do dig deep in their pockets at several junctures:

- When they are competing for a hit script or book
- For a script rewrite or polish when they have definitely committed a film for production. They think it's a form of insurance to pay an exorbitant sum to an A-list writer for a week or two or three to touch up or "punch up."
- To rewrite and reshoot a new ending after a disastrous preview (most often for an expensive film)
- To sign a green-light star or director

FOREIGN RIGHTS

There are sales agents who, for a fee, will pre-sell your film to various foreign territories, and that money can finance your film, but not fully. You have to discount those promised future payments to get the production money from a bank, and they tack on additional bank/finance costs. Moreover, pre-sales are nearly always based upon the name power of the stars, and sometimes the director. So you're back to square one. Everyone is pretty savvy: A hot star is worth so much, an up-and-comer or slightly over-the-hill actor less.

There is a virtual pecking order, and the players involved know what that order is. So-and-so is worth X in Europe, but only Y in Asia. Most foreign-advance deals are predicated on major U.S. distribution, which is not easy to get. Many countries have subsidies or tax breaks to encourage production, and wily entrepreneurial producers know how to stitch together multiple financing sources to get their films made. But it can be a long process, and the insiders have the edge. Often, getting a picture financed that way is like the ceiling of the Sistine Chapel, where God's pointing finger is but an inch away from Adam's outstretched hand, reaching for life—but it's a very long inch.

PRIVATE FUNDING

In today's digital world, many films are made inexpensively, for spit and glue. Producers go the route of raising money privately, through relatives and friends or a group of wealthy businesspeople. It's arduous and time consuming, but a lot of films do get made that way. And I don't mean dozens; I mean hundreds. The problem is, once made, many never see the light of day because it's so hard to get distribution.

Top young independent producer Christine Vachon knows a lot about raising money for independent films:

> A lot of the movies we're financing have a lot of moving parts. *Far from Heaven* had an equity financier, a North American distributor—Focus Films—and a foreign sales company—TF1. Each put in a third. It sounds easy, but was very complicated because everyone was recouping from different places. You really have to go after them [to follow up on financing], spend a lot of time having lunch.

Early in the nineteenth century, someone asked J. P. Morgan for a loan of $100,000 (a fortune in those days). J. P. Morgan replied, "Come on, take a walk across the street with me." The man said, "I'm pressured. What good will that do me?" J. P. Morgan smiled and said, "If you are seen walking down the street with me, there are a dozen people who'll loan you the money you need." It's not that easy today, and it's not that easy in the movie business because it's not a loan you want; rather, you want someone to give you a lot of money that you don't have to pay back. But the basic concept of the philosophy holds true: Hang out with the right people. And once you get a toehold, you'll know who those people are.

HOW DO YOU ACTUALLY PRODUCE THE MOVIE?

THE BEST WAY TO MAKE A FILM IS NEVER TO HAVE
MADE ONE BEFORE.

—JEAN COCTEAU

FINDING YOUR DIRECTOR

The director is the person who is going to make your movie. Choosing one is almost as important as choosing a mate. The consequences of a wrong director choice are not as severe or long-lasting, but I assure you the pain and the frustration will be as intense, 'til the end of the movie or death do you part. You've given life to your movie, but to make it walk, talk, and grow up to be president—or at least a rock star—is more up to the director than anybody else. Producing is a balancing act between your parental control (that word again!) and letting your child grow into a life of his own.

I've always felt that one of the hallmarks of a really good director is visual transitions. Just as every scene should be an arrow into the next scene, so should the last visual of one scene carry you into the next. A customary rule of thumb, oft-used, is cutting from outside to inside, from light to dark, from close to far, from quiet to noisy. My very favorite transition is from David Lean's *Lawrence of Arabia:* Peter O'Toole has just held a match to his bare skin, feeling the pain of the burn but not showing it, after which he blows out the match, and on the breath is a direct cut to the huge ball of the sun rising over the horizon (probably shot with a 1000mm lens). It's stunning and startling, and it's organic. The on-the-nose, pedestrian inartistic transition is what Billy Wilder used to make fun of—cutting from a doorknob to a billiard ball.

LOOK FOR A SIMILAR VISION

At a producing seminar I heard Bob Dowling, publisher of the trade paper *The Hollywood Reporter,* say "Producing is the only job where you hire the person you take orders from!" It would be funny, if it weren't so true. Directors in Hollywood are kings of the hill. It was James Cameron who, upon winning the Academy Award for directing *Titanic,* famously proclaimed, "I'm king of the world!" It was a big, nervy statement, but he wasn't far from wrong. Directors do rule the roost.

The big stars want the protection, and more, that working with the best directors can provide. The studios feel the director is the one who has the creative *vision,* a word I never heard uttered in the first half of my career. And they're right to feel that way about the top dozen or two. But in my experience, studios give even journeyman directors much the same due and power. This can be frustrating to a producer, so try to pick a director with whom you're compatible.

The director will—and you'll want him to—reinterpret every sentence, every page, of the script. If you pick well, he's making it better. Often, he's just making it different.
—Doug Wick

Writer Bill Goldman's mantra is "Bury me with a puncher," someone who can "knock you out." He's right, of course. Always go for talent first, compatibility second. But stick with talent that wants to travel the same road as you. Movies, like politics, are "the art of the possible," so you may have to settle somewhere in the middle of that bell curve, a theory of which I'm fond. Just as in everything else, I think there are only a handful of great directors, an equal amount of stiffs, and a much, much larger number of those somewhere in between. Jeffrey Katzenberg, lecturing my students, said, "Even at mighty Disney we hardly ever landed our first choice. Sometimes we'd end up with number fourteen." I would always rather have a middling director on a great script than a great director on a lousy script. I do not think Bob Zemeckis, Ridley Scott, and Kurosawa rolled into one could make a silk movie out of a sow's script. Cotton, maybe.

Sometimes directors, and writers, too, choose or don't choose you for their own, often odd, reasons above and beyond the script or book. When I submitted a book to horror maven Wes Craven, he asked me where I liked to eat. What? Yeah; if we liked the same restaurants, he felt he could work with me. We did like the same places, and so worked together developing a script that, unfortunately, never got made. When I lived in London and was co-producing Judy Garland's final film, *I Could Go On Singing,* I solicited Tony Richardson, a young, hot director *(Look Back in Anger, The Loneliness of the Long Distance Runner)* of the then-new (for England) working-class artists' movement. His first words to me were, "What films do you like?" He would read the book I had brought to submit only if we liked the same films. We did. I passed his test. So he read the book, but that test I flunked. He didn't like it. On to the next.

A FEW LESSONS I'VE LEARNED

Early in my career I micromanaged everything, including—God help me—sometimes placing or defining the activity of extras in a scene. It's counterproductive. My tardy apologies to those directors whom I bugged. Later, I had an epiphany: If I had the perfect director, a combination of the very best of, say, Francis Ford Coppola, Jean Renoir, and Ron Howard, I might still visualize a scene, or the reading of a line of dialogue, a bit differently than they would. So I made a 180-degree reversal. I figured if I selected the right director, and he and I basically agreed about the script and together chose the main cast, the movie would turn out damn well, essentially what I had hoped for. If I chose the wrong director—and I learned this through bitter experience—I could hang around him all day long and actually improve his work . . . but only the tiniest bit, and at the cost of such divisiveness on the set as to make it a lousy experience for everybody, including myself.

What I do in those rare cases when I feel I've made the wrong choice is encourage the director to shoot a lot of coverage, so when it comes time to edit we'll have more choices to improve the film. I had that experience when I chose Irv Kershner to direct *The Flim-Flam Man* at Twentieth Century Fox. I had gone first to Norman Jewison, a friend, because it was a comedy with heart and I thought (and still do) that he was a perfect choice. It was a contemporary story, but Jewison wanted to change the time frame and make it a period story in, say, the 1930s. He was probably right, but I didn't see it at the time. I was obdurate, recalcitrant, insistent on making it contemporary, so Jewison turned down the movie.

Irv Kershner was a gritty, documentary-type director. I greatly admired his work on *The Hoodlum Priest,* and his enthusiasm, so I committed to him for *The Flim-Flam Man.* An incident that should have been a warning sign was so small I didn't pay attention: In our meeting with studio head Dick Zanuck, Kershner, to sell himself, said, "I'm going in for comedy now." I know, it's a tiny thing, but it's like me saying I'm now going in for politics or opera. Kershner was, and is, very talented. (George Lucas—is there anyone smarter than he?—hired him for the second installment of his Star Wars trilogy, *The Empire Strikes Back.*) But as it turned out, Kershner had an elephant's foot when it came to comedy. What should have been funny wasn't nearly enough so, and he and I fought throughout the filming. At one point, Dick Zanuck brought us together in his office to make peace, but, as he told me later, Kershner and I began fighting again as we were leaving his office.

Kershner did shoot a lot of footage—a real lot. We had nearly three hours of rough cut, and ultimately I had to eliminate one entire sequence, of four increasingly elaborate con schemes. In those seemingly nineteenth-century days I, by contract, could re-edit the picture and have two more public previews after the director had finished all his work and delivered the picture, which I took advantage of. Try getting that today . . . they'll throw you out of the office. *The Flim-Flam Man* ended up getting reviews as good as those later for *The Graduate.* Kershner and I are now friends. Isn't there a proverb: "Success has a thousand fathers, failure but one"?

I knew the energetic, talented John Frankenheimer from his early, live-TV, *Playhouse 90* days when I was an agent. He went on to direct the excellent *Birdman of Alcatraz* and *The Manchurian Candidate.* John replaced an equally talented director, Arthur Penn *(Bonnie and Clyde),* on *The Train,* starring Burt Lancaster, who, rumor had it, engineered the switch (the power of stars, even then). John called to say he loved the book I had sent him, and would I please come to discuss it in the French countryside, where he was shooting? Off I went. We had what I felt was a very good dinner meeting, which ended with John telling me to see his lawyer to work out the deal. I left elated; I had nailed him. The minute I returned to Los Angeles, I met with his rep, Frank Wells, a smart, tough but good guy who later became Michael Eisner's right hand at Disney, until he was tragically killed in a heli-skiing accident. It was good that I was sitting because, had I been standing, I would've fallen over when Wells said, "John called me to say he doesn't want to do your project. He never did. He likes you and didn't know how to say no." Didn't know how to say no? He knew how to say "Fly to France to meet with me!"

Conversely, I didn't know Mike Nichols from Adam when I submitted *The Graduate* to him. I sent him the book via his agent, Robby Lantz. Only a few days later, upon returning to my New York hotel late one night, I found a telephone message: "A Mr. Nichols called. He said he likes the book." And I didn't have to travel the length of my hotel room to get a "yes," let alone across the Atlantic!

You might make the director your partner if it helps to entice him. When I made the deal for Mike to direct *The Graduate* I had no financing in place, no nothing. I offered to make him my partner. He committed, and we were off but not quite running, which I detail in a later chapter.

My partner, Stuart Millar, and I chose Franklin Schaffner to direct *The Best Man* based on a couple of TV shows he had done that we liked. After we closed the deal, but before we were to start preproduction, Franklin directed another live TV drama. My partner and I watched, of course—and it was simply awful. We were sick at heart. Halfway through the show we telephoned one another to commiserate. But the die was cast. Thankfully, that die was cast well; Frank delivered a terrific movie. We were right to choose him, despite our momentary insecurity. Frank Schaffner went on to win an Academy Award for directing *Patton.* The moral of the story is that everybody has some clunkers, but not everybody has successes. Having the best collaborators does not guarantee success, but have confidence in yourself to choose your collaborators based on their best work.

PREPRODUCTION

The movie business is unique in that you start a new business from the ground up with each and every film. You begin as a lone wolf, and by the time you're filming there will be 30, or 130, or more people on the payroll (thank God it's O.P.M.—other people's money). And when you've delivered your film to the financier/distributor, you're alone again, hoping to find and fund the next project that will allow you to start up a new business again. The path will be similar and familiar, but the personnel, the destination, and the roadblocks will be quite different.

> *Every picture presents different problems, different personalities. That's one of the wonderful things that keeps us all going, that we have jobs that keep being fresh ones because every project is different.*
>
> —**Dick Zanuck**

Preproduction nearly always determines how smooth or bumpy the ride will be during a shoot. A producer better know where he wants to end up and what kind of picture he wants to make in tone, style, and theme. Without this clarity of purpose (and this applies to many other fields, too), you can't get where you want to go because you don't really know where you want to go. Mike Nichols said it best: "Random is the enemy."

MAKING A GAME PLAN

Preproduction is where you and the director set the course for the movie. Like almost any project in almost any field, start with the big things.

> *If you understand the psychology of the idea, you can persist in its vision.*
>
> —**Brian Grazer**

Most subsequent decisions flow from the initial big ones. What kind of movie are we trying to make—comedy, drama, horror, sci-fi, or a hybrid? Beware of the hybrid; as one of the greatest and most commercially successful Hollywood screenwriters, Ernest Lehman, told me, "The audience comes to the theater and wants to get on a horse. They want to know what kind of horse they're getting on. A comedy horse, a drama horse, or what." That is simple and sage; I think he's right. Except I'm drawn to stories that have an underlying seriousness, yet have humor. I think *The Graduate* is that. In a less successful vein, I led the audience to laugh at the beginning of *Pretty Poison*, only to pull the rug out from under them when an alienated, rah-rah, Pepsi-Cola-ad-looking high-school girl murders her mom. I switched horses on the audience, yet the film actually won the New York Critics Circle Award for best screenplay that year. But, to support Ernie Lehman's thesis, even though I made it on the cheap, the public (as Samuel Goldwyn famously said) stayed away in droves. I always talk with the director about tone. If it's a comedy, do we want it to be wild and woolly, farcical à la the Marx Brothers or Mel Brooks, or do we want it to be more subtle and sophisticated, the kind of tone Woody Allen usually employs (which is more to my taste, even though Mel makes me laugh 'til my sides hurt)?

The director and I also talk about the look of the picture. Once we are in synch about the look, the director will deal more with the production designer and much more with the cameraman. I do participate, though; I like to sit in on the initial meetings, and then the director does the follow-through.

How you make your film is a function of the choices you, with your director, make about the script, casting, crew, locations, and schedule—all preproduction decisions. And you'd better make them with clarity and precision. In World War II, the Germans rained V2 rockets upon Britain. If they were but a fraction off at launch, they landed miles away from their intended targets.

> **[*A producer must have*] the ability to keep a very clear vision of the movie. Directors lean on you a little bit for that.**
>
> **—Christine Vachon**

LOCATIONS

We all like to shoot our movies at the locations that are called for in the script. But here, too, money rears its ugly head. That's why so many current American movies shoot in Canada—labor costs are cheaper, fringe benefits on that labor is less, our dollar is considerably stronger than theirs, and there are Canadian-government tax rebates. In fact, my last two TV movies were essentially forced to shoot in Canada or the financing entities wouldn't have green-lit them. Many European producers, and some enterprising American ones, utilize various government subsidies, which usually dictate where a film will be shot. You have to follow the money, which is why several states (e.g., Louisiana) now offer financial incentives to attract production.

You also go where you can get. You want an army? Some Eastern European countries will supply you with one for free. You want a skilled crew that you don't have to fly round-trip from Los Angeles, and pay for hotels and meals? Texas, Florida, and several other states can supply your needs. Most Hollywood movies do, however, bring key camera and design crew.

When you can't get, you improvise. Nineteenth-century New York no longer exists, so for *Gangs of New York*, Martin Scorsese and Miramax built it. But they built in Rome because of available facilities and cost. Likewise, Romania stood in for South Carolina in Miramax's *Cold Mountain*.

I have filmed in England, Spain, Mexico, and Canada, as well as urban and rural America, and all were, to use my son's syntax, "the same hard." The special issues unique to each country—like visas, work permits, and insurance—are usually handled by the studio, or the producer hires a local facilitator to ease the path. No matter how large the country or small the municipality, they all like the money a film company spends in their community, so most have film offices that are ready, willing, and eager to help. All you have to do is look them up in the phone book.

The Graduate was localed in Berkeley, but the University of California nixed our request to shoot on campus, so we used USC in Los Angeles. When I filmed *The Great White Hope*, the talented, imaginative production designer John DeCuir used Barcelona to simulate Berlin, Paris, and Havana, as we couldn't afford to travel and shoot in all those cities. In old Hollywood, producers and directors who wanted to film Westerns in authentic Arizona or Texas were told by studio moneymen, "A tree is a tree. A rock is a rock. Shoot it in Griffith Park [in L.A.]."

There's much to be said for shooting on sets built on soundstages. You don't have to contend with weather or gawkers, and you can move a wall to get the exact shot the director wants. Fellini, Kubrick, and Hitchcock had the technical know-how to match their talent, and preferred working in the quiet cocoon of the stage. Hitchcock would send a second-unit camera crew with actors' doubles to get any necessary atmospheric location shots. Stanley Kubrick did the same in *Lolita* to establish America as the locale. Stanley, the perfectionist, never left England. Ah, the magic of movies.

SELECTING YOUR CREW

Preproduction is no different from planning the dinner party I devoted an earlier chapter to. If you plan well and organize properly you'll be primed and in the best shape to deal with the many crises that are sure to crop up. As I've said, you start working backward from the planned start-of-photography date. Who is the first person you need? The entire crew is essentially there to serve the director. What does the director need? A camera to film what the actors are doing; sound equipment to record what the actors are saying; places, real or constructed, where the story takes place; and, of course, actors to play the scenes. Those are the major components of a crew, which on a big film can number well over a hundred, if not many more. But a small handful of people can also get together and make a film.

PD, DP, AD, ED

A production manager will do a preliminary budget and help facilitate hiring your key personnel. There are four key creative bulwarks—the production designer (PD), the director of photography (DP), the first assistant director (AD), and the editor (ED)—who, like corner pillars of a building, keep everything upright and steady. Ideally, the producer and director jointly chooses these crew members. But the director, appropriately, should get who he wants for his DP and AD. As producer, I will not (and likely cannot) force upon him my desired choice of production designer or editor. I always have an opinion: I recommend, cajole, entreat, and revisit my suggestions to my director. I win some and lose some, although it's never about winning or losing, but about what is best for the picture. And some I've won have proved to be a mistake, just as some I lost were wrong judgments on the part of the directors.

> *As a producer I can advise and guide or nurture and*
> *influence, but I don't have to make the final decision. I'm*
> *in service to a creative vision, but I share that vision, too.*
> —**Kathleen Kennedy**

Not only has Kathy Kennedy made more films than I, she's also had more major commercial successes. As I said in my preface, I'm continually learning from my peers. If I were working with Spielberg as a director, I would surely operate his way, as well I should. And, in reality, when I've worked with top-ranked directors, I've done just that. There's no way I would try—nor would I succeed—to ram an idea of mine down Alexander Payne's throat.

TECHNICAL HELP

You always want to go for the best technical help you can get, or at least the best your budget can afford. Which makes me reiterate: Trust *your* taste, *your* judgment. The director will often want the same people he's worked with before (as you yourself might). He knows and trusts their work, and can talk shorthand to them. It's his security blanket. Woody Allen seems to work that way, as do many other top (and not-so-top) directors. And the better the director, the easier it is to attract ace people to surround him with. That is, unless your budget limitation forces you to lowball on their pay.

Even if your budget does not allow for the absolute top line producer/production manager, production designer, cameraman, or editor, you can, if you are resourceful, do your homework, and use good judgment, still get a talented person in your price range at each position. Hire the very best people. They will make your picture better, and they will make your life better. In any part of life, nothing beats having a top professional. I could not be more pleased or secure than with my personal team of doctor, dentist, attorney, and accountant. If you choose the right movie team, they will in turn bring along their team, with whom they've previously worked and know to be good. That will facilitate communication. What you need is clear, precise, and timely information so you can make the right decisions, balancing the creative against the physical practicalities. You also want to give communication as good as you get, so everyone on the picture is on the same page.

> *You don't want to play games. You tell them the truth and you want the truth. Tell them to tell you what's going on, that you're not going to think they're a purveyor of bad news solely, but you have to know.*
>
> —**Saul Zaentz**

On the very first picture I produced, I learned that I didn't have to hire every single person on the crew, or tell every actor what time to show up for filming. After the key crew is set, picking the rest is like sending a chain letter: Each department head in turn selects—with the approval of the production manager or the producer—the people who work under him. It's just like General Dwight D. Eisenhower organizing the invasion of Europe in World War II. The cameraman will have his regular operator and his pet first assistant, who will have his favorite second assistant. The sound person, called a mixer, will have his regular recorder, boom man, and cable person. The production designer will have a voice in who is the set dresser, who in turn will have his regular assistant, and the prop man, with his respective regular assistants, and so on.

Which is good because if I were forced to take a test in defining the job of every single person on a film crew, I'd likely get—I'll bet to your surprise—a grade of B or C+. Really. I'm a good leader—organized, thorough, always worried, a people-skilled CEO—but I couldn't perform any single crew member's job. Nor, I'd bet, could Colin Powell, when he was an acting general, repair a tank. But I do have common sense, logic, and impatient energy.

I'm a guy who likes to shake up an equation. If I'm in a meeting with, say, eight people and we break for lunch, upon our return I'll take a different chair than I had before lunch, which then forces other people to do the same. Perverse? Maybe . . . although I surely hope not. But it does or can, I think, sharpen the focus. So it is, sometimes, when a director who continues to work with the same

DP and production designer just might be limiting himself—putting a governor on his creative engine, so to speak—so that he does not "see" beyond his normal horizon.

I chose Marty Ritt to direct *The Great White Hope* because he was an "actors' director," and the play and script was a tour de force for two actors, one portraying Jack Johnson, the black boxing champion, and the other his white mistress (both James Earl Jones and Jane Alexander came from the play to make their debuts in the film). Marty was known for gritty, realistic work. He began as an actor and was an Actors Studio alum. But *The Great White Hope* offered expansive theatricality, the story taking place in London, Paris, Berlin, and Havana, as well as in the United States. I decided to try to marry Marty to a production designer, John DeCuir, who was known for the imaginative size of his work. Marty was amenable, and I felt that the "look" of the film was the better for it. Marty thought so, too.

For less creative reasons I suggested a cameraman to Marty: Burnett Guffey, who was known to be fast, which Marty was not. But Guffey did shoot the wonderful *Bonnie and Clyde,* and that was my ammunition. *The Great White Hope* was expensive for its time ($8 million-plus in 1971, about $80 million today) and, as it was set in the early 1900s, needed thousands of extras, locations in Europe, and a huge crew. The studio, Twentieth Century Fox, and I were fearful of going over schedule. Each day could cost a small fortune. Happily, Marty agreed to Guffey, even though Marty had previously worked with one of the true greats, James Wong Howe. *The Great White Hope* would've looked a bit better with Howe as DP, but we finished very close to schedule. The movie looks fine, and I'm damn proud of it.

The director of photography, oddly, doesn't operate the camera, but sets the lighting according to the mood and requirements of each scene. Thus, he needs a camera operator. The operator needs someone to measure the action and movement to determine focus. And someone is needed to load and unload the film, and keep accurate records thereof. At the bottom rung, someone "claps" at the start of each scene so the sound and the film are synchronized, along with the scene numbers in the script and each "take," for later reference by the editor and director. Alongside that person is the script supervisor, who makes the same notations in the written script. This person also keeps track of directions and details so if scenes are shot out of sequence on different days, everything from hair to props to direction will match that which preceded it.

The camera crew needs electricians to place, move, and adjust the lights, as required by the DP. The chief of these is called a gaffer. Each cameraman has his own favorite gaffer. The gaffer's main assistant is called the best boy. The camera team also requires grips to lay down tracks, to enable the camera to move smoothly and follow a scene.

The sound team is smaller. Someone records the sound; someone places microphones; and someone holds the long pole—the boom—just out of photograph range. As with photography, scrupulous sound records must be kept of each shot and each scene for later editorial use.

The production designer, along with the DP, defines the look of the film, and suggests which locations should be real and which could be more effectively built on a soundstage. It is his job to find those locations, for which he uses an advance location scout, who also negotiates for the use of a particular selected site. Those decisions are first and foremost creative, but must also be practical. Each location needs to be accessible for equipment trucks. For a major sequence in *The River Wild,* we had our own helicopter fleet to ferry the crew and equipment—including crates of lunch boxes for the crew—to a tiny island in the middle of the raging Kootenai River in Montana. The sets built on soundstages are also designed by the production designer, in consultation with the director. Walls need to "fly," or be movable, for the director to get the movement and shots he wants.

A production designer will also work in close consultation with the costume designer so that the color scheme, as decided with the director and producer, is unified and creates the look and mood the director desires. In *The Graduate,* for example, Anne Bancroft's leopard coat was part and parcel of her being a predator seducing Dustin Hoffman, just as the over-the-top gaucheness of her home illustrated the empty materialism of her life.

The set dresser, who chooses the furniture, and the prop person, who selects the miscellaneous objects, both work under the direction of the production designer—who in turn requires the ultimate approval of the director. Each of these crew members usually has an assistant (or, depending on the size of the film, more than one). They do the choosing, but they need others to carry, place, and move.

The actors are the money and require a lot of tender loving care: wardrobe, makeup, and hair. Each of these is a separate department and, depending on the size of the film and the number of actors, can be handled by just one person or as many as twenty—all of whom are under the approval of the director. Not surprisingly, the most important star actors have a very large voice, if not final say, about their individual look and who is hired to achieve it.

On *Mass Appeal,* we had a very young prop guy; ours was his first major film. He was understandably nervous about showing his wares to Jack Lemmon. I tried to pump him up emotionally. A surprisingly short time later, he returned to my office, beaming. "You know what?" he said, "Jack Lemmon told me to pick whatever [prop] I want and he'll make it work." Nothing beats working with a real pro.

All these people and so much equipment require transportation trucks, cars, and enough drivers to compose a small army. The more times a movie company has to change locations, the more expensive it is. Even on a small-crew film, it can take hours, even half a day, to leave one location before the company is set up at the next. Oh, yes, and everybody has to be fed, too, and that is no small matter. Wasn't it General Sherman, during the Civil War, who said, "An army travels on its stomach"?

How do you marshal all these people and all this activity? I'm a bear about information, and communication. I want everyone on my films to know everything, and at the same time. I'll have periodic meetings with those hired, starting with the early handful of us and, later, including the whole army. Everyone must be on the same page, as in any other team sport.

Communication is a paramount skill. A movie's perspective comes down to the producer's ability to keep communication flowing, because you're often the one conveying the director's vision. Not only do you need to make sure people know what's going on, but that the information being passed through the departments via

the telephone game is current and accurate.
Communication falls apart with well-intentioned people
who think they have the right information, but never
understood what the director was asking for in the first
place. That breakdown makes things go wrong in both
minor and major ways, and it's up to you to solve the
problem usually on a tight time frame. I'm always
working toward following through with communication.
　　　　　　　　　　　　　　　　　　　—Kathleen Kennedy

CASTING

The reed that bends with the breeze, lives long. The reed
that stands stiff in the wind, breaks.
　　　　　　　　　　　　　　　　　　　—Chinese proverb

BIG-NAME STARS

As much as you always want the ideal actor for each role, there is the
practical consideration that the studio may insist on someone other
than your choice. In order to get the movie made, you may have to
compromise.

Talent and suitability for a role are not the only reasons actors are
chosen. In fact, these are not even the main reasons. To state the obvious, you have to put, as Harry Cohen said, "fannies in seats."
Every studio and distributor, and thus every producer and director,
are star fornicators. You heard me right. Almost any of the biggest
name stars can get a picture financed—on almost any script. The
more expensive the film, the bigger the names have to be. And, indeed, the bigger the names, the bigger the film usually is. The Mel
Gibsons and Tom Hankses of the world get tens of millions of dollars, and more millions on top of that in perks, which include everything from living and travel expenses for the whole family, plus
an entourage of nanny, secretary, personal trainer, masseuse, and
cook. Every studio wants the same stars. They are considered surefire because they can "open" a picture, so everyone chases them—
including me.

The problem is, you have a lot of competition trying to get those stars. When I lectured at the Polytechnic in Singapore, I truthfully told the students that $99\frac{1}{2}$ percent of the people in Hollywood spend all of their time chasing the other half-percent. They are pursuing the actors who can get a picture financed. You name them (and you can). Agents want to sign them for representation, writers want them to read their scripts, directors want to direct them, studios want them in their films, and producers really want/need them.

> *In comedy, often I create a partner in the star. In drama or thrillers, often I make the director my partner, and then get the star.*
>
> —**Brian Grazer**

The way to get one is to have a stunning script with an acting role that is different, more challenging, and somehow infinitely more appealing than any role the actor has ever played, or even been offered before. But first, you've got to get them to read it. That usually takes a firm money offer, unless you're buddies with the actor or a world-class entrepreneur.

The more important the actor is, the more complicated the negotiation and contract process (double that if both actor *and* director are A-list). The perk package—all the goodies the biggest, most powerful stars (and some directors) command—is in and of itself a protracted deal. If memory serves, when I was an agent for the Frings Agency, Elizabeth Taylor got something like fourteen round-trip first-class transportations to and from her location, to use as she chose—and that is kid's stuff compared to today, when perks can include everything the star's representative can think of. The studio puts up the show of a fight but usually caves because the star is not only the green light for the movie, but leads the marketing charge as well. Billy Wilder made that point about Marilyn Monroe when she was driving the entire production of *Some Like It Hot* crazy with her tardiness and absences, and even not knowing her lines. Wilder told the United Artists brass that he could get a replacement who he guaranteed would always be on time, always know her dialogue, and cause no trouble whatsoever. Who was that, the brass eagerly asked? His seventy-year-old aunt, Wilder replied.

The biggest perk of all is not called a perk, but I think it is one. If possible, the star's manager will often insinuate himself as one of the producers, at a large fee, as part of the negotiation. He will often make little or no contribution, but is thus able to tell the star client that he's not costing the star a penny, as he or she is getting the manager's services for free. This reminds me of a very old song titled, "Nice Work If You Can Get It."

A $40–$50 million movie will likely get off the ground and be very happy with Hugh Grant, Meg Ryan, or Kurt Russell. But for a $80–$90 million film (which also requires more marketing expenditure), you'd better snag Russell Crowe or Leonardo DiCaprio. Tom Cruise in *Mission: Impossible*—that's a no-brainer for any studio, at almost any price. What about Edward Norton in the same project, at the same budget? As good an actor as Tom Cruise is, I think Norton's a little bit better, and as physically skilled. But if I walked in with Norton and a top director, I don't think any studio would go the $100 million-plus for *that Mission: Impossible.*

Down the line, HBO wants movie actors who normally do not do TV. (And they're good at getting them; to paraphrase President Clinton's campaign team, "It's the script, stupid.") The networks—CBS, ABC, NBC—like prestigious actors who rarely do TV, or they like the safety of tried-and-true TV stars like Tom Selleck. Even a $1 million direct-to-video movie wants recognizable, marquee names. There is a ladder of value for name actors that is generally known and accepted, but of course it can change from film to film. John Travolta was down and out just before *Pulp Fiction,* but after, he zoomed right back to the top. Kevin Costner was at the top until *Waterworld,* and even though that movie did acceptable business, all the bad publicity hurt him. Will Ferrell used to be "just" an up-and-coming TV personality, but after *Elf* every studio tried to nab him. So it goes, and likely so has it always gone. Even the NBA is working overtime trying to create and pump up stars to match the golden attendance years of Larry Bird, Magic Johnson, and Michael Jordan.

The right actors can make or break a film. One of the greatest directors of actors, Academy Award–winner Elia Kazan *(On the Waterfront, Viva Zapata!, Gentleman's Agreement),* told me, "Any good actor will know his character, his role, better than the director." Another Academy Award–winning director, George Roy Hill *(The Sting, Butch Cassidy and the Sundance Kid),* wrote me as I was preparing to direct for the first time: "The most closely guarded of directors' professional secrets is that if you put together a really good script with really good actors, seventy-five percent of your job is done."

Even the best script in the world cannot survive a serious error in casting in any major role.

—**Frank Pierson**

In 1998, Jack Lemmon agreed to a television script I had. The material was soft, and I didn't think any network would touch it without a major star attached. But when I walked into CBS and said Jack Lemmon had committed, they fell over themselves telling me how wonderful the script was, and damn if they weren't right to be in the star business; soft script and all, we got huge ratings. Mind you, it was a lovely story, and *The Long Way Home* was a TV movie I'm quite proud of. Jack was, too.

We held out for Meryl Streep for *The River Wild* and the studio, Universal, acceded even though they preferred other, bigger, box-office names. On the other hand, CBS insisted on Patty Duke for my last TV movie. Happily, she liked the role and proved to be wonderful—as always—in *Miracle on the Mountain*.

I once developed a Latino gang story for United Artists. I chose Evan Hunter to write it. He's a pal, but also an ideal choice, having ignited his early career with a similar-themed story, *Blackboard Jungle*. We did the research together at Venice Beach—discovering that the real gang members could be alternately charming and scary. United Artists liked Evan's script, but wouldn't make the film, even at a modest price, given its provocative subject matter. Later, when I was making pictures at Universal, Ned Tanen was head of production, and liked the Evan Hunter script. I wanted a wonderful Latino actor, A. Martinez, for the lead. Tanen nixed that idea, as he, like most, wanted a name.

The young white actor Robby Benson had had surprising success in a small basketball picture, so I sent the script to his equally young agent, Rick Nicita (then starting at CAA, now head of their motion-picture department). He liked the script, and Robby did, too. I invited Ned and Robby to my home for dinner. Ned, a bright, good guy, was a straightforward exec with a sense of humor. Referring to Robby's recent basketball picture, Ned said, "So this kid is a thirteen-million-dollar grosser." (That was a large number for 1985!) I made my picture, but with Ned's actor, as spoon-fed to him by me.

But I paid for it dearly—a white guy playing a Latino! Robby Benson wore brown contacts and skillfully affected a slight accent. Surprisingly, and fortunately, the critics didn't go after us for racist casting. They didn't have to; I was hard enough on myself. I felt I was in the ugly tradition of Al Jolson in blackface singing "Mammy," and the fine Jewish actor Sam Jaffe wearing brown body makeup to portray Gunga Din. However, I had such an emotional investment in the script, I didn't want to give up on it. That's my rationale for the Faustian pact I made. You pay for everything in life, one way or the other.

Another casting consideration is money. You may have $100,000 in your budget for a certain role, but the actor you want might cost twice that. As an inducement, you can try to give an actor better billing than he previously had. Or perhaps the role you're offering is so different, the actor may be willing to cut his price. It's always worth a try. They say that deep down everybody wants to be a director, or thinks he can be. So some producers have nailed the actor they wanted by offering him or her a chance to direct the film. Many actors have jumped at that opportunity, but not all have delivered the goods. Generally, your alternative is to find another actor, just as you do when the actor you love, and who may even want to do your film, is already busy on another film. Who ever said life was fair?

CASTING DIRECTOR

Let's expand my list of key hires to include the casting director. A good one will

- Give you suggestions/ideas that never would have entered your mind.
- Save you time by bringing in a handful of choices close to the mark, rather than dozens of actors who are totally wrong for the role.
- Be skillful in negotiating deals favorable to the production.

There's a reason Woody Allen uses Juliet Taylor again and again. I worked with her on a small Paramount film, *First Love,* and she brought us Beverly D'Angelo and Swoozie Kurtz for their first film roles, as well as a young new actor, John Heard, who to our amazement turned down the lead to take instead the third role in the film. Everybody Juliet Taylor brought in was not only talented, but on the money for their role. Her work with Woody Allen has become progressively easier, although I'll bet she doesn't agree, as every actor would kill to be in one of his films—and often would take a big pay cut to do so. On the other hand, she has to keep coming up with fresh ideas for Woody so the same faces don't appear again and again. You, as an audience, may not be consciously aware that a film is well cast, but you "feel" it when even the smallest role is real, and interesting.

TRUST YOUR GUT INSTINCTS

Casting, again, goes right back to *your* taste. I think it nearly always is gut, emotional, even if, after the fact, you can articulate why you chose a particular actor. I remember Mike Nichols and I were interviewing a great-looking, sexy actress for *The Graduate*. When she left the room I told Mike, "It's hard to judge her, I'm so damn attracted." He said, "Use what you feel, if it's right for the role." She didn't get the part.

I often interview actors together with the director, but sometimes not. Many directors like to be alone with an actor. It's more intimate, and they are better able to judge the actor's inner qualities and to assess what it would be like working with them. That's fine with me, as long as I get to judge for myself, seeing the director's choices on film or a reading they videotaped. I like that modus operandi. It keeps my judgment fresh, and the director doesn't feel I'm always looking over his shoulder. We then together make the final decisions about whom we want. If you've used the right criteria to choose your director, you will readily agree on the actors. The casting director will also have an opinion worth listening to.

When casting my comedy idea *Caveman*, the very first girl we interviewed was Shelley Long. She hadn't yet done a film, but was (and is) funny and talented. I loved her. But how could I see only one actor for the role and decide to cast her? Well, I couldn't. The director and I must've seen thirty or forty others before realizing Shelley was our girl. She went from *Caveman* to starring in films and, ultimately, on the TV series *Cheers*.

I had much stronger conviction than that, however, about casting Jane Alexander for *The Great White Hope.* I had seen the play four times on Broadway, where it won the Pulitzer Prize. (Talk about guts: The playwright, Howard Sackler, used his own million dollars from the sale of the play to Twentieth Century Fox to finance the Broadway production.) All four times I saw the show, Jane gave a knockout performance (as did James Earl Jones). She had power and vulnerability—and, of course, great talent. Marty Ritt and I were salivating to have her. But Fox wanted to screen-test her before agreeing. In those days I had real chutzpah (you'll have to learn the lingo if you want to work in the biz), and told them, "No. If we test her, you're gonna tell us she's not pretty enough." Jane is very pretty, but not in a conventional Hollywood way. We stood firm, and the Fox brass ultimately caved. Jane, first time out, got an Oscar nomination for her performance and went on to a stellar, quality career. Our casting two fresh, brand-new faces (James Earl Jones, too), both mesmerizing performers, brought great attention and acclaim to *The Great White Hope.* Even though I feel we weren't quite smart enough in translating the play to a film script, it's a picture I love and am very proud of.

I'll bet we saw a hundred or more young men for *The Graduate,* and the bell I always insecurely long for did not ring when Mike Nichols and I first saw Dustin Hoffman. But we did make a sterling choice in him—history proved that—the why and how of which I'll detail later on.

When trying to cast the male lead opposite Judy Garland in *I Could Go On Singing,* our first choice, Peter Finch, turned us down, as did our second choice. The director, Ronald Neame, and my partner and I weren't enthused about any other possibilities, and reluctantly made a compromise choice. When he, too, declined, I remember saying, "What could be worse than when the actor you don't even want turns you down!" But sometimes you get lucky: We ended up with the best possible guy, Dirk Bogarde—a fine actor, a British star, and a pal of the mercurial Judy. The picture still bombed.

Sometimes you get saved from your mistakes. As reliably told to me, Michael Sarrazin was the first choice of United Artists and the director to play opposite Dustin Hoffman in *Midnight Cowboy.* However, after I had first used Michael in *The Flim-Flam Man,* Universal

Studios signed him to a contract, and *Midnight Cowboy* producer Jerry Hellman and director John Schlesinger couldn't successfully negotiate for his release. They "settled" for Jon Voight. Settled?! He gave a great performance in a great, Oscar-winning film, and was off and running toward his own Oscar in *Coming Home.*

Each director has his own method for interviewing actors. Many choose to have the actor read a scene. Often the readings are taped for the producer, for the studio, or for the director himself. Some like to look at film of the actor's previous work, and some just like to sit privately and talk with the actor, to get a sense of what qualities he could bring to the role. That's not how it's done with major stars, though. *They* interview *you.* They're right to do so; Tom Cruise or Julia Roberts will nearly always "open" a picture. Others can be a gamble: For instance, Bruce Willis and John Travolta, both highly paid and sought after, have each had back-to-back bombs.

But, in fairness, who hasn't had bombs? Even back-to-back ones? We all have. But what we all have not had is success. So judge Allen Iverson for his league-leading scoring, not for the number of shots he's missed because he's fired so many.

Edward Norton, a hot, young, talented actor ever since his first screen role (in *Primal Fear*) earned him an Oscar nomination, was so eager to play the lead in *American History X* that he volunteered to do a test. I admired his work, but was dubious because he seemed slight, borderline frail, and the role called for a physically tough neo-Nazi. But his test knocked my socks off. He had trained and buffed himself to the point that I'd be afraid to meet up with him in a dark alley. However, the director, Tony Kaye, was unimpressed; he wanted an authentic street person. The studio, New Line, allowed Tony time for open auditions in New York and Los Angeles—because all studios are director fornicators, and they don't want to get a rep or rap for seemingly foiling creative talent. (Producers rarely qualify in that category for them.) One month later, New Line production chief Mike De Luca (a bright, straightforward exec, one of the best I've dealt with) and we producers looked at the tests of the actors Tony Kaye liked and wanted. They were *not* impressive. Tony asked for more time to continue his search, but enough was enough. We were fearful of losing Edward Norton, so we sat Tony down, and Ed Norton was cast. On the second week of shooting, Tony sauntered up to me on the set and said, "[Edward Norton] is the best piece of luck I've ever had." Luck?! Norton got his second Oscar nomination for *American History X,* though he and Tony's relationship ended on a sour, acrimonious note in the process (more on this later).

BUDGETING AND SCHEDULING

Almost any movie can be made at almost any price. If Roger Corman and Francis Ford Coppola were given the same script to budget and shoot, I guarantee you would see two very different results. I don't mean just creatively. Francis would, almost assuredly, take months to shoot, whereas Roger's schedule would be measured in weeks, perhaps even days. Francis is used to all the goodies (in fairness, he's made some modestly priced films, such as *The Conversation*), whereas Roger is one of the inventors of down-and-dirty. Francis always seems to be going for art, and by gosh he has achieved it many times. Roger seems to be going for commerce, although he surely likes quality, and also achieves it. Each has an amazing nose for talent. Just look at some who got their start with Roger: James Cameron, Jonathan Demme, Jack Nicholson, and many more. And Francis threw his weight behind George Lucas, when Lucas couldn't get *American Graffiti* financed.

My admonition to you, would-be producer reading this book, is this: "Cut your garment to fit the cloth." If you can convince someone to give you $10 million worth of cloth, make your garment— your picture—for that price. And if you can only obtain $2 million worth of cloth? Find a way to make that garment. And you can.

At best, budgeting and scheduling are inexact sciences, just as a budget for a week-long trip is. If you have $500 for a family vacation, you're not going to the Taj Mahal in India. Your common sense tells you you're not going to have Nicolas Cage starring with Matt Damon and directed by Jonathan Demme in your $3 million movie.

The professionals are darn good at estimating budgets. Although the studio sets a budget figure when they green light a film, and likely have done a preliminary budget, once the director is on board, he begins to work on a shooting schedule with the production manager. I vet it, but it's up to the two of them. The length of the schedule is a big determinant of cost, of course. The math is easy: You have to pay a crew and hold actors other than your stars for, say, eighteen weeks versus ten. A little more guesswork goes into how much a set is going to cost to build, or an actual location to rent. But part of the production designer's job is to estimate that, and end up at, or close to, the projected figure.

Production is always like that push-me, pull-you animal in *Dr. Dolittle*. Can you save money on casting and put it into the sets? Is it cheaper to build the sets or to find a location? A million questions like that must be answered, with the final decision resting with the director or producer—and, ultimately, if they choose to exercise their power, the studio. In a crunch, they will.

A smart producer or director, with some connivance from his production staff, will squirrel away a little money in some category that's hard to detect to use as a cushion in case of emergency, which, I guarantee you, occurs 100 percent of the time.

Though I feel responsible to the studio and their money, and indeed they hold me responsible, often they do not empower me with the necessary authority or control. The budget of *The River Wild* began to gradually creep up as we neared the start date. The studio, Universal, was understandably nervous because the star, Meryl Streep, great actress though she is, is not considered box-office magic. The head of business affairs, Jeff Korchek, was sent to meet with director Curtis Hanson and me to ask us to put up a portion of our fees as a contingency in case we went over budget. I knew Curtis was going to say no, thus I could have—should have—let him answer first. But that's not my nature, so I spoke up and asked Korchek if the studio would give me the authority to pull the plug on Curtis if he were taking an excessive amount of time to shoot a scene. I knew what the answer would be (okay, I'm a bit of a wise-ass), and he didn't disappoint me. Korchek said, no, that the studio couldn't do that. Remember, the director is king; he is the one with the vision, he is the filmmaker. I asked how Universal could ask me to put up my hard-earned producer fee when the control is in the hands of the director? Having no answer, Korchek merely shrugged. But he's truly a good guy and, hey, you don't kill the messenger. Curtis then chimed in to say that he wouldn't put up any of his salary, anyway. Case closed.

The day before filming was to begin, Casey Silver, the production head of the studio, flew to our location in Boston to caution us to adhere to budget, but he chose to meet only with Curtis Hanson. Maybe I'm thin-skinned, but I asked Casey how he expected the director to listen to and respect me, when he, the studio head, hadn't bothered to include me in that meeting. Casey must have studied with Jeff Korchek, as he, too, merely shrugged.

I find the better the director, the slower and more reluctant he is to make decisions. Whether it's picking locations or deciding about actors, the good directors seem to like to keep their options open; there might be something better around the corner. But perhaps that's as it should be, even though sometimes it can be maddening for the producer. After all, you, too, want the best movie possible.

Even if you are the most responsible producer on the planet, you must remember to shoot the movie, not the budget. If you finish right on budget, or indeed even under budget, you're only a hero until the film is released. If it's a flop, you're a bum, and so labeled.

Conversely, if you're over budget, you're only a bum until the picture comes out. If it's a hit, you're a hit, and all is forgiven. Early in my career, I officed at the old Goldwyn studio, next to Bobby Wise, who was in the midst of co-directing *West Side Story* with Jerome Robbins. United Artists, which financed via the Mirisch company, was on Bobby's fanny throughout the entire shoot because he ended up exceeding the approved budget by nearly 50 percent. But then the picture was released. It was a commercial success, and won several Academy Awards, including one for Bobby himself. He was the hero of the town, and it couldn't have happened to a nicer, more self-effacing director. As a steadfast pro, who began his creative life as editor of *Citizen Kane*, Bobby knew to shoot his movie, not his budget.

A movie, any movie, should be, and always is, insured. The big insurance needed is a completion guarantee, so the film will be finished and available for distribution no matter what. The major studios are rich enough to always self-insure. Independent films buy completion bonds from companies that specialize in them. The fee is negotiable—usually 5 percent of the budget, with half being returned to the production if the bond money is not needed. Customarily, there is a 10 percent over-budget contingency before a bond company can contractually take over a film. They rarely exercise that power, choosing instead to work with the filmmaking team.

Insurance, of course, is purchased to cover various unforeseen emergencies and, obviously, for the major actors and the director; an injury to such a key player would force the production to shut down. For the producer, insurance is where you confront your position in the firmament: No studio, no independent, no film ever insures the producer.

> *The only one allowed to drive a car on location is the producer because their death or injury will not impair the picture. The smallest actor who's established for any number of days is driven to the set. So is the director. The producer can go off a cliff, but basically the show will go on.*

—David Brown

PRODUCTION

> *Miles to go before I sleep . . .*

—Robert Frost

If you've done your job well during preproduction, the producer shouldn't have much to do during actual production. Of course, that's never the case. However, the producer is the one superfluous person on a movie set. Everyone else has a very specific task. Not the producer; his job is crisis-management. Problems pop up all the time. The producer's main job is to solve those problems, to keep them off the director's back so he can concentrate on making the movie, to keep problems from arising in the first place, and to solve problems quickly and efficiently when they do occur. This means the producer better be on top of everything and everybody, especially the production manager and line producer who are ramrodding the production.

> *The ideal producer is able to get the best out of everybody who's working on the picture. The key is asking the right questions, and helping to create an environment of trust and positive energy.*

—Curtis Hanson

COMMUNICATING WITH YOUR TEAM

The thing that's important to me during the shoot—and I think this can be a major producer contribution—is to be able to talk about each day's work with the director, after we've seen dailies. But only afterward, and in private. During dailies, the director can make his comments to the editor, DP, and other crew members. The producer's comments, if observant and sensitive, can help the director and the picture stay on the track agreed to in tone, style, and performance.

> *I don't interfere on a set. I'll watch dailies and make suggestions.*
>
> —**Saul Zaentz**

I've also worked with directors who would rear up on hind legs at a wrong-headed or untimely suggestion. As long as you and the director remember it's only about the work, you should be able to say anything to each other. Just don't personalize. Easier said than done, of course.

The gifted screenwriter William Rose (*Guess Who's Coming to Dinner, It's a Mad Mad Mad Mad World*) described his script for *The Flim-Flam Man*, which he wrote for me, as being "one foot off the ground," meaning larger-than-life humor. Nonetheless, I constantly and vehemently disagreed with director Irvin Kershner for allowing the actors to play as broadly as they did. The picture was not a success commercially but got fabulous reviews. So who was right, Kersh or me?

Conversely, director John Badham took heed when early on in filming *Short Circuit*, I suggested that he tone down the actors, who I felt were over the top. Even with his many successful credits, John was always open and accessible. Happily, *Short Circuit* was so successful, the studio wanted a sequel.

> *I count on a producer. It's so easy in directing to lose your way and maybe go off-track. It's very important to have somebody whose judgment you trust. A producer not only knows the project very well but also has just enough distance to have a perspective that, in the heat of battle, is not just helpful, but essential.*
>
> —**Frank Pierson**

Directors each have their own way, their own style, of communicating with actors. Woody Allen told me that early in his directing career, he talked to his actors a lot, but now pretty much all he says is, "Do it once more, please, just a little faster." David Lean, two-time Academy Award–winning director, was asked in an interview, "What's the most important thing for a director to know?" Lean, to my surprise since he was one of the most commanding visual directors ever, replied, "How fast the actors should speak."

I make it a point never to talk to actors, other than to pay them a compliment if I'm happy with their work. I'll say anything critical only to my director. Simply defined, the producer is in charge of the movie (or used to be); the director is in charge of the set.

However, talking to actors during filming is sometimes unavoidable. Judy Garland, during the filming of *I Could Go On Singing*, approached me on the set and complained bitterly that Ronnie Neame, the director, was doing too many takes of each scene. She had already attempted suicide during the first week of filming, so I was eager to keep her on an even keel, emotionally. Ronnie, who was slightly intimidated by Garland (who wasn't!), was only too happy to comply. So in the next scene, after a single take, Ronnie yelled, "Cut! Beautiful! Let's move on to the next scene." Judy immediately rushed to me, saying, "So that's the game the son of a bitch is going to play." Sometimes you can't win.

There's also a great—very different—William Wyler story. Willy was notorious for doing many, many takes of each scene. He was not an articulate man, nor very communicative with the actors, but he had unerring taste and invariably knew when an actor had captured the moment. On one film he was summoned by the studio head, who told him, "Willy, your actors hate you. You go for take after take after take. They can't stand it. They hate you." Calmly, Willy replied, "They'll love me at the preview." And he was right.

For *I Could Go On Singing*, we began Judy's shoot at the famous London Palladium, with her singing the title song by Harold Arlen. Judy hadn't done a film in a while and was eager to see herself, so the next day she watched dailies with us. There had been an undetected hair wiggling on the lens. Judy was marvelous, and the scene was definitely usable, but not visually perfect. That night she took too many pills and had to be hospitalized. I immediately called her then-manager, David Begelman, in New York, telling him we were starting out with Judy problems and he'd better get to London as fast as he could. He said he could arrange to come, if I'd pay him $25,000. I was stunned. He and his partner, Freddie Fields, were making a ton of money as Judy's managers. (Had I a crystal ball to see his future behavior, I wouldn't have been as surprised. He later embezzled money from the actor Cliff Robertson and, ultimately, after an enormously successful career, first as agent and then studio head of Columbia and MGM, committed suicide amid personal financial chaos.) Although I was seething. I answered that I probably could handle the situation myself, The next day, David arrived in London. I guess he figured it was worth a shot to try to extract some money from me.

Judy's erratic behavior should not have been a surprise. Her reputation was that of a brilliant but complicated and unstable performer. The tip-off came the night before we were to start filming. I was awakened just after midnight by a phone call from Judy. "I just want you to know that I'm going to show up tomorrow," she told me. That was a first (and, happily, a last). Show up? We're all paid to do that.

I'd earlier taken her passport for the British authorities, and I calculatingly chose not to return it to her, as I had real concerns that Judy would leave the country before we finished shooting. Judy often seemed to be hanging by a thread emotionally, and my partner and I worked hard to buoy her spirits. Near the end of shooting, trying to make her feel good, I enthusiastically said, "Only six more days to go!" After which, she repeated back to me, "Six more days to go!" with such despair in her voice, as if she had just been sentenced to life in prison. Thank God I had thought to steal her passport. When she finally did leave England, we had to hire a body double to shoot some linking footage (long shots on her back) so our picture would stitch together. It was on that picture that I learned a hard truth: You can categorically improve a film by imaginative editing, you can make it better, but it doesn't mean you can make it any good.

The United Artists brass flew to London to view our final cut. When the film ended and the lights came on, one of the executives was actually asleep. He was prescient, no matter how jet-lagged. The film was not a success, even though many liked Judy's performance. Some of those, who knew the hell I went through, commented that it must therefore have been worth it. It wasn't. I regret to this day canceling a planned vacation with my wife and son to the Danish island Bornholm, a short trip from London. I felt I could not afford to be away for a week during production, even though I had a partner holding down the fort. Wrong decision—life is more important than art. And anyway, this didn't turn out to be art, other than the art of survival. As much as I love making movies, time with my family would have been more valuable.

Charming, funny, and bright though Judy was, she usually left wreckage in her wake. Dirk Bogarde and she were close chums, but halfway through shooting they were pissing ice water at each other. I don't know if their friendship was ever repaired. He was a talented pro who later wrote a memoir and a novel, both well received. To repair myself I moved with my family to Paris during post-production. I'd fly to London for four days every other week for editing. However, nothing could save the picture, although I did learn a smart maxim from Ronnie Neame, who was a brick throughout. He taught me that you have to work harder on a bad picture than on a good one. Don't give up on it. A valuable lesson, without which *I Could Go On Singing* would have been even less good.

I also learned what I am trying to impart to you: Trust your own taste. The title song was, I suspect, pulled by Harold Arlen from his trunk, rather than written specifically for our film. I thought the lyrics by the renowned Yip Harburg were clunky. "I could go on singing 'til the cows come home!" 'Til the cows come home . . . that's romantic? Not to me, but the highly credentialed music maven Saul Chaplin, our associate music producer, convinced us the lyrics were fine, and I was too intimidated to disagree.

A bonus: I met Liza Minnelli, who was living with Judy during filming. Only a teenager then, Liza once did an impromptu imitation of her mother for me that was so good and that oozed such talent I knew she would become the great entertainer she is.

I did say that producing is crisis-management, didn't I? Some pictures have more crises than others. My hair started turning gray with *I Could Go On Singing*.

ON LOCATION

It's heresy to some, but I dislike being on location, away from my family. I dislike being on the set even if filming is being done in my hometown because there's so little to do. Many of the top producers I interviewed for this book will surely downgrade me in their estimation for that remark, but I stand by it. Of course there is stuff to do, especially the handling of crises. But I find it labor-intensive in the wrong way. If we're shooting a nine-hour day, I may have several occasions to offer input, a couple questions to answer, and once in a while I may have to figuratively put out a fire or be involved in a change-of-plans decision. But the rest of the time I'm standing around, giving rise to some crew grumbling about "that fat cat."

When I am on location (and I have been, too many times), I'm constantly monitoring how smoothly our ship is sailing, checking the physical aspects of production and the money being spent, and interfacing with the director creatively. But all of that notwithstanding, for me it's too many hours of standing-around time, even though I can go to the office trailer provided for me, make phone calls, and work on future projects. But that is hit-and-run, not the most productive way of working.

As I've already forewarned you, many of the best producers disagree:

I am on the set of all my movies. Every day.
—Saul Zaentz

I work on the set. I go out with the crew, actually. If they have a question, or if something comes up, they don't have to go more than five feet.
—Dick Zanuck

Frank [Marshall] and I like to be very hands-on. We're there every day doing our part. It's what I believe fundamentally is the creative process, and more importantly I enjoy it. It's fun.
—Kathleen Kennedy

On the other hand, I am not alone in not wanting to be on location:

> *I was on set every minute of every day on my first two movies. I learned from being there every minute of every day that you don't need to be there for every minute of every day. I look at it kind of as a luxury to do that. It's really fun to be there, but is it necessary for a producer? I think it's not.*
>
> —Brian Grazer

> *I get very bored on the set. You'll learn to be there at certain pivot points—key scenes, key moments. Otherwise, if there's a problem, they call you.*
>
> —Doug Wick

I have read and heard that Jerry Bruckheimer makes only brief visits to the sets of his films. He hasn't won an Academy Award yet, but I'm sure it's on the horizon for him. His many enormous successes have made him a household name, like Hitchcock and Cecil B. DeMille were years ago.

I personally think some producers like to hang around a set for their ego. As producers have slowly and inexorably been devalued by so often being forced to share credit, being on set visibly justifies their existence and importance. It makes them feel important; they think it proves that they are creatively contributing. This is tricky ground, because this opinion makes me vulnerable to potshots from studio executives and fellow producers. But these are my true feelings, and that, after all, is the purpose of this book.

The tightrope a producer has to walk during shooting stretches between his loyalty to and protection of his production, and his responsibility to the studio or financing entity. The movie comes first, always, yet you never want to be anything less than candid, honest, and communicative with the company that put up the millions to make the movie. It's the right ethic. Besides, pragmatically, you may need to go back to them for money next time.

> *Your loyalty is to the movie. It's not to the director, it's not to the studio. It's to the movie. And, ultimately, to the audience.*
>
> —Doug Wick

POST-PRODUCTION

> *You get three cracks at every film: once in the writing,*
> *once in the shooting, and then a whole new crack in the*
> *editing.*
>
> —George Stevens (two-time Academy
> Award–winning director,
> *A Place in the Sun, Giant*)

EDITING

I told you earlier that the script is all-important, the blueprint for the movie, and yet, no matter how smart you are, you only really know how good the script is once you've seen the film put together.

> *You can like a script and it can work, but, until you see it*
> *on screen, you don't know.*
>
> —David Wolper

That's a little late, but because of the post-production process, it's not altogether too late. You can't make or break a film in post-production, but you sure can help it. Astute editing can clarify a story line, change the energy and pace of a picture, even enhance a performance. A wonderful example of enhancing a performance is what Mike Nichols did with editor Sam O'Steen on *The Graduate.* Throughout the film, Dustin Hoffman periodically whimpers—sweet, plaintive, charming, very funny whimpers, all but one of which were inserted into the film during editing and sound mixing.

The editor for *Pretty Poison* was an Academy Award winner. After our disastrous preview, I took over the editing. But I experienced great frustration in communicating and working with the editor. I wanted some flash cuts of only six or eight frames, but the editor would give me three feet, then grudgingly cut it down to two feet, before finally, after the fourth or fifth go at it, we would get it to where I wanted. I reexamined the editor's credits and saw something that had initially escaped my attention: Although he had worked on good films with good directors, none of them worked with him a second time. Most top filmmakers go back to the well time after time, to the same people they like and respect. Stellar credits may not be quite enough reason for you to hire someone.

The producer, since he initiated the project, can and should have clear and fresh opinions about theme, clarity, storytelling, performance, and pacing, among other things. However, the producer should not be so cemented in his earlier vision that he is blind to the new, different, added values the director and actors have brought to the project. I, as producer, may have impregnated the film, but in the making, in the womb, it develops a life of its own. The finished film, even in a rough-cut form, tells you something—which is why I always like to see the first rough-cut assembly done by the editor, even though the director has nearly always selected the specific takes and may have put together sequences along the way.

> *Post-production brings a whole new life [to the film]. You have to clear your head, put aside your original ambition, and see what's in the room.*
>
> —Doug Wick

The most exciting times on a film for me (that is, *after* I get a green light) are the table reading, where the director has the cast first read the script aloud, then the first day's rushes, when suddenly the picture becomes a reality and when I see it all put together for the first time. My first view of an entire film nearly always depresses me. My anticipation is so high from my passionate dream that I'm always disappointed. I think the first viewing is where you truly see the story, and know whether it's working. Happily, merely excising the weak scenes, *if* they don't contain vital story information, makes the picture better. With more editing and some creative imagination, the film gets better and better. Usually. But not always. I've been there.

Film is essentially a realistic medium, despite what genius and magic directors bring to it. Gore Vidal's play *The Best Man* was a biting, very funny political satire. But when I saw the rough cut of the film (photographed in black and white by the great Haskell Wexler, his first union film), it was more a trenchant drama than a comedy. We shouldn't have been surprised because my partner and I had selected Franklin Schaffner as director, and his forte was male confrontation. (He later directed, very successfully, both *Planet of the Apes* and *Patton,* for which he won the Oscar.) Gore Vidal, who wrote the screenplay, was dismayed upon seeing Schaffner's cut; he felt his funny repartee had been muted. After all, it was he who gave birth to the play. Without losing what humor was there, though, editing enhanced the drama the film had turned out to be. That drama got amazing reviews, and was a big hit at the Cannes Film Festival.

Although I'm going to address *The Graduate* chapter-and-verse later in this book, I want to comment that when I first viewed the rough cut of that film, I felt that Mike Nichols had delivered a tougher, stronger, edgier, and more penetrating telling of the story than I had envisioned when I optioned the book.

Just as in a script each scene should be an arrow into the next scene, so should it be in editing. Because what is editing, other than story telling? The difficulty is that you are limited to what you've shot, unlike in scripting, where you're only limited by your creative imagination. A classic exercise to show the power of editing is to cut from a delicious hot-fudge sundae to a cut of a person's face. You, the viewer, will perceive him as salivating in anticipation. But precede that same shot of a person's face with a shot of a child being slapped, and the face will seem to register shock, anger, or sadness. Does that support the axiom "Beauty is in the eye of the beholder"?

I think editing is where you get the most bang for your buck. With a very small payroll, you're making your picture better—that is, if you're making smart decisions. Sometimes I find it pays to not look at your picture for a week or two, then come back with fresh eyes to see how it plays and where it can be enhanced. It's often a struggle to get as much editing time as you want or may even need because when you initially make a budget, the studio or financier will limit that time and then, when shooting's finished, will often push for final delivery so they can release the film and start to get their money back. Obviously, the very top-of-the-line directors and producers can get all the time they need.

With Brian Grazer on 8 Mile *and Scott Rudin on* Wonder Boys, *neither of them was in the editing room. I mean,*

*nowhere near the editing room, and neither expressed
any desire to be there. I like input. I truly do, as long as it
is well-intended and thoughtful. I very much looked
forward to screening the movies for them, and did so for
each of them prior to screening for the studio. I wanted to
hear what they thought, and I also wanted to protect
their reactions by not showing the film to them
prematurely. I wanted the picture to be in good shape
when they saw it the first time because you can only give
a fresh reaction once. Both of them had very thoughtful
things to say. It worked well in both cases.*

—Curtis Hanson

In the old Hollywood days, when pictures cost less and the studios
had everybody under exclusive contract, many films would do
weeks of reshoots or add scenes after the film previewed and got an
audience reaction. That is rarely feasible today, although a handful
of filmmakers, if they have the power, allocate some contingency
money for possible reshoots.

Sometimes a preview reaction is so negative, the studio will push
the filmmakers for a rewrite and reshoot of a particular scene or
two, nearly always the ending. A classic successful case of this was
Fatal Attraction: Paramount ordered a more upbeat, revenge ending, which everyone feels led to that film's enormous commercial
success.

The final cut, having the final say, is the most sought-after, highly
prized creative perk. A handful of directors have it, and you can
name them: Spielberg, Lucas, Scorsese . . . Still, it can be difficult to
exercise it with impunity. If the studio top dogs and marketing department are unhappy with the final cuts, you'd better listen. And
even the best do.

SOUND DESIGN

Music is so accessible and universal that its power in film cannot be
overestimated. Since the days of silent films, music has been an important component of the emotion a film can generate. Back then,
each theater had an organist to accompany the on-screen action with

appropriate dramatic, romantic, or humorous music. It is my opinion that, today, nearly every really good or commercially successful film has music that is first-rate, that enhances the film. My biggest success, *The Graduate,* is no exception. The Simon and Garfunkel score was so emotionally right, the feeling so strong, it helped the film. Unfortunately, the converse is not true; a great score will help a poor film very little, and surely will not save a lousy film. The most used convention, if you think you have a catchy, strong theme, is to use it repeatedly throughout the film so that by the climax its familiarity makes the audience feel they're with an old friend. It's like saying kitchy-coo while tickling a baby. After doing it several times, you don't even have to touch the baby to start it laughing—shades of Pavlov's dog.

Even though we had a very successful preview of *The River Wild,* foretelling its later success, the head of the studio, Sid Sheinberg, told the production head, Casey Silver, that he didn't like the music score. Sid did not mandate that Casey do anything about it, even though he had the power to do so, but Casey nonetheless picked up on that post-preview comment and ordered a new score. I was not unhappy about the decision because although the score was very serviceable, it didn't exactly hit the ball out of the park. So $1 million was spent on a new score, which definitely helped the film somewhat—but it also didn't knock the ball out of the park. *The River Wild* was a hit, but I don't think any more so than it would have been had we kept the original score and saved the million. This is unprovable, of course, but I do have my strong opinions, and this is one.

Sound design is an art unto itself. As movies have become bigger and more special-effects-laden, sound has become increasingly important: new sounds for new, futuristic worlds; new voices for mutants and aliens; car crashes and explosions that make you feel that you're the one being targeted. Sometimes it's too much for me; I feel like I'm at a Laker playoff game and a Rolling Stones concert all in one.

The sound mix, combining the dialogue, redubbed dialogue, sound effects, and music, is usually supervised by the director. As producer, I like to see each completed reel to offer my comments, and from time to time I wander down to the dubbing room to check out what's going on. I've even supervised the entire dubbing process myself. On

The Great White Hope, director Marty Ritt, a huge horse-racing fan, said, "Kid, the racing season at Del Mar is on and I don't want to miss it. You mix the picture." I did, but that's really a story about trust and collaboration, which I'll deal with in a later chapter.

PREVIEW SCREENINGS

When it came time to preview *Pretty Poison,* the neophyte director and producer were understandably very nervous. They had a lot riding on the film—it could truly launch, indeed make, their careers. Although the subject matter of the film was "difficult," edgy, and dark, I nonetheless reassured them with my "truth" (at the time): "Relax. Nearly every picture previews well. It's not a guarantee we'll have a hit or the critics will embrace it, but I assure you we'll have a good preview." Our preview was a shocking lesson for me, a disaster. People started walking out early on, and after the matricide they left in droves. By the time the picture ended, half our audience was gone. To compound matters, though it was only ninety-five minutes long, the film seemed to drag interminably. I was shaken, the studio was shaken, and the young producer and director were in shock. So much for my cockiness.

But I learned from that disastrous preview; that's what previews are for. I got a loud, clear message that the audience hated that the young girl had gotten away scot-free, having killed her mother in cold blood. I felt I knew how to fix it: just adding three brief new scenes, explaining the characters better, and letting the audience know that the murderer would indeed be caught. And it wouldn't cost much. The problem was that Twentieth Century Fox did not want to spend a nickel more on what they had just seen with their own eyes to be an unmitigated dud. But I convinced the studio brass that I could get the reshoot done in a single day and they relented, *if* I agreed to change the title from *She Let Him Continue* (which I loved) to *Pretty Poison.* It was a supportive, fair, pragmatic trade-off.

> *I'm a fresh voice. That was one of my fortes, seeing something and telling them how to fix it.*
>
> **—David Wolper**

I "took over" from the inexperienced producer and director team, which sounds unseemly—and was, though it was common practice in those days. (Darryl Zanuck took over *Cleopatra* from Joe Mankiewicz, a two-time Academy Award winner—took over but did not save; *Cleopatra* almost sank Fox.) I did the re-editing, but insisted that the director sit with me so I could explain the reasons behind my decisions and hear his arguments against my changes if he disagreed. I supervised the music and the dubbing (mixing all the dialogue, sound, and music tracks together). The results? Superlative reviews, no business. Needless to say, that method of working, with the producer taking over the picture, was "old Hollywood" and would not, could not, happen today. I myself never worked that way again.

Another time I got pulled into an editing situation was with Edward Norton on *American History X*. Edward is very bright, very involved, and articulate. He was frustrated with how the editing was evolving in the hands of director Tony Kaye. I was, too, but for a different reason. Edward felt—correctly, in my opinion—that Tony was cutting to the bone and losing the emotional nuance and build of not only Edward's character but others as well, and thus his character's relationship to them.

My frustration was that Tony blew like a stinkweed in the breeze, being continually influenced by whomever he'd last spoken with. Edward was a major star and the studio, wanting to please him, gave him his own editing time. Tony was very upset, understandably. And right to be so. I had to mediate. Although I sided with Edward creatively, I had the unpleasant task of telling him he must cease and desist and let Tony finish. He accepted that, and graciously.

However, Tony ultimately shot himself in the foot. After editing for nearly a year—compared to the customary four months—Tony announced he wanted new scenes written by a new writer. That was finally enough, even for New Line. As well it should have been; we had already had a gratifying, successful audience test-screening. New Line had to relieve Tony of his duties, even though no studio wants to be perceived as unfriendly to creative talent. Edward went back in the editing room, and I believe he enhanced the picture without violating the content or essence of Tony's work. Tony had, after all, directed every moment in the film. He nonetheless went ballistic and personally paid for a series of trade ads blasting everyone at New Line, including the producers. (Though his trade-ad attacks were as fuzzy and unclear as I felt his editing was.) Tony wanted to use the nom de plume Humpty Dumpty as his credit, but his own guild wouldn't allow it. He trashed our film in the press, causing us to be disinvited from the Toronto Film Festival and negatively impacting those critics who are director/auteur-minded.

Although it had been Mike De Luca, New Line's then–production head, who had originally suggested Tony Kaye for *American History X*, I had been an enthusiastic supporter. Tony shared my feeling for the delicacy and importance of the neo-Nazi racist subject matter. However, Tony proved to love the camera more than he loved his actors. He was his own DP and a helluva good shooter, but was so in love with his "toy" that he shot and shot and shot. He used more film the first day than most directors do in a week. And again the second day. New Line became cost-nervous. They, and we, spoke to Tony, and he cut it down, or tried to. There was still a ton of footage at dailies each night, and Tony insisted on seeing every minute of it. I mean literally hours. I thought he should have been spending more time reflecting on the next day's work. But, in fairness, he made what I think is a wonderful, if flawed, film. The good parts are real pearls; there were just not quite enough of them to form a necklace. Still, I'm very proud of and mostly happy with the picture.

The reviews were mixed. Those who liked it loved it. Those who didn't were offended. Tony's execution was as raw as the subject. I could barely get my wife to see it and I myself always close my eyes during one particularly graphic, brutal scene. Edward was magnificent, receiving his second Academy Award nomination. If Tony Kaye had kept his mouth shut and not lambasted everyone within range, he'd be a very hot director today.

My first partner, Stuart Millar, was fond of saying, "It's a business of inches," meaning a lot of little things can add up to a big thing, whether it's storytelling or an actor's performance. And one of those "inch" things was vitally, critically important to me in *American History X*: the ending, what the audience was left with. The original script, scooped up by my then-partner John Morrissey, ended with the reformed neo-Nazi seeking to avenge his brother's death. I steadfastly lobbied for moral uplift and redemption, and was able to

ensure our film ended with Norton accepting responsibility by utter-
ing, "What have I done?" as he cradles his murdered brother in his
arms. It's a small change, but major to me and, I submit, to the raison d'être of *American History X.*

The talented, tough George Roy Hill offered me his "rule of thumb":
"The first man who says to you, 'They'll never notice it,' fire him, because he's your enemy."

HOW DO YOU GET PEOPLE
TO SEE THE MOVIE?

NO ONE EVER WENT BROKE UNDERESTIMATING THE
AMERICAN PUBLIC.

—H. L. MENCKEN

MARKETING

You don't sell it, they do—"they" being whoever puts up the money.
The distributor has the power and authority to decide the marketing/
advertising campaign and the distribution pattern, as well as the
amount of dollars to be spent. If you have a lot of muscle, if you're
Steven Spielberg or the producers I've interviewed for this book, you
can have enormous influence, bordering on control. All studio heads
and marketing departments will listen carefully to the valued,
courted filmmakers at the top of the heap who the studio hopes will
bring them their next project. Brian Grazer has the track record and
clout to get pretty close to the marketing budget and distribution
plan he wants.

> *They let me [have what I want], probably because I care*
> *so much. I've had a lot of success. That helps for sure. On*
> *my first movie,* **Nightshift,** *we had a poster that was so*
> *horribly embarrassing. I was just so overpowered by the*
> *powers-that-be in marketing, I had to live with it. I vowed*
> *I'm not going to do that again, I'm not going to let people*
> *overpower me so much that I can't have a voice that*

*properly identifies a movie commensurate with the way I,
at least, see it. Whether the way I see it is right or wrong
is subjective and remains to be seen, but it will reflect my
taste. That's all I want—for the movie to reflect my taste.*
                                                    —Brian Grazer

You, the producer, should know better than anyone what the story
is and what feeling, what emotion, perhaps what message, you want
an audience to derive from the film. That's why you have to communicate, and hopefully persuade, the distribution and marketing executives to your point of view. Remember, every month they're releasing
a new movie, and there's no way they can have the same level of excitement and conviction about each one. So you have to pump up
their enthusiasm. Even if you do not have the power and authority
by contract, then by force of personality and persuasive logic, do
your best to make the marketing team follow your lead.

*The ideal producer would be focusing on [marketing] at
the time that the director can't, way back when we're
shooting the movie. I always find it amazing to sit down
at the studio marketing meeting, after the movie's not
only finished shooting, but oftentimes you're well into the
editing, and they're just starting to think about
marketing. [You think] why not be coming up with great
[marketing] concepts way ahead of time so you don't have
a gun to your head.*
                                                    —Curtis Hanson

MOVIE POSTERS AND PRINT ADS

The studios have always paid lip service in listening to me, but how
much of what I want and actually get from them varies. And, to be
fair, some of my ideas may be lousy, and they are experienced marketing pros. I, along with the other producers of *American History X*,
liked the strong, bold-print ad showing Edward Norton bare-chested
and with a large Nazi swastika tattooed on his chest. In retrospect, I
ask myself, Was that scary image the right ad to entice people to see
the film? I fear the answer is "no."

The other side of that *American History X* coin was thirty years earlier, when I produced the equally race-themed *The Great White Hope*. The ad image I wanted and fought for was a large head shot of James Earl Jones with the buoyant smile he often displays in the film, and which captures the impudent character of a man who is totally his own person. But the studio, in its infinite wisdom, used a very somber photograph of him with a white woman and the tag line, "He could beat any white man in the world, he just couldn't beat all of them." Looking at an ad that labels all white people as racist, would you like to go see that movie? I doubt it. No, I know it, because not enough people did see it. My peers loved the movie, though, and it was thus a step forward, not back, in my career and, more important, in my psyche.

Mike Nichols and I chose the famous *Graduate* image (the ads for the big successes nearly always become famous) of a cap-and-gowned young man under the sexy, bare, inverted V of a woman's leg. It was created by a gifted British graphic designer, Richard Williams, who Mike knew of and suggested. It was such a distinct design that the paperback version of the novel utilized it.

> **Jaws *is an early example of working with the book publishers. . . . On the art campaign, that symbol of the shark coming up toward the lady swimmer above went from the hardcover book jacket to the soft cover to the movie screen.***
>
> —Dick Zanuck

DON'T FORGET, YOUR AUDIENCE IS GLOBAL

The marketing tail wags the whole dog. Two-thirds of the revenue for most films comes from outside the United States. Even within the United States, the studios want a film they can sell with succinct clarity and immediate impact. A perfect example is *Twins*, a film of years ago, starring Arnold Schwarzenegger and Danny DeVito: A picture of those two actors standing side-by-side (one a muscular Mr. Universe, the other short and rotund) bearing the title *Twins* immediately told the audience it was a broad comedy. More recently, *White Chicks*, starring the popular black brother team Shawn and Marlon

Wayans employed a similar tactic. Get it? Black guys playing white chicks, and the poster showing that. You'd have to be deaf, dumb, and blind to not know that it's a wild comedy.

Moviegoers in Berlin or Tokyo do not want to pay their hard-earned money to go to a movie theater simply to read subtitles. Give 'em action, give 'em special effects, give 'em spectacle, and give 'em something they already sort of know, like *The Lord of the Rings*, Harry Potter, *Star Wars*, James Bond, *Spider-Man*, etc. Ads and TV spots for those films don't have to waste time and money *explaining* what the picture is about because the audience already knows. So the advertising blitzkrieg is selling, "We're here, we're in town, and we're playing in so many theaters there's definitely one near you."

The international market has grown significantly as a revenue base. As a result, the good news is the audience base has become larger. The bad news is because there's an opportunity to make more money, people are spending more money, and that increases the stakes in what you're doing. That in turn increased the number of people you have to answer to, which can ultimately dilute your vision. With that many people on the battlefield it simply becomes more difficult to maintain a belief in your vision. Tenacity and stamina become your virtues.
—**Kathleen Kennedy**

From the business perspective the studios are right—huge world-wide grosses are generated by the pre-sold (a favorite studio term) film. You know which films they are and can add titles yourself: *Lethal Weapon 5*, or is it 6? *The Mummy 3. Jurassic Park 4. Spider-Man 3.* So the search continues, each studio looking for the next "tentpole" (another favorite term), or for sequel possibilities.

Sid Sheinberg, when he was head of Universal Studios, told me, "All our marketing research [and research plays an ever-increasing role in movie decision-making] shows that the public wants clear, honest information about a film and its content. They don't want to be misled, lied to, or tricked." Come to think of it, that's pretty good life advice, too.

Hollywood has become so institutionalized, so researched, so marketed to death because there seems to be more predictability to what people worldwide will pay to see. I don't know whether it's cause or effect or both, but the studios' desire for spectacle, action, and big-name stars, is understandable. Those films travel well for the very reasons studios make them. *The Matrix Revolutions* did much more business overseas (in the United States, too) than did *Mystic River,* not only at the box office but also in all ancillary venues. The third *Matrix* film is well-made and entertaining, but *Mystic River,* in my opinion, is a truly superior one. I believe it was the British philosopher C.E.M. Joad who wrote, "I cannot prove that a Beethoven symphony is a better piece of music than 'How Much Is That Doggy in the Window?' but it is."

Without marketing clout, many a fine, smaller film barely sees the light of day. Mega-marketing dollars are put behind mega-budgeted films. *Lost in Translation* is a film I loved but, with all its kudos, did less business than many inferior, muscular action movies. There were not enough advertising dollars spent or enough pizzazz in visuals to compete with *The Matrix* or James Bond. It was, however, a commercial success on its own terms because of its low cost. The studios are probably right: Only the "cognoscenti" seem to really want to see "slice-of-life" films dealing with real people in real situations. Many critics are so surfeited with bloated, empty epics that, in their hunger for meaningful, quality films, I believe they overpraise some well-intentioned but mediocre "small" pictures.

Since the major studios want to be all things to all people around the globe, art and commerce are too often mutually exclusive. In fairness, it requires a huge investment to produce and market films. The very biggest stars and directors can, by their very clout, make the studios put their muscle behind a pet, so-called vanity project, and all credit to those stars and directors who exercise that clout; they often reach for the artistically ambitious. Warner Bros. supported Mel Gibson's *Hamlet,* albeit reluctantly. They chalked it up to the cost of being in business with Mel Gibson and did it because they wanted to keep him happy for their *Lethal Weapon* franchise and more. But even superstar Mel Gibson was forced to put up his own money to make *The Passion of the Christ;* no studio would touch it. Fortunately, he happened to have the necessary $20 million in spare change. But I shouldn't make fun because he showed the courage of his convictions. And he made movie history in the bargain, plus a nice bundle for himself.

NONSTUDIO FILMS

Other small, nonstudio films do sneak through and show that audiences *are* hungering for genuine, accessible emotion. They sure found it in *My Big Fat Greek Wedding,* not exactly an artistic triumph, but wonderfully identifiable and satisfying. It, too, struggled to find financing (so often the case), yet without huge initial advertising support, it grew into an amazing, enormous commercial success. But that's a rarity, an anomaly. A couple of thousand films are submitted to the prestigious Sundance Film Festival each year, nearly all without distribution. Sundance selects and exhibits maybe a hundred. Of those, a dozen at most are picked up by distributors. The odds may be against, but that does not deter real filmmakers. That's where and how *Sex, Lies, and Videotape* was launched. And two recent Peter Stark Producing graduates had their first produced film, *Napoleon Dynamite,* bought at Sundance by Fox Searchlight, a top specialty distributor. Ingenious marketing helped it become the most successful specialty film of 2004. Films big and small, expensive and modest, all make a publicity push where they can get a big bang for a small buck.

What Dick Zanuck said he and David Brown did for their big studio film, *Jaws,* applies even more to smaller independent films:

> We went up to twenty states in twenty days before the domestic release. One state a day, going on everyday radio and television shows. And then we went to foreign markets—South Africa, South America, Japan—selling it.

My favorite poking fun is that the three biggest growth industries in America are bottled water, company retreats, and film schools/festivals. Virtually every young person (and beyond) loves movies and is interested in film as an art form. People think that because they read, write, and understand English, they can intelligently judge a movie. Those same people wouldn't dream of judging a painting, and do not know enough about music to judge a composition, yet have no hesitancy whatsoever about judging a movie. Studio executives get paid handsomely to do so, although currently very few of them are in the business of looking for art. They judge commerce, or try to. The current climate is one in which the artistic content of films is not front and center or uppermost in the hearts and minds of the studios that finance films. Marketability is. I'm a sucker for good writing. However, I tell my Peter Stark Producing students that good, quality writing is number three on the list of two things the studios are looking for. What they *are* looking for is a simple, clear, high-concept, marketable story and/or (preferably *and*) a role to attract a big-time, world-famous movie star so they can advertise and "sell" the film. The great Spanish director Pedro Almodóvar echoes my thoughts: "I don't want to be offensive, but I get the idea that Hollywood is not demanding about scripts. And what most concerns me is the value of the script."

> *Unfortunately, story is not in the number one position as far as the studio is concerned anymore. It used to be we would sit around and say, "We can make a great picture!" Nobody says that anymore. It's "How will it play overseas? What are the demographics?" All those questions that we never asked. We just said, "Jesus! That's a great story! Let's make it! We could make a great film." We don't talk in those terms anymore.*
>
> —Dick Zanuck

As a grown-up in today's world, on any given Saturday night, I find surprisingly few films that I'm eager to see. But I keep going because hope springs eternal. I love films, both making them and seeing them, and sometimes my expectations are realized. Take, for example, *Maria Full of Grace*, an HBO independent film that was released theatrically. It blew me away; it was so real, so powerful, so emotionally true—and shot for a mere $4 million. That should make hope begin to spring in you, even though it can be as difficult to raise four million dollars as forty.

WHAT DOES PRODUCING REALLY TAKE?

THERE ARE ONLY TWO KINDS OF CAREERS IN
HOLLYWOOD: LONG AND SHORT.

—BOB BOOKMAN, CAA AGENT

The film world is not round, it's flat. People fall off the edge: Michael Cimino after *Heaven's Gate,* producer Ross Hunter when soapy melodramas were no longer in fashion. Both had far more than the Warhol-declared "fifteen minutes of fame," but in each case a highly visible clunker pushed them off the edge.

I liken producing to being on a luxury cruise ship with a thousand other passengers when it springs a massive leak and begins to sink. Everyone rushes for the lifeboats, only to discover that just one is seaworthy, and it holds but twenty-five people. You can imagine the melee to secure a place.

Producing takes two things: taste and tenacity. They're at the top of everybody's list. That's it, only those two things. But they're the things that separate the people I interviewed for this book from the pack.

TASTE

Taste is the single most important thing.

—Brian Grazer

What stories excite you about what characters is what differentiates you from everybody else on the planet. Except you're part of the human race, so hopefully the emotion, the excitement, the pleasure you feel about a particular story will be shared by others—by paying customers.

> **What makes a good producer? The first word that comes to mind is taste. It has to do with the kind of stories you want to tell. The next things are courage and persistence.**
> —Frank Pierson

TENACITY

The greatest taste in the world will do you no good if you're not prepared to do everything short of killing to get your story made into a film. I'm being a bit of a wise guy here because I am a moralist and I strongly believe in not doing anything illegal or even unethical. But the point I'm making is that you have to be totally passionate about getting your film made. The coach of the Russian Wimbledon tennis champion Maria Sharapova said of her, "She's just very focused on what she wants to do, extremely committed. She has that mental toughness; she's determined to make something out of herself." Any high-profile, seemingly glamorous profession has many more people wanting to be part of it than there's room for, so it's fiercely competitive. You better be as tenacious as the clamp of an alligator's jaw.

Writing this book, I solicited advice from Neal Gabler, respected social/media critic and author of *An Empire of Their Own: How the Jews Invented Hollywood.* "Stamina is the most important attribute of an author," he e-mailed. That same shoe fits producing.

Tenacity means persevering when your project has been rejected a dozen (or perhaps two dozen) times. You think of a new angle, maybe a new piece of talent to approach, another financing source. Tenacity is hanging in there; if they knock you down you get up, and if they tell you "no" you go somewhere else. When you've gone through all the somewhere elses, you think up a new angle to pitch and then start going through the list all over again. One of my Peter Stark Producing Program teachers expressed it best: "A project is only dead if you quit working on it."

> **You believe in something, and you go for it.**
> —Christine Vachon

Paramount bought for me Bernard Slade's play *Tribute* before its scheduled Broadway run, in part because of Slade's previous smash success, *Same Time, Next Year.* The out-of-town tryout for *Tribute* in Boston wasn't that successful, and the play didn't knock 'em dead in New York, so Paramount backed out and cut me adrift. But I had an option on the rights in turnaround, so I immediately solicited all the other studios. Even with my strong track record, there were no takers. What was I to do? I loved *Tribute,* the play dealing as it did with a fractious father-son relationship. (Remember, I said I select material of personal relevance. . . . I have three sons.)

There was no way I was going to give up trying to get the picture made. A year earlier I had briefly met a New York financial guy, Richard Bright, who had an associate producer credit on a film that he either put some money into or arranged for. I called him cold and told him of my plight. Bright said he couldn't help but that he would arrange to have me meet a Canadian, Garth Drabinsky, when I was next in New York. Yes, the same Garth Drabinsky who now can't even come to the United States because he's wanted for criminal embezzlement. But this was before Drabinsky founded the multiplex theater chain Cineplex Odeon and started the multiplex trend. He was an ambitious, smart mover-and-shaker who desperately wanted to be big in the movie (and later legitimate theater) business. To me it says a lot about his ego that, although he's a generation younger, he always called me "kid."

Drabinsky arranged Canadian financing, with the aid of government subsidies and tax shelters. I had to take executive producer credit rather than producer (due to Canadian content-tax-law requirements), but *Tribute* got made (starring Jack Lemmon, Lee Remick, and Kim Cattrall in her very first film role). And I'm damn proud of the movie. It was sold to Twentieth Century Fox for distribution and, as a bonus, got me a trip on the Concorde to the Cannes Film Festival. Front door, back door, side door, window, skylight . . . get there any way you can. John Guare wrote a wonderful play, *Six Degrees of Separation,* illustrating how one person you know leads you to the next, and that person to the next. In this case it was who I knew—and who that person knew—that got the picture made. Oh, yes, and Richard Bright got an executive-producer credit on the film, just for the introduction. Believe me, he deserved it.

> *[I attribute my success to] some luck, some talent, and definitely perseverance. It took me a long time. And times were not always good. Sometimes far from it. I kept at it and I kept at it.*
>
> —Curtis Hanson

Of course you really, really have to love films, theater, or TV to be a producer. When you see Brando in *On the Waterfront,* or Meryl Streep in *Sophie's Choice,* or Gene Hackman in almost anything, you have to be riveted, and then exhilarated. I'll never forget when I first saw *Hiroshima Mon Amour.* It contained the first flashback I had ever seen that was a direct cut instead of a shimmering screen that said, in effect, "Hey, folks, we're flashing back in time." It was electric, and I nearly jumped out of my seat with excitement. After seeing *Bonnie and Clyde,* I didn't want to go to sleep that night, I wanted to go out right then and make a movie. Those feelings I had, and continue to have, are pretty much shared by all top producers: the excitement of reading a story, script, or book you think would make a great movie; the nervous energy involved in figuring out how to tie up the material before someone else does; being a little jealous of, even while admiring, a fellow producer's fabulous film. (I congratulated producer Jerry Hellman for *Midnight Cowboy* with the line, "Congratulations, you bastard!" He understood.)

Completing a film that turned out pretty darn close to what you wanted, and knowing it's going to be around forever, is a little piece of immortality, if you care about such things. Sometimes, though, films don't turn out as you envisioned, and they hang around to haunt you. I've had those, too. One critic, reviewing a film of mine that he hated, negatively invoked an earlier film I directed that I thought—hoped—had quietly disappeared. Yet there I was, lambasted in print again for all my peers to see. But I admit that at the time, I had believed wholeheartedly in both films and was glad to have made them.

ORGANIZATION

Now, let's talk. . . . What else really makes a producer? For one thing, you better be organized. You're running a business. You're the

CEO of a company whose job it is to manufacture a couple of minutes of film each day that will become a prototype product you hope a lot of people will want to see.

> *What producers must have, that directors can sometimes get away without, are superb organizational skills, the ability to look after the finances of the picture and also keep tabs on how everybody's doing in terms of what they're supposed to be doing.*
>
> —Curtis Hanson

PROBLEM-SOLVING

You also have to be a psychologist and a therapist. You're dealing with big-time personalities who have big egos. How you deal with them is not teachable. You need people skills, which Daniel Goleman has written about in his fine *Emotional Intelligence.* Some people are blessed with that sensitivity and some are not, but being aware how important it is, and training yourself to be a really good listener, will give you a big leg up. I'm still learning to do just that with my wife and grown children. I highly recommend Goleman's book to anyone who needs to hone their self-awareness and sensitivity to others.

> *You have to be a master psychologist because most people that you're going to be dealing with in this business will have tremendous egos. You have to be able to negotiate around those egos. It's not always an easy task.*
>
> —Dick Zanuck

I've had my failures as a psychologist, too, cases where I wasn't sensitively attuned. Working with Judy Garland, as I've recounted, was like walking on eggshells all the time. At the end of one day, she asked my partner and me what we were doing for dinner that night. I told her we already had plans. As we drove away, my partner said, "Do you think maybe we've made a mistake?" "Nah," I replied. "And besides, I really do have plans." At about one A.M., I was awakened from a sound sleep by Judy, in a vituperative rage, using expletives I hadn't heard before (or since). "Larry, you SOB [one of her milder expletives], I'm at the airport about to leave for the United States because you're such a ******!" But fortunately, presciently, I had her passport. She was a prisoner in England, at least temporarily. And she did indeed show up for work the next day. I felt I earned the equivalent of a Ph.D. in psychology in dealing with her mercurial moods.

Immediately after the success of *The Graduate,* I thought I would try to be a real entrepreneur, setting up financing for a project, selecting the main creative elements, including a producer who would organize and supervise the shoot but not be in the trenches myself. As luck would have it, I simultaneously fell in love with the novel *She Let Him Continue,* and saw a twenty-minute first film effort by a young director and producer team. I glued the two together, and off the heat of *The Graduate* made a swift deal with Twentieth Century Fox. I say off the heat of *The Graduate* because the subject matter of the novel was dark, almost off-putting. But I was flavor of the month (or year); they might have financed the phone book for me. And, as an added enticement to the studio (which I calculated), it was to be a very inexpensive film—about a million bucks. The screenwriter, Lorenzo Semple, Jr., delivered a wonderful script, and he did it swiftly because the novel was powerful and succinct. So I was a relaxed, happy camper at David Wolper's dinner party, bragging that I had a picture starting in several weeks, with a solid script and a superb cast (Anthony Perkins and Tuesday Weld) and that I didn't plan to even visit the location in Great Barrington, Connecticut. I had hired a producer for that. Oh yeah?

Not halfway through dinner, I was summoned to the phone. It was my producer and director team, telling me key crew members were in mutiny, and they were unable to start the picture. I was on a plane the next morning. I arrived to find a disaster. Very little had been prepared. The production manager, Steve Keston, had been a beginning production assistant on my first film, *The Young Doctors,* nine years earlier. He was now a top New York physical production guy, and gave me an ultimatum that unless I fired the director he would quit and take his entire crew with him. Can you believe it? I can't, even now. He thought the director was too inexperienced and unprepared—and he was, unfortunately, right. But choosing a production manager over the director? No way. What a mess . . . I wanted to be back in L.A., in my own bed.

After talking things over with my producer and director team, I immediately went to the first AD and successfully convinced him to stay with the picture and, moreover, got him to ensure that many of the New York crew would hang in there with us. With that in hand, I summarily fired Steve Keston. I then did my producer detective work, found an available New York production manager, and got him up to Great Barrington the next day. And I lucked out. He was strong and experienced, just what we needed. I went around to all the department heads and the people under them, and gave them all pep talks, like any good football coach would. The young producer and director team couldn't believe I was so buoyant and upbeat. Just the night before, had I not lamented what a mess we had on our hands? My producer and director were so unsophisticated, they didn't see the obvious: I had to rally the entire crew, get them on board emotionally, and raise their confidence to work together as a team with 100 percent enthusiasm. And I did.

> *When people are butting heads, and the director won't speak to the writer, the movie is losing some valuable energy. You have to facilitate their communication. A tough, fair debate can lead to the kind of breakthrough that takes a movie to the next level.*
> —Doug Wick

The shooting started smoothly, but immediately fell behind schedule, and continued to do so each passing day. Our schedule was tight, but it was essentially a dialogue picture and, hey, the director had approved the schedule. And I had, too. After the third day I sat with the director as he prepared his shot list for the next day's work. "How many setups do you have?" I asked. "Twenty-two," he said. I then showed him that he'd been averaging about a dozen each day. I mandated—sensitively, I hope—that he figure out how to shoot the next day's work with a dozen setups and have four to six other "gravy" shots in his hip pocket in case he had time for them. We ultimately finished close to our budget, but we paid for it in the editing room. We had very few editing alternatives. I never worked harder on a film or in post-production, and I wasn't even the producer—I was only executive producer.

The net result? We made our film, which I pridefully loved, warts and all. Lorenzo Semple's screenplay was voted best of the year by the New York Film Critics Society, and we got a rave review from Pauline Kael, the most respected critic in the country.

IS THERE A RECIPE FOR SUCCESS?

You could line up twenty people in a row and ask them how they became a producer and they'd each tell you a different story. People think there's some formula, some ladder or a set of steps to go through, but that's just not the case.

—**Kathleen Kennedy**

But there are some things it really does take to become a successful producer. Taste and tenacity. Being organized. Taste and tenacity. Being a psychologist/therapist. Taste and tenacity. Common sense. Taste and tenacity.

A top Hollywood agent, Ari Emmanuel, said an older New York agent, Robby Lantz, taught him four lessons: You have to have taste, you have to be aggressive, you have to be fearless, and you have to have the ability to sell.

The plain fact is that the qualities that make a successful producer are essentially the very same qualities that make someone a success in any field. There is virtually no difference, excepting those few careers that require specialized knowledge such as brain surgery or rocket science.

A producer is a generalist—a jack of many trades, and hopefully a master of some. He or she must have the creativity of an artist, the mind-set of an entertainer, the people skills of a politician, the business acumen of a real-estate developer, the insights of a psychotherapist, the ebullience of a cheerleader, the charm of a snake-oil seller, a stomach and psyche as strong as Arnold Schwarzenegger, the organizational skills of a CEO, the ability of a five-star general to delegate, the malleability of a chameleon, the dedication of a monk, and the tenacity of a bulldog. And, be several of those at any given moment.

These days I am pretty much a full-time academic. I keep my hand in producing, but teaching, which began as my moonlighting job, now takes precedence. I'm pretty darn good at it. And you know what? I use the exact same skill set to run an academic program as I do in producing. I like being good. I like being thought of as good. So I bust my fanny to assemble the best possible team, whether it be teachers or a film crew. I try to imbue each and every team member with the idea that we're a family, that we have a common goal and will help each other to reach it. I work hard to instill pride of product, knowing that, in small measure, it will live after us. I'm a rah-rah cheerleader, but I'm also, when necessary, a diligent critic. I see myself as a sheepdog, scurrying from side to side, barking once in a while to nudge my flock into the pen I've selected. When they're all safely and happily inside, it's a great feeling for me, of course, but for them as well. My taste is utilized in the students I pick and the courses I design, as much as in the stories and creative personnel I choose to make movies. As I've happily learned, the satisfactions and rewards in academia are equal to those in making a film. That is, except for the money—the movie business is feast or famine; academia is a smaller paycheck, but a steady, reliable one each and every month.

HOW HARD IS IT?

IT'S WORSE THAN DOG EAT DOG, IT'S DOG NOT
RETURNING OTHER DOG'S PHONE CALLS.

—WOODY ALLEN (FROM *ANNIE HALL*)

f it were easy, everybody would be doing it. Sometimes, it seems as if everybody is making or trying to make movies. But maybe that's because I live in L.A., a company town. Whatever restaurant I go to, every good-looking waitperson is a would-be actor, or they're a would-be producer, writer, or director. In truth, getting to produce is not easy. In fact, it's damn hard. But so is anything worthwhile. We producers live on hope. I used to practice basketball at home with a tennis ball and an empty coffee can for a hoop, so I could make the basketball team in high school. And that was worth it, too. I loved playing the game and being part of a team, synchronizing my individual skills to mesh with those of my teammates. Again, as I write this, I see the consistency, the parallel of basketball with what I'm doing today—consistency in the desire, the doing, and the satisfaction.

Someone once asked me if I was a gambler and I immediately responded, "Absolutely not. I can't stand to lose a nickel of my hardearned money." He responded by saying, "So why are you in the movie business?" Good question. It is a hell of a gamble. I guess, buried beneath my insecurities, is a nugget of confidence. Maybe even a large nugget, because usually I'm stubbornly convinced I'm right, and that the studios or talent who turn me down are wrong. My psychotherapist wife would call that "denial."

The master Pulitzer Prize–winning playwright Arthur Miller (*Death of a Salesman, The Crucible*), when asked by a *New York Times* interviewer what it takes to be successful, replied, "The hide of a crocodile." The bestselling novelist Karen Joy Fowler (The Jane Austen Book Club) corroborates in her own *New York Times* interview: "I was not the most talented. I succeeded because I was the toughest."

The hardest part is mental, gearing yourself up each day to throw yourself into the fray. And a fray it is, just as in any fiercely competitive field—too many bodies trying to squeeze through too narrow a door. Many get trampled emotionally along the way.

> *It's really a manic depressive world for a producer. . . . Dick Zanuck and I would sometimes sit around in our office in Beverly Hills, having had all our projects wiped out in a single day, and you have to pick yourself up from that. [Longtime producer] Joe Wizan tells a story about a man who gets kicked in the balls every single morning when he goes to work and somehow stumbles through that day. And that's the life of a producer.*
>
> **—David Brown**

Producing makes me think of my dentist's office. If I have a ten o'clock appointment with either my dentist or a creative executive at a studio, I always arrive five minutes early. The door to the dentist's or CE's office opens, and someone comes out and leaves. A few minutes later it's my turn. I present my newest movie project, or have my teeth cleaned, after which I leave. Upon leaving, I see the next appointment sitting in the same chair I was sitting in a half-hour before. That goes on all day long, five days a week. And there are several more creative executives at that same studio taking similar meetings, plus the other studios/financiers on their own merry-go-rounds. My dentist, however, administers to everybody who has an appointment, whereas each studio will finance only a dozen pictures a year. You do not need to be Einstein to compute the math. If you want to be assured that you will be able to pay the rent and put food on the table, I recommend you be a dentist.

It's the only business where in one year you can go from the **New York Times** *Best Ten list to the one hundred neediest cases.*

—Billy Wilder

GETTING PAID

"You can get rich producing, but you can't make a living." That wise-guy quote has occasionally been attributed to me, wrongly. But the statement, although exaggerated, is true. You can make millions on a single film, and I have. But you can also go a long time between films. Today, the top producers make $1 million and up as a fee for producing a film, even if it's a failure. But profits, even though I've tasted them several times (and they're delicious), are elusive.

You've all read or heard about the creative accounting practices in Hollywood, and they do exist, but much, much less so than popular opinion would have it. The studios don't need to cheat. Contracts for producers so favor the studio in every way that, as one wag said, "Profits are like the horizon. As you approach, they recede." Most producers have little or no bargaining power. A handful do, of course, and you likely know those names: Bruckheimer, Rudin, Grazer. They get money from dollar one—the gross receipts, the same as the studio itself. The rest of us—the mere mortals—share in the profits after those gross participants: the stars; often, the director; the studio's distribution fees, marketing costs, and departmental overhead; and, of course, the actual cost of the movie, with interest added on. Even the hugely successful, rich Alfred Hitchcock once complained to me that Cary Grant's gross participation delayed and diminished his own for *To Catch a Thief.*

My most clarifying experience about profits, or the lack of them, concerned *Short Circuit.* Our film was a well-received success—not a runaway hit, but still a hit. Everybody knew it. Nonetheless, after many months in release, I received an accounting from the studio, TriStar, showing that the film, though modestly budgeted at about $18 million, was still in the hole, with a loss of roughly the same $18 million. That very same day—I repeat, that very day—Jeff Sagansky, TriStar's chief honcho, called, urgently asking, "How quickly can you make a sequel?" You are ahead of me here. Would anyone in their right mind in any business do a sequel to a product that had lost money? The answer, obviously, is that they would not. I never did see a single penny of profit from *Short Circuit,* but TriStar must have, because we did indeed, at their behest, produce *Short Circuit 2.* There's gold in them thar hills, but not everybody gets to mine it.

> *The film business is a cruel, shallow money trench, a long plastic hallway where thieves and pimps run free and good men die like dogs.*
> —**Hunter S. Thompson**

Most producers live on their fees—a tiny amount while developing the script, which they cannot live on, and a substantial amount when a film actually gets made, which you can live on handsomely, sometimes for several years if you're wise and prudent. Early in my career I often felt the need to calculate exactly how long, how many months, my savings would "carry" me . . . that is, my wife and three sons. One time, mid-career even, I sold a favorite Milton Avery watercolor, a Matisse lithograph, and a beautiful Morris Graves drawing to cover my living expenses rather than use up my savings. Why? Insecurity, fear. I recall separate conversations I had with two great actors, Jack Lemmon (with whom I did three films) and Henry Fonda (with whom I did *The Best Man*). Each had an amazingly prolific, wonderful, long-lived, nonstop career, yet each told me that after every single film he was fearful he would never get a job again!

REJECTION

> *If you can't stand the heat, get out of the kitchen.*
> —**Old saying**

Like I've said ad nauseum, all of life is producing. In producing this book, I got some of the same rejection I've gotten from day one in the movie business.

On my first few TV films, I worked with a very bright young exec, who later moved on to be a real mover-and-shaker in feature films. We had an excellent working relationship, and I could see the exec was headed for bigger things. The exec actually exceeded my expectations and went to the very top. Soliciting an interview for this book, I sent my usual fax, but to my surprise I did not get even the courtesy of a response. I took that as more dismissive than the rejection I got from the producer whose story follows.

I know an über-producer (name withheld to protect the guilty . . . or myself), as good a producer as there is, a prolific, high-quality, prodigious worker. I faxed him ahead of my New York arrival to solicit a brief half-hour meeting. We aren't buddies, but we have known each other for years. I called immediately upon arriving in New York on a *Monday* (important story point) morning. His assistant called later that day, apologetic: His boss was going to be out of town the entire week I was in New York and couldn't possibly meet me. I got that call on my cell phone while having lunch with my investment guru, Tom Russo, to whom I turned and said, "I'll bet he's not going out of town." Tom replied, "Why would you doubt him?" "You're not in the movie business," I said. Two nights later, on *Wednesday* night, my wife and I were walking down Broadway to see a show, and who do I bump into? You guessed it, the guy himself, who couldn't have been friendlier or nicer. I was equally friendly and nice. I never brought up the subject of my desired interview. My wife later complimented me on being so "classy." I may be an aggressive, assertive guy, but I would have felt demeaned had I the need to even mention my desired interview. It was simple ego self-protection, and anyway my scar tissue, after many years and rejections, is pretty tough.

Smug though I was, there's no guarantee that I actually was right in my self-serving judgment. His plans might have changed, or some urgent business might have arisen that kept him in town. I say that not because I'm generous of spirit in such matters, because I'm not, but the longer I live, the more I learn that whenever I think I know the reason why someone disappoints me, it often turns out to be something wholly different.

The funny thing about rejection is that we give it as often as we get it. Whenever you choose a particular script, restaurant, or boyfriend or girlfriend, you are automatically rejecting the others. I learned, almost by accident, that my attitude toward rejection is different than most. I was part of a seminar panel at UCLA on the topic of rejection. The panel also included an actor, a studio executive, and an agent. Each of them shared the same view: If they couldn't get the job, sell the script, sell the actor, they felt horribly rejected. For me, the rejection of my project by agent, actor, or studio head never bothers me. Oh, of course I prefer a "yes," but I anticipate a "no," and I am rarely surprised. As they say, "Many are called, few are chosen."

However, I can't stand rejection that I consider personal; an unreturned phone call, fax, letter, or e-mail, or the person who volunteers to read my script that very weekend, and six weeks later I haven't heard from him. Or the exec who tells me he personally would read my submission only for me to get the turn-down later from an underling. I wish that stuff didn't bother me, but it does. I have devised my own defensive/aggressive measures to assuage my feelings of rejection, which frankly are powerful and demeaning. If, after what I consider an appropriate amount of time, I haven't received a response to my submission, I will call that person's assistant and ask that the script be returned. That sends a message that I do not wish or accept to be treated that way. Further, it often results in that person reading my submission immediately, or doing so the next time I submit a script. I also make it a practice to never telephone anyone more than twice without getting a return call. If they choose not to call me back, they are sending a very clear message. Actually, this is an accurate thermometer by which to judge your hierarchal temperature. After *The Graduate*, anyone on the planet would call me back immediately. At other times in my career, I was mid-list on return calls. Now that I'm more an academic than a producer, I'm moving toward the bottom of some return call lists.

You can win the producing war and have a successful career (as I feel I have, with a forty-five-year career and many movies to show for it), while nonetheless losing a number of battles along the way. My longtime pal, writer William Goldman, himself the winner of two screenwriting Academy Awards and author of numerous novels and nonfiction books, said so many showbiz books are self-congratulatory ("and then I wrote/did/made . . .") that he advised me to include in this book a failure or two, some rejections. Unfortunately, that is all too easy to do.

IT DOESN'T ALWAYS WORK

Let's start with Bill himself, and our working together. I'd long been a fan of his fiction, and after reading his novel *Boys and Girls Together*, I arranged a lunch with him. We got along famously, even though I told him that compelling as I found the characters in his novel, I didn't think the story added up to a meaningful, successful conclusion. We parted as new friends. Relationships are important to a producer. I think of a producer as a gardener, planting lots of various seeds, conscientiously watering and nurturing them, and once in a while getting a flower.

A few months later Bill called and asked me to read *Archer*, a detective/crime novel by a master of the genre, Ross MacDonald. I did so immediately, but didn't like it. I told Bill it felt like a series of talky interrogation scenes about events that happened twenty years previous. Bill said, "Schmuck. I'm going to write the script on spec." I said, "I don't care. I still don't like the book."

I should've listened when he called me "schmuck." Bill's script became the movie *Harper* and made a ton of money for the producers, rocketing their careers. When I finally did read the script and saw the movie, my stomach sank. It was so damn good. I immediately called Bill and said, "How the hell was I supposed to know you were that talented to make a colorful, action-packed, slam-bang script/movie from that static book?" Well, in fact, I should've known. Wasn't it I who solicited Bill in the first place because of his talent?

That's a producer's stock-in-trade—recognizing talent. And the earlier it's recognized, the better, because the talent is cheaper, and you develop a working relationship for the future.

I like to think I do have an eye for talent. When I was an agent, the first assistant I hired, Marion Rosenberg, was crackerjack, and later became an agent herself—a good one—then a personal manager, and is now a producer, as the outgrowth of representing big-time director Paul Verhoeven.

> *One of the major things a general manager [substitute producer for general manager] has to do is know talent and not be afraid to take risks. You can't teach evaluating talent—you either have it or you don't. As for taking risks, you need the courage of your convictions.*
>
> —Kevin McHale, general manager of the Minnesota Timberwolves, in a *New York Times* interview

But in the case of Bill Goldman and *Harper,* I simply didn't listen clearly enough to my first instincts. So much for my true-to-oneself mantra.

Having learned the hard away and now fully a convert to Bill's talent, I sent him a novel I'd just optioned, *The Graduate.* But he didn't like that book, so he in turn said "no" to me. (No one's infallible!) Next, Bill told me he wanted to do an original script based on two Western outlaws at the end of the cowboy era, when our country was starting to become industrialized. Being a huge sports fan, Bill's template was Mickey Mantle and Roger Maris at the twilight of their careers with the Yankees. That idea excited me, and we immediately set to work on *Butch Cassidy and the Sundance Kid,* but sporadically. Bill lived in New York and I in L.A. so we met intermittently over the next year or two and exchanged lengthy letters (no brief e-mails in those days). At the end of this book is a summary extrapolation of some of those letters, as compiled and published by the Producers Guild of America magazine.

This time Bill and I struck gold, or at least he did. The *Butch Cassidy and the Sundance Kid* script was bought by Dick Zanuck and Twentieth Century Fox for what was at the time the highest price in the history of the movie business for an original spec script. But I did not get to produce the movie. Bill and I had a "friendship" deal, nothing on paper. His Hollywood agent (a business marriage I brokered, no less!) maneuvered his biggest commission-paying TV client to be the producer. This, after I had done the most important work a producer can do—developing the script. No matter, I was left out in the cold. (Welcome to Hollywood!) I should've listened when Stanley Kubrick told me, "I don't trust anyone who doesn't put it in writing." Small justice that the TV client himself was bumped to executive producer when Paul Newman chose a friend of his to actually produce the film.

The details of the *Butch Cassidy* saga are even worse. It was I, while still the common-law producer, who sent the script to Paul Newman. Paul loved it from the get-go and agreed to do it, except he wanted to direct, and I demurred. I sent the script also to Jack Lemmon (trade secret here), who was Bill Goldman's first choice for the Butch role. Yep, he was. But Jack's publicist/friend/manager, who ran his company, turned it down for him. Though I subsequently did two pictures with Jack, I never thought to ask if he had read the script himself. I'll bet not. I submitted the script to director Norman Jewison, who not only turned it down, but added, "There's no way you can spoof the Western genre." Yep, this was the same guy who has had such an enormous commercial and critical career, including winning the prestigious Thalberg Award.

If you dig deep enough, all of us belong to the same mistaken-judgment club. Here's the final irony: While I was still operating as the de facto producer, I submitted our roughly 190-page script to Dick Zanuck, who passed. The version of the script Fox subsequently bought for the record-setting price had been cut by about forty pages, but otherwise was exactly the same in every other respect as the one I had submitted to him. As Zanuck recalled, "You sent me this script of *Butch Cassidy and the Sundance Kid* and said it was terrific. I remember reading it over the weekend—it was huge! It was like four hundred pages. And, in there, which you spotted initially, and I could see vaguely, what became the picture. But there was a lot of muscle play going on with the agent all the time, by the time he rewrote it."

Is there a moral to this story? Yes; there are several:

- Get it in writing. If I had signed an agreement with Bill, I could not have been pushed out. (Samuel Goldwyn, not kidding, said, "A verbal contract isn't worth the paper it's written on.")
- Editing is important. The shorter version of the script was cleaner, clearer, more accessible. So it is with most scripts and films.
- Star power matters. By the time Zanuck and Fox bought the script, the whole town knew that Newman and Steve McQueen were both interested (although McQueen didn't do the film).
- Life goes on.

Bill originally titled his script *The Sundance Kid and Butch Cassidy.* I convinced him to reverse the names.

So I was batting 0 for 3 with Bill. I was down, but not out. *Yet.* Now the final installment, at-bat 4. I prevailed upon Twentieth Century Fox to option for me a tough autobiographical novel about a deserter from World War II, not the most promising commercial subject, but this was right after *The Graduate* and I was, as I've said, hot stuff. Who would I want to write the script other than Bill? No one. And he said "yes." Bill, as nearly always, wrote an amazingly theatrical script with a great leading role. I signed Martin Ritt to direct. He wanted Paul Newman to star, having worked so successfully with him in *Hud*. Having originally solicited Paul for *Butch Cassidy*, I was on board with that idea. However, Paul turned down the role.

Next on our list was Steve McQueen, arguably as big a star as Paul (their inability to agree whose name should be first helped derail Steve's involvement in *Butch Cassidy and the Sundance Kid*). Paul, as the story was told to us, saw Steve at a party and said, "I just read a script I'm not going to do, but it would be great for you." Steve McQueen had an ego, too, and he wasn't about to do something Paul had turned down. Then came the final blow; we got the news that sunk us: Darryl Zanuck, famed film pioneer and studio head, was to produce for Fox his World War II epic *The Longest Day*. He wanted and needed U.S. government and army support, which the studio felt (probably correctly) they couldn't obtain if they financed my movie about a deserter from that same war. So Bill and I, and his script, were down for the count. Our picture never got made. He and I have steadfastly remained close friends, despite never having made a movie together . . . but it would've been nice to have had both!

I have been successful enough that I've been asked to write a book on producing, but I can't believe how many more tales of nonsuccess I have in my dossier. Not once but three separate times, I've developed scripts that I was unable to get produced, yet some other producer got made.

Countdown, an original script by Loring Mandel, was based on research he and I did at the Houston Space Center and Cape Canaveral (as it was then called) about the first capsule to land on the moon. Loring is an Emmy Award–winning writer who received a lifetime achievement honor from the Writers Guild. I was unable to get his script made into a movie. But producer William Conrad did, with Robert Altman no less, directing his first feature.

Burnt Offerings was a metaphysical horror story I couldn't get made, despite having two of the best directors on the planet (Bob Fosse and George Roy Hill) sequentially attached. I met Bob Fosse when he was directing his first movie, *Sweet Charity*. I thought him hugely talented as a Broadway choreographer, and watched with interest as he moved into directing. The brief times we were together, I found him smart and tough-minded as all get-out. I marked him as someone I wanted to work with. *Sweet Charity* proved to be a bomb, after which this terrifically talented director was persona non grata in Hollywood—but not with me. I prevailed upon a new movie company, CBS Films, a branch of the network, to option *Burnt Offerings*, by New York playwright Robert Marasco. Running CBS Films was Gordon Stulberg, a former business-affairs exec at Columbia whom I had negotiated with when I was an agent. We were sort of pals, and that helped me convince him to hire Bob Fosse.

Bob was as tough-minded as I had sensed, always focused and relentless about the work, yet developing the script with him was full-time fun. As a teenager, he had worked in burlesque, and every day Bob would show Marasco and me a different burlesque routine or share some arcane lore. I learned, for example, that a "skull" is when the comic lifts his hat off his head with both hands as his body does a wiggle to emphasize a joke. It doesn't read funny, but seeing Bob do it was.

But I had unfortunately and mistakenly enticed Bob to the wrong project. This time my favorite quote—"You only make one mistake—deciding to do it in the first place"—bit me in the fanny. We never did crack the script. *Burnt Offerings* was moody, compelling, and well-written, but it was a mystery without solution. Crazily enough, I was nonetheless subsequently able to entice director George Roy Hill to develop a new version with me. Alas, at that point, CBS decided that feature films were not for them, and they folded. The option lapsed, which proved to be the end of *Burnt Offerings* for me, despite my having nailed two back-to-back future Academy Award–winning directors (Bob in 1973 for *Cabaret,* and George in 1974 for *The Sting*). It wasn't the end of *Burnt Offerings,* though. Yet another talented director, Mark Rydell, picked it up, or rather had Fox pick up the stage play, and he made the movie—without me, obviously. He knew of my early involvement and even talked to me about it. But, in my experience, Mark's not a guy who is keen to work with producers. He's a capable producer himself, as well as a first-rate director. I couldn't bring myself to ever see the movie, but I do know it was a flop, albeit a flop that attracted three top directors, who saw in it what I did, and what the audience didn't.

For *Destiny Turns on the Radio,* I actually had a green light for production, only to be shot down—first by the schlocky financing company, and then by the writers, who were disgruntled at my inability to get it on-screen swiftly enough. It was eventually made and released (with Quentin Tarantino as Destiny) by Rysher Entertainment, now out of the production business. Perhaps *Destiny* was one reason why.

Happily, it sometimes has worked in reverse, to my benefit. David Susskind, the successful TV producer, owned a story about an alcoholic, *The Morning After,* that he could not get on the air. When his option lapsed, I picked it up and made a television movie for ABC, starring Dick Van Dyke in an Emmy-nominated role. But I only got to do it once—they did it to me three times.

You can do everything seemingly right and still have something bite you in the fanny. I got an early read of a rip-snorting action novel, *First Blood* by David Morrell, which centered on the character John Rambo. The book had movie written all over it. I thought it was perfect for writer-director Richard Brooks, a crusty guy who had a long string of quality, muscular action hits under his belt. I sent it to him via his agent, the colorful Swifty Lazar. Richard, at that point in his career, no longer worked with producers, but he responded strongly to the book. Lazar told me, "Richard has such respect for you and your films, Larry; he's willing to make an exception in your case." I was thrilled, not only because Brooks was the best writer and director for the job, but because of the compliment he'd paid me.

Lazar set up the deal in ten seconds flat at Columbia Pictures. Richard wrote the screenplay without input from me. I was comfortable with that, for a first draft, because of Brooks's talent and because the novel was structured in such cinematic fashion. Months later, when Richard gave me his screenplay to read, I found it to be excellent and told him so, effusively, with compliment after compliment, before concluding with a suggestion that the ending didn't quite work yet. Richard seemed fine with everything I had to say, but early the next morning Swifty Lazar called to relay to me the message that Richard thought either he should do the movie or I should do the movie, but not together. I understood why he didn't like working with a producer. I was stunned, but agreed to bow out because Richard had made the enormous investment of his creative time and energy. Columbia paid me the customary $25,000 development fee, and I was out.

But Columbia never made *First Blood* with Richard. They didn't make it at all. Their option lapsed, and it was picked up by Warner Bros. for director Marty Ritt. But Marty came up empty in developing a script, and Warner Bros. let the project go. For the first couple of years of this saga, with top creative people and studios involved, I was the only one to make any money—my $25,000 development fee. Then a couple of enterprising, entrepreneurial producers, Mario Kassar and Andy Vajna, not only filmed *First Blood,* they made an action star of Sylvester Stallone. The film's success spawned two Rambo sequels, making the producers rich enough to buy their own Gulfstream jet. I had the prescient nose for the material and the skill to set the project up with an ace writer-director, but I still ended up out in left field. You win some, you lose some.

Should I go on? I developed a movie-of-the-week script for ABC with Dick Wolf *(Law and Order),* who only is one of the most successful writer-producers in television history. I failed to get that script on the air. I also read the novel *Rosemary's Baby* in galley proofs before its publication, but I didn't "get" the ending or understand it, so dismissed it out of hand. It became a wonderful film, a classic.

You want more? Marvin Josephson, then head of top talent agency International Creative Management, had been, as Dick Clark's manager, our partner on *The Young Doctors,* my first film. He telephoned me about an exciting new novel he was representing and said he had chosen me to present it to, as he selected his sales targets qualitatively and carefully. I was so cynical and cavalier, I didn't believe his flattering pitch for a moment. I merely glanced through the book, and then rejected it and him. It was *True Grit,* which became the film starring American icon John Wayne, and it was so successful it spawned a sequel, directed by my ex-partner Stuart Millar (which, unfortunately, was not as successful as the original). Like I tell my students, the hitter who leads the league bats only in the mid .300s, and Babe Ruth struck out as often as he hit home runs.

I was playing tennis doubles and my partner was Sidney Poitier (the best-looking guy near eighty I know . . . okay, he's tied with Paul Newman). Our opponents were writers Peter Stone, who has won an Emmy, a Tony, and an Academy Award, and the one and only Neil Simon. After the match, we were shooting the breeze, and discovered that each of us had a project that director Herb Ross had committed to for the next year. A director can do only one picture a year. We were trying to puzzle out whose project he would do, until we realized, simultaneously, he was shining all of us on and that it probably wouldn't be any of ours. Part of producing is great, but part of it is crappy. You can't get one without the other.

> *One of the amazing things about the movie business and Hollywood to me is how everybody lies. I say believe nothing until the money changes hands.*
> —Bill Goldman

SUCCESS DOES HAPPEN

> *Mazel (luck): that which only a competitor possesses.*
> —Yiddish dictionary

I've had enough successes to keep me going, and that's not a casual comment. As most old pros will tell you, survival is the name of the game. Of course, any producer worth his salt aims for meaningful, entertaining, lasting work, but that is hard to achieve consistently. Even three-time Academy Award–winning producer Sam Spiegel *(On the Waterfront, The Bridge on the River Kwai, Lawrence of Arabia)* had more than his share of flops. Single-minded dedication and plain old stick-to-it-iveness sometimes counts for more than creativity and taste in getting a picture on. You have to treat rejection like a fly on your face: Brush it off. So many successes happen because a producer won't take "no" for a final answer, even after getting literally dozens and dozens of rejections. And even though success smoothes the road, there are always potholes.

Producer Dick Zanuck's odyssey to get *Driving Miss Daisy* made is a gutsy example of overcoming rejection:

Driving Miss Daisy was definitely the toughest. Nobody wanted to make it. Absolutely nobody. It wasn't a question of money. Nobody wanted to make it. Period. We would go from studio to studio, and sometimes you could literally see a person's eyes glaze over, about thirty seconds into the meeting. You could see a little sneaky look at the watch, a little panic in the face, wondering "How am I gonna get out of this one?" We were told "no" so many times. Warner Bros. finally took it on. . . . *It was our third time there.*

Driving Miss Daisy won Academy Awards for best picture, best actress, and best supporting actor, and likely cemented Dick's being annointed with the ultimate recognition, the Thalberg Award.

I told Dick about my similar difficulties with *The Graduate.* He replied, "Yeah, but that to me had such commercial prospects. That had sex!" (I could not have greater respect and affection for Dick, personally and professionally, but he was production head of Twentieth Century Fox at the time, and he, too, turned down *The Graduate.*) Had the roles been reversed, I'd likely have said no to *Driving Miss Daisy.* Go figure. That's why I earlier quoted Socrates' axiom, "Know thyself." Your own taste may be different, surely *is* different, but stick to it and stick with it. There is nothing else. Which is an added reason why you better know and love your project going in— it is not a hundred-yard dash, but a two-mile run. And frequently it's a marathon.

SELLING

> *Son, they don't kill you, they worry you to death.*
>
> —Jack Turman

Selling is not really the most important thing, but it's the thing you'll be doing all the time: selling an agent, publisher, or writer to choose you over someone else to make his story into a film, perhaps even with your lesser offer; convincing a studio, a moneyman, or an acquaintance to back you in acquiring an option; convincing a writer to do a script; selling a writer, a director, actors, to commit to your project, rather than another; selling your ideas, your concept, to your creative collaborators; selling the marketing/distribution departments on your thoughts for how to best present your and their finished product. And selling your audience—that's the ultimate target. Then, like painting the Golden Gate Bridge, when you've completed the film, you start all over again when you fall in love with the next story.

There is no one best way to sell something, so don't be daunted if you're nervous at the thought of it. Selling is totally individual. It depends on your personal style. H. N. Swanson was a legendary book agent in Hollywood's heyday. He would guide studio executives to "see" the movie possibilities in literary works by Faulkner and Fitzgerald by putting a spin on their characters thus: "When Burt Lancaster and Kirk Douglas ride into town the first person they see is their old nemesis, sheriff Spencer Tracy." Not only could he sell, but Swanny had great taste. After reading Elmore Leonard's first book, he called him up and said, "Kiddo, I'm going to make you rich." And after 84 rejections, that's exactly what he did. That story surely supports the Greek chorus of "taste and perseverance."

I know producers who literally jump up on an executive's desk and act out every role in the story they're pitching. My style is straightforward, which means I quietly say what it is I've got, and why I believe in it. I personally go for no hyperbole. I will even offer my realistic assessment, such as, "I don't think this particular project can go through the roof, but I can make it inexpensively, and with the level of name actors I think we can attract, the downside should be very limited." My reputation is important to me. Indeed I think it's the most important thing anyone has, and I never want to sully mine by suggesting something I do not wholeheartedly believe in or can't deliver.

> *One of the producer's jobs is closing the deal. Sometimes some of the scripts lying around are great; they just don't know how to get them made. I was a salesman for the early part of my life, so I had the ability to sell.*
> —David Wolper

When I was first trying to break in the business, I managed to get a job interview where the opening question was, "Tell me about yourself." God help me, the first words I heard coming out of my mouth were, "There's really not much to tell. . . ." Needless to say, I didn't get the job and my memory of that interview is still vivid today. Earlier in this book, when I talked about "planning ahead" and "working backward," I also meant, and should have said, "thinking ahead." I should've prepared for that hard-to-get interview and thought about my strong points, what would "sell" me, and been at the ready. But I didn't, and I wasn't. Generally, you get just one bite of the apple so, as the Boy Scouts say, be prepared. Which, if I'd known then what I know now, would have included doing some homework on the guy interviewing me.

In my job interview with a small TV-production outfit, I shouldn't have volunteered (silence is not lying) to the guy interviewing me that I was earning $200 per week (a lot of money in 1954) selling fabrics for my father's textile business. When I didn't get the job, I realized that he himself likely wasn't making that much. Ah, if we only had our wits about us all the time. . . . But there's something called luck, maybe I would not have had the movie career I did if one of those early interviews had resulted in a job.

Sometimes a subtle soft sell is called for. While I was an agent, Ernie Lehman was working with Hitchcock on what turned out to be the classic *North by Northwest*. I tried to get an appointment with Hitch, but his assistant told me, "Mr. Hitchcock doesn't see agents." Ernie confirmed that Hitch was protected, enveloped by his powerful agency, MCA. I begged Ernie to get me in a room with Hitch. Ernie's a pal, and he did it. I figured the reason that Hitchcock didn't want to see agents was that they assaulted him, trying to sell him actors. With his reputation, he could get whoever he wanted, and likely he usually knew who he did or did not want. So I decided upon an oblique approach. I had learned (I did my homework!) that Hitchcock loved wine, and was a great connoisseur. I knew a little bit about wine myself, and that's what I chose to talk about with Hitch. Ultimately, of course, we did get around to talking about his movie. I sold him five—count 'em, five—actors: James Mason and Eva Marie Saint, the two leads opposite Cary Grant; Martin Landau, who had just moved from New York to start his L.A. movie career; and a couple of others. Not bad, huh? I didn't think so, either, and my sons still get a kick out of that story. No good deed goes unpunished, however. . . . Before the movie was even completed, both Eva Marie Saint and James Mason left our agency for another. Tarzan ain't the only one who operates in a jungle.

I watched my boss, Kurt Frings, and his client, director Stanley Donen, maneuver the made-in-heaven combination of Cary Grant and Ingrid Bergman into Stanley's memorable *Indiscreet*. They sold

Ingrid Bergman based on Cary Grant's being definitely set for the picture. (He wasn't.) They then told Cary that Bergman was going to do the picture, so he signed on as well. That dream combination surely helped the film's great success. Would you call that "selling" or "finagling"?

> *I can be very, very convincing when I believe in something. I can breathe life and currency into either an idea or a script.*
>
> —Brian Grazer

I was a real eager beaver as an agent. I was so exhilarated to be in the biz, and so happy to be selling Christopher Plummer rather than periwinkle blue satin, that I worked like I was shot out of a cannon. I remember having the chutzpah to write to an important executive, "I saw so-and-so going into your office, and wondered what he has to talk to you about that I don't." And, to another, I wrote, "How can I get to be as important as Lew Wasserman if I can't even get an appointment to see you?"

COLLABORATION

> *If three people say you're drunk, lie down.*
>
> —comic Ed Wynn

Collaboration is a double-edged sword. At its best, it's wonderful, resulting in better work than that of any one individual. Even not at its best, teamwork generally elevates the results of a movie. And emotionally it can be very nurturing. As has been said about love, all joy is doubled, all pain cut in half.

> *When you're existing in a collaborative art, you need a number of people to embrace an idea and share a point of view. That requires clear communication.*
>
> —Kathleen Kennedy

As in love too, the downside of collaboration, however, is that it's too rarely between or among equals. One person usually has the dominant power. It could be the star, the director, or the studio/

financier. Less often it is the producer, and it is virtually never the writer. If the person with the most muscle chooses to exercise it, collaboration becomes a sham, mere window-dressing. And, in truth, in my experience, most everybody wants the final word. I know I do. Whether it's politically correct to acknowledge it or not, especially in a field as collaborative as filmmaking, the plain fact is that nobody really has full, complete control.

> *It's not an auteur's game. It takes many people to make a picture. Collaborative effort is the whole key. Even the guy moving things on the set can come up to you and give an opinion.*
>
> **—Saul Zaentz**

One of the discoverers of DNA said, "The essence of true collaboration is brutal honesty. Anything less does not serve the goal." Honesty can lead to friction, but better that than swallowing your true opinion. The guru producer Sam Spiegel observed that creative collaboration actually needs abrasion, much like the friction that causes an oyster to produce a pearl.

I like to think I'm enlightened, so in those cases where I have had nearly absolute authority, I have not only listened to and taken into account other opinions, but have actively solicited them. But the choices were mine. Years ago, then Secretary of State Henry Kissinger was at my home for dinner. A guest asked, "Dr. Kissinger, surely you've thought about being president yourself." With alacrity, he replied, "I have, but for a single reason only. That'd be one less person I'd have to convince." That says it all.

> *No matter how much anyone wants to say "I'm the auteur, it was me," it's always a group dynamic. The good version of the group dynamic is thrilling. It's like playing on a great sports team. And the bad version is like someone who always steals the ball and misses the shot. I've experienced both.*
>
> **—Doug Wick**

WHO'S IN CONTROL?

If a producer finds him- or herself overmatched, outgunned, when someone else has final say, he or she must utilize smart, sensitive people skills. Do not come on too strong or down too hard on a particular opinion of the power player be he the director or studio exec or the star. Pick those issues that are important to you, the ones you're willing to go to the mat for. Be judicious about when and how to confront your issues. You get what you want by the logic, clarity, and compelling force of your point of view. Mike Nichols and I, by contract, were equal creative partners on *The Graduate,* yet in practice, he had much more control than I in directing the actors, in editing, and with music and sound. However, I initiated the project, and on those issues of great importance to me, I made sure to be heard and have impact.

Willy Wyler told me he was halfway through directing *The Big Country,* a Western starring Gregory Peck and the lovely Eva Marie Saint, for whom, as her agent, I made the deal. Also in the film was well-known, excellent character actor Charles Bickford, who had a reputation for being a mean guy. One day in the middle of filming, Bickford was scheduled to be in the first scene after the lunch break. Lunch break was over at two o'clock, but no Bickford. By three o'clock he still hadn't shown up. At four o'clock, after the AD had frantically searched for him everywhere, Bickford sauntered in. Wyler angrily approached him and said, "You're two hours late! You held up the entire company." Bickford calmly replied, "Yeah, what are you gonna do about it?" Wyler said to me, "Here I am, arguably the most important, powerful director in Hollywood, and what could I do about it? Nothing! Bickford had control. It's character was established in nine previous scenes. I was stuck. I swallowed it and finished the picture." It continued to rankle Wyler; he never forgot it.

Several years later Wyler was in Europe to film Audrey Hepburn (he directed her first starring role, in *Roman Holiday*) in *How to Steal a Million* opposite George C. Scott (who, although hugely talented, was not known to be the easiest actor to work with). Smiling, Wyler told me his story: "The very first day of filming, Scott was an hour late to the set. I fired him immediately. The studio went crazy. They begged me to reconsider. But I stood firm. His character had not yet been established on-screen. All I could think of was what Charles Bickford had done to me years earlier." In the end, Wyler replaced

Scott with Peter O'Toole, who was romantically a better match for Hepburn, although O'Toole, too, was considered a bit of a hellion.

Years ago, I ran into the great writer Paddy Chayefsky in New York at the same time his screenplay *Altered States* (from his novel) was being filmed in Hollywood. Surprised, knowing he liked control, I asked what he was doing in Manhattan when his film was being shot in L.A. Paddy answered, a bit smugly, "I have total control. My contract says they cannot change a single word of my screenplay." That's power; I was impressed. Except the British director, Ken Russell, was such a jazzy shooter that in many scenes he had the camera pointed at a piece of furniture or a tree instead of the actor delivering Paddy's brilliant dialogue. The sad result? Paddy removed his name from the credits of the finished film.

ACCLAIM

If it doesn't matter who wins, why do they keep score?

Producers are hot stuff to most everyone *not* in the movie business. Producing seems more glamorous and exciting than most other jobs. And it is. That's why "civilians" are more interested in talking to me about what I do than what they do. It's nice; I'm not knocking it. A producer's salary, perks, and restaurant seating are good. But the respect is not. Within the movie community, the producer is the low person on the above-the-line totem pole. As I write this, the Directors Guild of America has just published its manifesto of a director's bill of rights:

> A director, every director, has the primary responsibility [read authority, control] over all creative matters in preproduction, production, and post-production.

Every director? All creative matters? What does that leave for the producer? Only the most important thing—getting the project greenlit and in production. I immediately wrote—even knowing it to be futile—to the President of the DGA, Michael Apted *(Coal Miner's Daughter, The World Is Not Enough, Gorillas in the Mist):* "If I, as producer, option a book or script, develop it with a writer, and arrange the financing for a film, does the director deserve to have *the* primary role or *a* primary role?"

I've still received no answer, all these months later. And Apted is one of the good guys. De facto, the director is in the superior position. In a movie world of very large egos, I admire Woody Allen for *not* taking the "A Film By" credit when virtually every director does, even first-time directors. Since he writes as well as directs his films, he's far more entitled to take the credit than most of those who do.

Growing up, my sons saw me interviewed by the *New York Times,* play tennis with the likes of Robert Redford, Barbra Streisand, and Teddy Kennedy, go to glamorous premieres and parties, enjoy the studio-sent limousines for airport pickups, freebie trips to the Cannes Film Festival, and more. What they didn't see was what happened between nine in the morning and seven in the evening: rejection after rejection; the ugly spirit of competitiveness that made people lie to me, or even cheat; the people who pretended to be my friends when they thought I could do them some good. My sons are now in the movie business, and learning for themselves what really goes on. Nevertheless—and this reaffirms my major point—none of them would rather be doing any other kind of work.

Back to who thinks what about producers. Take a careful look at some movie reviews. Most prominently feature, and talk about, the director and the actors. The writer will sometimes get a mention, but the producer rarely will—unless the producer is a brand name like Cecil B. DeMille used to be, and Jerry Bruckheimer is now. I remember Mike Nichols's agent, Robby Lantz, excitedly telephoning me about the rave review for *The Graduate* in the *New York Times* (merely the single best, most prestigious place in the world to get a good review). "They mentioned your name!" he exclaimed. And why shouldn't they? I caused it to be made. But it was a big deal to Robby because it was out of the ordinary. If you want to be a producer, you better have a strong sense of yourself, and be able to give yourself the appropriate stroking, because you aren't going to get much of it elsewhere.

The Los Angeles County Museum of Art, whose collection has been enhanced by major gifts from prominent producers Hal Wallis, William Goetz, and Ray Stark, has a year-round classic-film program. In the brochure listing the films, only the director and the actors are named, not a single producer or, for that matter, writer. Right here in the company town.

> **As a profession [producing] is woefully misunderstood
> and really discredited as the force that it is. Going to the
> Cannes Film Festival in competition for the first time, my
> name wasn't even in the catalogue. I would have to grub
> a ticket just to be able to walk in with my director. It's
> like, "Why do you think this movie's here?" If you're in it
> for the gratitude, you're not going to get it. If you're
> waiting for it or expecting it, you're in the wrong
> profession.**
>
> —Christine Vachon

Many think of the director as God. Director adulation began long ago, and was given currency and impetus by the French *Cahiers du Cinéma* auteur theory, which held that each film has an author, and it is always the director. Alongside the acknowledged greats, the French also extolled the virtues of the likes of Jerry Lewis and Sam Fuller. They do like to be *au contraire*. In the old days, when producers ruled the roost, the esteemed director Frank Capra (three-time Academy Award winner) was lauded constantly in the press for his so-called Capra Touch. His perennial favorite screenwriter, Robert Riskin *(It Happened One Night)*, was so pissed about the adulation for Capra he once angrily threw a dozen blank pages on Capra's desk and famously said, "Here, give these the Capra Touch!"

Has there ever been a more self-congratulating business than movies? Every single guild, from screenwriters to costume designers, every film festival (and there are scores, from Toronto to Podunk), and most film critics compile "best" lists. I'll bet there are more organizations giving out best-picture, best-actor, etc., awards than the combined Nobel, Pulitzer, and all-star college and professional sports teams combined. They all call attention to themselves by giving out awards and honors. I have seen reviewers call a film "a masterpiece" or "an unsurpassed achievement" in March or April, yet by the end of the year that film doesn't even make their Ten Best list. Weird.

When I worked in my father's textile business, the only award given was for the winner of the annual TALA (Textile Association of America) golf tournament. Conversely, if you survive for any length of time in the movie business, you're bound to receive an award for something. I got a "starter" award for my very first film, *The Young*

Doctors, a modest little drama that was barely a success. Some exhibitor organization named it "Picture of the Month," and I received an engraved plaque, now rusted. Walk into any Hollywood office, you'll see the walls adorned with plaques and scrolls recognizing achievement and almost always flanked by posters from the occupants' films (and not only their hits). You will also see a lot of reflected glory on those walls: a photo of Producer A with Steven Spielberg, Tom Hanks, Jack Valenti, or maybe the president of the United States. (I've got one of those; I keep it in a drawer, but I'm not pooh-poohing it; I just don't feel the need to put it on display for whomever walks into my office.) There are also those who practice reverse-chic, and use their Academy Awards as doorstops. (Alas, I do not have one of those.)

My own ego is probably as large as that of those who decorate their offices in such a fashion, but I have a need to be different, to separate myself from the pack. Art posters that I've collected over the years adorn my walls—same ego; different manifestation. I have Picasso's self-portrait staring at me, instead of Dustin Hoffman's face. My pet theory is that the movie business attracts people of low self-esteem, looking for their place in the sun. And that is not said to denigrate the genuine artistic passion that many possess or are possessed by.

Even though my preceding comments are somewhat derisive, they are about some folks in Hollywood, not all, and certainly not about the movie business itself. I am not cynical, cavalier, or denigrating about what I've chosen to do and what I'm encouraging you to do. Every field has some practitioners you would not like to have dinner with. In the textile business I would take a telephone order for, say, four bolts of fabric at thirty-five cents a yard, write up the order, and schlep on my shoulders that eighty pounds of cloth a football-field-length to the manufacturer's factory, only to be told upon arrival that he was canceling his order as he had since bought the same fabric from somebody else for half a cent less per yard. I'd rather deal with someone who has a photo of himself with Pamela Anderson on his wall.

Art and satisfying one's soul are wonderful, but the money is also not so bad. I went the way of all flesh after *The Graduate* and bought a big Hollywood house, the former home of Dore Schary, legendary head of MGM in its heyday. Hollywood is very big on celebrity-labeled homes; no matter how much success I had over the years, my home, ironically (and unimportantly), was always referred to as "the old Dore Schary house," never "the Larry Turman house." Before I started in the movie business, I had a date with the daughter of a prominent agent. When she gave me her home address, I told her I didn't know where it was. "Sure you do," she replied. "It's right past David Selznick's house, a block up from Fred Astaire's place." I had not a clue what or where she was talking about. And the topper came when I picked her up. I was chatting with her parents and they began talking about a film I hadn't heard of. "That film's not out yet," I said. "Sure it is," they replied in unison. "We saw it at William Goetz's home last week!"

In those days, all the mucky-mucks had home projection rooms. I did, too, after *The Graduate*. This was before videotapes; it was a big deal. The film I would show on a Friday night would be picked up by, say, producer Jerry Weintraub on Saturday morning so he could show it that evening, while I'd arrange a pickup from, say, Mike Medavoy or Peter Guber to screen on Saturday night. We'd serve dinner (I went the Chinese-chef route) before or after but, amusingly, some friends wouldn't come to dinner because they'd already seen the movie at someone else's house! Aside from the sociability, it was a good way to keep up with the current work of creative and technical talent. For some, it was a competition; it was a coup to be the first to show a hot new film. With the advent of videocassettes and then DVD, much of that life—bicycling a print from one home to another—is gone.

Those home screenings were used to extend one's reach and access in the who-you-know department. Movers-and-shakers like meeting and mingling with each other. Tom Brokaw was anchoring a Los Angeles station in those days, and mixing him with Barry Diller, director Mark Rydell and überagent Sue Mengers was a kick for me and for them as well. Sue told me that for her dinner parties she would use one big name as a lure to get another she wanted to meet or get to know better. I recall her telling me Jack Nicholson had first come to her home to meet Mick Jagger.

Hollywood social life is inextricably mixed up with business life. Many young agents, studio execs, and producers don't consider the twelve-to-fourteen-hour days they put in as work. That's because the last four hours of most days are spent at a screening, often followed by a party or a leisurely expense-account dinner at a fine restaurant, furthering a relationship with someone who can do you some good. It's glamorous and seductive. For me, that aspect quickly wore out its welcome. I had the advantage of being born in Los Angeles; my friends were and are my friends of long standing. Most in the film business, however, come from somewhere else; they meet people primarily through work. Their social life becomes incestuous and narrow. One has to make a conscious effort to have and maintain a full and varied real life. As with moviemaking, I recommend the effort. It's worth it.

If you're looking for fame, I suggest you be a rock star or a U.S. senator. Yet, despite the preceding candid, truthful, legitimate gripes, I wouldn't trade my profession or the career I've had for any other. Nor would any of the professionals I interviewed who, when asked, "Do you like producing?" to a person replied enthusiastically, "I don't like it. I love it."

THEN VS. NOW

"Fings Ain't Wot They Used t'be."

—Lionel Bart song title

Back in the so-called Golden Age of Hollywood, even as recently as three decades ago, things were better. Certainly for producers, but overall as well. Everyone in America used to have the movie habit; going to the movies on a Friday or Saturday night was a regular (and less-expensive) activity. Professional football and basketball were not the big draws they are now. Fewer people worked through the weekend. There was no Internet or cable. And, believe it or not, there was a time when there wasn't a television set (or two) in everybody's home. For producers, it was like having your own personal oil well in a field that Standard Oil owned and ran, and they supplied all the equipment and workers you needed. Today, producers are "wildcatters," on the lookout, scrounging for a piece of land they can make their own, where they can sink a well and maybe once in a while strike oil.

When I started in the business, each studio had under exclusive year-round contract a dozen or more producers, each enjoying a fat weekly paycheck. And that was a time of low income taxes. Heaven. Better yet, the studio would send a memo to all their producers saying something like, "Today we have purchased the Pulitzer Prize–winning novel by so-and-so. Please register your interest if you would like to produce this project." And each studio had writers, directors, and actors under contract, and all the physical production personnel and equipment to make the film. Today it's a full-court press, full-time hustle, to get your hands on a hot novel or script.

And if and when you do, there's the next hurdle: trying to attach actors. I'll never forget meeting with Dick Zanuck, then head of Twentieth Century Fox, after I turned in *The Flim-Flam Man* script, written by the renowned, and talented, William Rose (*The Man in the White Suit, It's a Mad Mad Mad Mad World,* and *Guess Who's Coming to Dinner*). Rose's script was excellent so I was feeling good, even cocky. But Dick Zanuck had a very long, sad face. I was startled. "What's the matter, Dick? Don't you like the script?" He replied, "I love it, it's great." "So why the long face?" "Larry, you see this desk I'm sitting at? My dad sat here for many years. When he got a script he liked, he looked at the typewritten list of actors and directors the studio had under contract, faceup under glass on his desk. He would say, 'We'll start shooting in three months with Henry King directing, and put Tyrone Power, Don Ameche, and Alice Faye in the movie.' I, his son, on the other hand, sitting at the same desk have nobody under contract, so I have to go to Jack Nicholson's agent, hat in hand, and plead with him to at least consider *The Flim-Flam Man* over the dozen other scripts he has by his bedside." That said it all. We ended up with George C. Scott, every bit as good an actor as Jack Nicholson, but having nowhere near the box office allure. *The Flim-Flam Man* got better reviews than *The Graduate,* but you, dear reader, likely never heard of the film.

Today, the motion-picture business is bigger, better, smarter, and more successful than ever. Now the whole world is our market, in a way it never was before. Most of the revenue used to come from right here in the good old United States of America. Today, the film industry's marketing reach is so great that the cognoscenti in England, Germany, and Japan learn what the grosses are for hit pictures at the same time we in America do. And every day, more foreign markets have access to American-made films on video and

DVD. The latter has proved a gold mine. And that old enemy, TV, seems to provide everlasting financial return for old movies. In fact, mass-produced entertainment is one of America's top exports. It's big business, and has thus—for better or worse—become institutionalized and acquired corporate mentality. There aren't any stand-alone movie companies like there used to be. Now they are all part of entertainment empires: Vivendi Universal, News Corporation, Sony, and Viacom.

The producer's authority more and more has been usurped by studio executives, many of whom have never written, directed, acted, never really had a job in the industry over which they preside.

—**Frank Pierson**

In the old days, I would meet with the head of the studio who, after reading my script, would say, "I like it; let's make it," or, "This one is not for me." Those bosses were true seat-of-the pants mavericks like Jack Warner (Warner Bros.), Harry Cohen (Columbia), Louis B. Mayer (MGM), and Darryl Zanuck (Twentieth Century Fox). Today, each studio has many layers of executives under the studio head, each of whom has the power to say "no" but not "yes." If this committee, or the studio head herself, says, "I like it," it is not followed by, "Let's make it," but by, "Let me see what foreign has to say about its potential in Europe, Asia, and South America," or "I want to show it to marketing, to see if they feel confident about advertising this concept."

One of the things that make it tough today is the people who really pull the lever to go or not to go, in most cases have very little actual experience, and know very little about the mechanics. But they're in charge, so you have to deal with that, which we never used to. When we used to go to a studio and see a Darryl Zanuck or a Harry Cohen or a Jack Warner, whoever it was, they were picture makers. And you couldn't hustle them because they invented the goddamn business. They knew more than you knew about how to do it. But today, you go in and it's the old Fred Zinnemann story.

—**Dick Zanuck**

Here's that story: Fred Zinnemann (two-time Academy Award–winning director), toward the end of his career, met with a young, twentysomething studio executive, whose first question was, "Tell me, Mr. Zinnemann, what have you done?" Zinnemann, older but still steely-sharp, replied, "You go first." That young executive should have read my section on homework.

I remember precisely the epiphany I had that things had changed, that it was now all about marketing. I had a meeting with Alan Ladd, Jr., a taciturn good exec, when he was production head of MGM. I had submitted a project to him that he simply did not like or get. No problem for me; I've long been used to turndowns. After all, it only takes one "yes," one buyer; he clearly wasn't the one. At least he was straight-ahead candid, as always. As I was leaving his office, my hand on the doorknob, he said, "But if you attach an element, a star or a director, please come back to me." The pugnacious me felt like saying, "I thought you hated the script," but the pragmatic me said nothing. "Don't bite the hand that feeds you," is a thousand-year-old piece of wisdom. I knew that if I was indeed able to attract a marketable star, or a director who could in turn attract a star, Ladd would be a potential financier of the script, the very script he didn't like.

When *The Graduate* was first released in late 1967, the subject of a young college graduate sleeping with the wife of his father's partner while romancing her daughter was considered racy, sexually provocative. Brief flash cuts of a woman's bare breast (Anne Bancroft's body double) was pretty strong stuff then. When the film was re-released in 1977, with the rating system instituted, *The Graduate* received but a mild PG rating, not being rough enough to get an R. In the wink of an eye, society had undergone a dramatic change, and the movie industry quickly followed suit.

I had a similar experience about how fast things change with *The Great White Hope.* In the climactic dramatic moment black heavyweight champion Jack Johnson, hounded out of America, living in forced exile, reluctantly, angrily agrees to fight the "white hope," who was to take his title. "Set up dat fuckin' fight," he says. Even though that line of dialogue was taken right from the Pulitzer prize–winning play, the ratings board insisted that the use of the "F-word" would mean an automatic X rating. The studio, Fox, felt that such a rating would be box-office death for this expensive picture. So we had to excise the "F-word" and substitute *damn* (I wanted, vindictively, to use *darn,* but I would only have hurt myself). Not two years later the same studio released *M*A*S*H* and every third word seemed to be *fuck.* It got an R rating! As passionate and upset as I was at the time, losing the F-word didn't exactly ruin *The Great White Hope*—but seemingly overnight the use of that particular expletive became acceptable to mass audiences (and to studios).

At roughly the same time, *Midnight Cowboy,* with a dreaded X rating, won the best-picture Academy Award. In fairness, *Midnight Cowboy* cost considerably less to make than did *The Great White Hope,* and had a known star, "my" Dustin Hoffman, whereas James Earl Jones and Jane Alexander had been making their film debuts. As good as *The Great White Hope* is, I have to admit *Midnight Cowboy* is a better picture.

In the old days, the credit roll before and after a movie generally took less than a minute. Today, the credit roll often takes up to four or five minutes, and in a handful of cases even longer. The credits for *Sky Captain and the World of Tomorrow,* starring Gwyneth Paltrow, Jude Law, and Angelina Jolie, listed 896—count 'em, 896—names. Such long credits seem ridiculous and boring, except to those who worked on the film and their immediate families. Computer-generated images (CGI), which constitute a large part of many films today, require added teams of workers, who need to be, and should be, duly credited. Nonetheless, wasn't it a lot better in the old days when, after just a few seconds of credits, you were into the movie? I think so. If I were king of the universe, I would mandate that everybody get credited one time only for doing the specific job of producer, director, writer, whatever. No "A Film By," or "So-and-so's Production of," etc. Now we all have to sit through an interminable list of credits fore and aft. And all the so-called creative people are named on the posters and billboards. Often there are so many, in fact, that their names are bunched and scrunched and virtually unreadable.

Here's how it is now, and it didn't used to be this way. In April 2003, I met with Bingham Ray, then head of United Artists, and pitched him the idea of doing a new version of Gore Vidal's political play *The Best Man*. Since UA had financed the 1964 film I produced with my then partner, it seemed logical to solicit them to do a 2004 version. Bingham Ray sparked to the idea with genuine enthusiasm. Indeed, he even suggested a director, Burr Steers, who was not only Gore Vidal's nephew, but who'd had attention-getting success with his first film, *Igby Goes Down*. Bingham said he had loved *The Best Man* and wanted to look at the old film again. I left his office elated. I didn't hear from him for a couple of weeks, so I telephoned, only to learn he was at the Cannes Film Festival for the first half of May. A week later, he called me to say he couldn't get hold of the original *Best Man*, a film his company had financed and distributed, and assuredly had a copy of. A month later, at the end of June, he called raving about the film, which he had now seen, citing to me chapter and verse how much he liked the acting, directing, script—the whole movie. I was pleased with his effusive compliments, and thought I was on my way. But then he told me his boss, Chris McGurk, head of MGM (UA's parent company), wanted *The Best Man* for MGM, not UA. That was fine with me. It was better, actually, as MGM made bigger-budgeted pictures.

I called Chris McGurk, who I knew well, and after a week of telephone-tag connected with him. He wanted to hear Gore's "take" on the new version, which was not unreasonable, except two and a half months had gone by, and Gore had returned to his home in Italy. I tried to arrange a conference call for early July, timed to my annual visit to Italy, when I often visited Gore. Easier said than done.

With so many bodies involved, I had to wait until Gore returned to Los Angeles for knee-replacement surgery. The inimitable Gore wanted McGurk to come to his home for the meeting, feeling that he "outranked" him. I couldn't pull that one off, so we all agreed to have our conference call, which I was able to finally pull together the end of August. The call went great. Gore was dazzling—smart, clear, funny. Except, after all that, Bingham Ray at the last second wasn't able to be on the line with us.

As fortune would have it, the very next night I ran into McGurk at a screening. I attacked, meaning I walked across the aisle to confront him. He'd loved what Gore had to say, but said he thought it should be a United Artists film, not MGM, exactly the opposite of what Bingham had told me. The good news was that McGurk had already told

Bingham to move ahead with the deal. Again, I was pumped, even more than four months earlier, when I first broached the idea. McGurk's mouth was the horse's mouth, so I thought I was off and running. But a week passed and I heard nothing from Bingham. I called him. He didn't call me back. I followed up with a fax. Again, no response. I then faxed McGurk, asking if he could move things along. Bingham was, after all, his employee. No response. I called Bingham again, only to learn that he was away at the Toronto Film Festival and couldn't be reached.

I decided, perhaps later than I should have, to involve Gore's powerful Creative Artists Agency. It took Gore's agent a week to reach Bingham, who confirmed that UA was indeed going ahead with the deal. The agent then tried to contact the head of business affairs of UA to negotiate Gore's deal—first things first. When the agent finally did reach him, he was informed that UA had to confer internally before making an offer. I personally knew that business-affairs guy, so I got into the act. He promised me he would make the offer for Gore, after which he would negotiate for my services as producer. But by mid-October, half a year after I'd presented the project to an enthusiastic response from the head honcho, the deal for Gore Vidal's writing services still had not been closed. That's how it is now. I assure you it wasn't like this then. As poet François Villon wrote, "Where are the snows of yesteryear?"

> *The lousy part of producing, especially nowadays, is making deals. It's become so incredibly complicated. Contracts and negotiations are a frustrating component of my job, and I think it stalls the process in a way that can hurt a project's momentum. You need lawyers talking to lawyers, and there's no grassroots component to deal making anymore. I find it tremendously time consuming in an unnecessary way.*
>
> **—Kathleen Kennedy**

This story I've recounted is not about people—Bingham Ray is a solid citizen, successful and smart, although he was recently fired, ostensibly (as stated in *Variety*) because he was more concerned with art than commerce. Chris McGurk, meanwhile, has breathed life into the moribund ex-giant MGM. Indeed, this story is about the world of movies today, where even small films cost a lot, and then cost a lot more in finding a place in the marketing sun. Every bet on every film is a big one. The rewards for the winners are humongous, from the tiny *My Big Fat Greek Wedding* to the monster *Lord of the Rings* trilogy. But the downside for the losers is also humongous. It's all big stakes, big decisions, so unless there's an auction mentality, things move slowly—too slowly for my taste, but I have no choice. At least I'm on my feet, still bobbing, weaving, and moving forward, like all of us in the ring.

In the old days, the studios used to want both art and commerce. They still do, but the scales have tipped and commerce is the goal, with art sometimes being a fortunate by-product. I'm reminded of the story about the uneducated Samuel Goldwyn selling himself to the world-renowned intellectual playwright George Bernard Shaw to get Shaw to entrust one of his plays to Goldwyn for filming. Shaw reportedly said, "Mr. Goldwyn, you seem to be interested in art, whereas I am interested in commerce!"

> *The big difference is the costs are so horrific, and they didn't used to be. I think it's great that stars make money. I want us all to make money. I think the problem is that when the costs get astronomical, it limits the kind of movies you can make. And, you tend to make mostly shit, which is what Hollywood has been doing.*
>
> **—Bill Goldman**

I'm well aware that every generation thinks things were better in "their day." I've never met a person who didn't think his high school graduating class was the best the school ever turned out. Does this sound familiar? I think it was Socrates who complained that the children of ancient Greece were slack and slothful compared to his generation. So I'm in good company, and I will stick by my guns. Producing, the life of a producer, was indeed better then—much better—than it is now. But I bet you wouldn't get that answer from Jerry Bruckheimer, Scott Rudin, or Joel Silver. And dammit, even I continue to say producing is a noble profession—it's just not for the faint of heart.

AGEISM

Old soldiers never die, they just fade away.
—General Douglas MacArthur

Here's a question I ask myself: Why did two of the very greatest directors—Billy Wilder and Elia Kazan—not direct a single film during the last two decades of their lives? Kazan's last was when he was sixty-seven, Wilder's when he was seventy-five. I do not believe it was because they chose not to direct. I knew each of them, and both were physically rigorous and mentally sharp into their eighties. Was it because, after making studios richer, each made a last film that was not a commercial success? Was it, as my wife suggests, that their interests and their sensibilities were out of touch with the world in which they were living? This is hard to believe, as Kazan continued to write novels and Wilder amassed yet a second cutting-edge art collection. Without being able to prove it, I think that surely there was more than a modicum of ageism involved.

When I was deciding upon a director for *The Great White Hope*, I considered George Stevens, whose work from the early *Gunga Din* through the masterful *Shane* and *A Place in the Sun* ensured his position as one of the greats. When I brought up his name, the Twentieth Century Fox front office said he was "past it." Past what? I don't think they just meant artistically; rather, they felt he had bloat and would take too long to shoot, would spend too much money. In most professions age is venerated. But not so in the movie business. Ronald Reagan was not exactly a kid when he was running our country. But pop culture is for the young. And even though the best films are indeed art, their raison d'être is pop-culture commerce.

Many of us, myself included, evidently think of ourselves as younger than we are. During the first day of filming on *The Young Doctors* in Poughkeepsie, New York, a crowd gathered outside our hotel. Our star Fredric March sought me out. "It's my first day. Tell them I'll sign autographs later." I didn't have to tell the crowd anything; March got into his waiting company car, and no one in the crowd even noticed him. But two minutes later, when Dick Clark walked to his car, the mob went crazy and surrounded him. It's hard for an aging star to compete with "young and hot." Of course, today

Dick Clark is himself an aging star but is still competing successfully with the young and hot. Nonetheless, Bette Davis was on the mark when she said, "Old age ain't for sissies." Neither is producing.

The beauty of being a producer (as well as the difficulty) is that you're not for hire. If you have a great idea or control a great property, you'll be the producer of that film no matter how old you are because they can't legally make it without you. Although I'm getting up there in years, I've never experienced age discrimination, nor do I expect to. As long as my brain is working and I still have some fire in my belly, I can produce. Studios, moneypeople, don't go into business with a producer for his talents (although they recognize and prefer the good ones). Rather, they get in business with a producer for what he or she brings to the table . . . an unusual story, a top director they can't say no to, a box-office star over whom they are salivating. A few of the younger people will "shine me on." It doesn't feel good (reread my chapter about rejection), but it does not deter me. Sometimes an agent will say, "Of course, Larry baby, I'll send your script to movie star so-and-so. You have great taste and a track record." But often, that script does not find its way into the hands of the actor I desire. So I have to be ingenious. Does that actor have his own production company to which I could submit? Perhaps a personal manager? He has a publicist or a lawyer, for sure. I live by the mantra I preach to you: front door, back door, side door, climb in through a window.

Dino DeLaurentiis and David Brown are both in their eighties and still at the top of their game, each having been honored by their peers with the prestigious Thalberg Award.

> *I attribute my success to my editorial creativity, which doesn't die with age. The kind of quality that can keep you working through many, many years, if your brain holds up, is your ability to think up ideas. Ernie Lehman and I used to meet at the beginning of the day. We'd think up something goofy, an article, an idea or something, which we sold. We were able to be self-employed. Producers are self-employed, with all the disadvantages.*
>
> —David Brown

TRICKS OF THE TRADE

Peter O'Toole, as Lawrence of Arabia, while holding a lighted match to his palm for what seemed an interminable time, is asked, "Doesn't it hurt?" "Of course," he replied, "The trick is to not mind the pain."

There are no tricks. There's only character. Who you are and how you conduct yourself will determine how you are perceived and how you are treated. Me writing about character in this book will likely do you no good, as your character is surely well-formed by now. When I am in my wise-guy mood, I feel there are only two kinds of people in the world: those who are on time and those who aren't; those who are neat and orderly and those who aren't; those who tell the truth and those who don't. Clearly there are shadings. C.E.M. Joad, a British philosopher, said, "Everybody lies, even the nuns when they have to take a pee excuse themselves with, 'I have to go wash my hands.' " Little things matter and do add up (like never jumping to the front of the food-truck line at mealtime, even when perks and position allow you to).

My own personal style tends to be aggressive, but I acknowledge it, to take the edge off ("Dear So-and-So, I don't mean to press you, but . . ."). Or I'm aggressive, and defuse it with humor—however, this can be dangerous, as humor is often misunderstood. Another tack I take is to be assertive in making the call or writing the letter or fax, yet give the person a way off the hook ("I need/want something from you, but if you are unable to accommodate, I'll of course understand").

Pamela Harriman, famously married to Winston Churchill's son and later to Avril Harriman (with pit stops along the way with the likes of the Agnelli scion) was rumored to have special sexual prowess. When asked about it point-blank, she answered, "There are no tricks. There is only enthusiasm."

STAY ORGANIZED

My so-called trick is that I'm obsessive-compulsive. I like a clean desk, nice and neat—not that I ever achieve it. Working on several projects at the same time and trying to find and scare up new ones means there's always lots of activity like a mouse on a treadmill. There's more clutter than I'd like in my head as well as on my desk, but I work hard to keep everything current. Like many, I complain from time to time, but I do seem to thrive on the hectic hustle. My compulsiveness serves me well.

RESPOND PROMPTLY

I answer every phone call and letter, even those from strangers, and I do it right away. I do it for my own peace of mind, to get it off my desk and know I don't have to think about it anymore. And it's common courtesy. When I receive or solicit a new piece of material, I respond very quickly. Agents and managers like that. Their clients, writers and directors, like it, too. It helps put you high up on their list for the next time they submit a book or a script. I even ask, when I'm finished, if they'd like me to return it. Good manners are good business. That philosophy got me a reputation for being reliable, which I am. And I appreciate people who respond similarly when I'm the one doing the submitting.

BE RELIABLE

I think reliability is one of the best traits a person can have in any business, and in life. Do what you say you're going to do, and do it when you say you're going to do it. I've lived by that rule, and I like to work with people who have the same credo.

Clarity and *consistency* are watchwords: Be clear about what you want, be clear about how you go about getting it, and be clear with everybody with whom you communicate. And be consistent within that clarity. Allow people to count on you and what you say without a questioning thought. I'm talking about following your personal moral compass and work ethic, which will dictate your way of working. It should allow you to say "I don't know" when indeed you don't have the necessary skill or information, and it will enable you to admit you're wrong when you make a mistake. Surprisingly, you will find that will actually increase others' respect for you.

When you're producing a film, many people working for and with you have to be able to count on your reliability, your consistency.

They need to know what to expect from you. There's great security in that. It allows people to respect you, trust you, relax with you, and function at their best.

PEOPLE SKILLS

Do you like it when someone thanks you for something you did for them? Or if someone compliments you on your new sweater or the meal you cooked? Sure you do. We all do, even if the praise is dutiful rather than sincere. Who can judge, after all? Who can tell the two apart? As you make your way, remember to acknowledge those who helped you or showed you a kindness. It's the right thing to do, and you'd be surprised at how it can smooth your path.

Sam Goldwyn, Jr., who has his own specialty production and distribution company, told me his father's advice was, "Son, be nice to everybody, because you will meet them all twice. Once on the way up, once on the way down." I think the older Sam Goldwyn was right, not only because it's good business, but because it's being a good person. Jealousy, anger, fear, and competitiveness are all pernicious emotions, and the less we feel and have of them, the better our lives will be. Okay, so I'm preachy. Maybe it's destiny that I ended up as a teacher. The older Goldwyn's words of wisdom are clever, but some people do go up and up and up, and don't ever come down.

Nothing is more important, more valuable, than so-called people skills. I do not mean the particular skill set a person has (like an engineer or a computer wizard), but rather being tuned in to other people. People at the top of almost every field are blessed with that talent. It means knowing when to push and when not to push, and how to do it with tact and style. I've been turned down by Hal Ashby and Sydney Pollack with such grace and charm that they made me feel I had just won the lottery rather than having had them say "no" to a script I wanted each to direct.

That kind of tact and sensitivity can be deceptive, though. Some of the sleaziest, most untrustworthy people I've had to deal with were oozing likability. Indeed, I've heard many colleagues remark that so-and-so is such a nice person. What they mean is that he or she is beguiling and charming. Alas, many people are fooled by that, unless and until they are on the receiving end of a dirty deed. Those charmers, of course, are not restricted to the movie business. They abound in every field from advertising to politics.

Fortunately, they're in a minority; unfortunately, some of them do get to the top. This does not mean you should adopt their tactics. Your reputation is your most important possession; it's based on character, *your* character (not that your unconscious gives you much choice in how you deal with people), or what stories you choose to tell. As an atheist Jew, I believe nonetheless in Jewish folk wisdom, "What is hurtful to you, do not do unto others. That is the law; all else is commentary." But enough preaching; as you have likely already discovered, integrity to yourself is as important as integrity to others.

> *It's all about character and common sense. Someone once said, "I can hire professionals, I can hire mechanics. But you can't hire common sense, you can't hire character."*
>
> —Saul Zaentz

MODES OF COMMUNICATING

I love the fax. It's a way of expressing yourself clearly, succinctly, and without fear of interruption. Plus, it has the advantage of the recipient being able to reread your message. And it's immediate. In the movie business, you can play telephone tag with someone for a week (unless, of course, Gwyneth Paltrow or Brad Pitt places a call). When you do connect on a call, at the other end two other buttons are probably lit up and, with the rampant, ambitious anxiety residing in so many Hollywood players, you may not have the listener's undivided attention. I do make phone calls, of course, many of them . . . but I love the fax and utilize it often.

My favorite use of the fax was for a meeting I had scheduled with an HBO executive. He had canceled and rescheduled three or four times, and when I showed up at his office for the appointment he did not cancel, I was still kept waiting. After half an hour I called my secretary (that's what they were called in those days; today, it's "assistant") and dictated a fax to be sent to that HBO executive: "By the time you read this I will have left your office; it is unprofessional and unconscionably rude, after canceling three previous appointments, to keep me waiting so long." By the time I got back to my office there was an apology waiting, with an entreaty begging me to give him another chance. I did, and now we have a good business relationship. As my friend Stanley Kubrick said, "You make people treat you the way you want to be treated."

As much as I love the fax, it's Pony Express compared to e-mail. I was late getting into the tech world, but once there, I became an e-mail junkie. For swift and reliable communication, nothing beats it. E-mail hasn't really changed anything in show business, except it makes everything faster. I've already noted that I'm an impatient guy, so e-mail is right up my alley. But the very speed of e-mail does increase the pressure of the business. My attorney complains that when he marks up a proposed contract for suggested changes, he used to have a couple of weeks' respite before hearing back from the opposing attorney. Now it's right back in his face after a couple of days, giving him no breathing room.

If I'm diligent and a good enough detective to get someone's e-mail address it gives me a leg up. I can contact that person directly without being blocked or shunted aside by a protective assistant, as so often happens. Among the truly powerful in Washington is the appointment secretary to the president, with his own battery of assistants. But if you can get the president's personal e-mail address, you'll have his ear.

I recently traded phone calls for over two weeks with the manager of a big-time actress. The manager was scrupulous about calling me back at eight in the morning or eight in the evening, a standard Hollywood trick. I sent her an e-mail and within a day received a reply: "Please send me your script." She promised to read it promptly. Good. That was three months ago and I haven't heard back. Bad.

So e-mail does make me a tad more productive. I'm a superb typist, from my early Navy training, and can knock out a dozen e-mails in no time at all, although my wife (correctly) admonishes me to think before pressing the Send button. But is faster always better? Not if you're engaged in sex or having a fabulous meal at a fine restaurant.

Better than a fax or e-mail, of course, is a personal, face-to-face meeting. Today, everyone's so busy, so pressured, that a lot of people do business without ever having met. I'm a great believer, when possible, in having a face-to-face meeting very early in a relationship. Meetings are nearly always positive, even if you don't have a specific project to sell. That's why, in the days before television, politicians took trains from whistle-stop to whistle-stop to shake as many hands as possible. However, everyone's so busy these days that you better have an agenda if you want to get back in the door again or have the person take your future phone calls. I've sometimes used "fishing expedition" as an excuse for a meeting, meaning I wanted to find out more about the company, what their mandate is, what kind of projects they might be looking for. If you're a beginner, starting out, you'll need something more imaginative, more concrete. (I can do it because I'm an established producer; they know me and my track record.) And make sure the meeting is brief. A tiny bit of schmooze is good, but too much and you'll be labeled a time-waster.

PRODUCING *THE GRADUATE*:
A CASE STUDY

Ah, *The Graduate*. It changed my life. But not in any major, important way. It made getting my movies financed a bit easier . . . for a while. I was offered important studio jobs. I began to be invited to dazzling dinner parties by the likes of eminent director William Wyler, and at the Malibu mansion of Paul Ziffren, an entertainment lawyer who was a power in national Democratic politics. And I made an awful lot of money—more than I'd ever dreamed. All that was heady and good, but it did not make me a better husband, a better father, even a better producer. Nor did it make me less obsessive-compulsive.

I first read about *The Graduate* in a *New York Times* book review of the novel, just as my partnership with Stuart Millar was breaking up. I was so avid in those days, I myself, not some assistant, read all the book reviews in the *New York Times*, the *Times* of London, *Publishers Weekly*, *Kirkus Reviews*, and other publications, along with keeping up with all the new Broadway and off-Broadway playwrights. I was constantly on the lookout for writing talent and story material. The *New York Times* review made it sound like Charles Webb, the author of the novel, would make a good screenwriter. After reading the book I didn't think so, but the book itself haunted me. And *haunted* is the right word. The weird dialogue and situations were funny and nervous-making at the same time. Webb's dialogue reminded me of Harold Pinter, whose quirky plays I loved. Two scenes from the book jumped out at me: a boy in full scuba suit and diving mask in his family swimming pool and, even more so, the same boy, disheveled, his shirttail hanging out, on a public bus with a girl in a wedding dress. I've already acknowledged I'm more a word person than a visual one, but those two images struck me and stayed with me.

I simply had to get my hands on that book and control it. And I did so by putting up my own money—for the first and only time in my life. Luckily for me, the book was published to little acclaim, and few sales. I had no competition to acquire the movie rights. The price was modest—$1,000 for a one-year option, against a $20,000 purchase price. But $1,000 wasn't modest for me at that point in my life, in 1964. Plus, it was against my religion to put up my own money.

I sent the book to a couple of writers—William Hanley, whose play *Slow Dance on the Killing Ground* I had liked, and Peter Nelson, a budding writer I knew from when he was a creative assistant at CBS's *Playhouse 90*. I also sent the book to Frank Perry, who had recently directed the successful indie love story *David and Lisa*. Nothing productive came of my meetings with the two writers, and my lunch with Frank Perry was a bust. I did not like his response to, or take on, the book. I was always a fan of Mike Nichols's smart, mordant humor in his act with Elaine May. When I saw *Barefoot in the Park* on Broadway, it was oozing Mike's directorial insight and style. I did not know Mike, so when in New York, I submitted *The Graduate* to him in a simple, conventional way: through his agent, Robby Lantz.

On that same New York trip, a very social press agent pal of mine, Mike Mindlin, invited me to go to a party with him at the apartment of famed photographer Richard Avedon. I was, of course, eager to go. And what a heady crowd was there: Stephen Sondheim, Betty Comden and Adolph Green, Leonard Bernstein, and, of all people, Mike Nichols. It was a very exciting evening for me, during which Mike acknowledged he had received the book. When Mike and I got together, I told him the truth: I had no deal, no nothing, so I proposed that we be fifty-fifty partners, and share everything—fees, profit percentages, and creative control. It was simple, clean, and fair; we shook on it. Of course, that was before he became Mike Nichols.

Making that deal reminded me of the Jewish joke about the marriage arranger who, after finally convincing the poor orthodox parents that Princess Margaret of England would be a suitable wife for their ugly, pimply son, muttered to himself, "Vell, that's half the battle." Vell, I had a novel that I loved, and a fresh, exciting director, but as I learned all too quickly, that was only half the battle. No studio liked the book. At all. They didn't get it. Or rather, the readers who covered the material at each studio didn't get it. I submitted *The Graduate* to every single studio. They all said no. No one thought it was funny. No one thought it was any good. In short, no one liked my taste. During the many months of my unsuccessful attempts to raise money to get a screenplay written, Mike directed another smash Broadway success, *The Odd Couple*. It didn't help our cause. Mike Frankovich, production head at Columbia, said, "Who's Mike Nichols?" Paramount's top studio guy, Jack Karp, a business type, merely said, "My people don't like the book." David Picker, my smart, savvy, United Artists exec, said, "What's funny about it?" Everybody, every company, beat my brains out.

The last stop on the line was Joseph E. Levine's Embassy Pictures, king of the schlockmeisters. He was a larger-than-life character, a throwback to old Hollywood, an uneducated, great salesman—but a salesman of schlock. Joe's stock-in-trade was to buy a finished foreign film, Americanize the title, and then do a marketing blitz, with his own name plastered on larger than the title itself. Two Italian films—*Hercules* and its sequel, *Hercules Unchained*—were his claim to fame. He took on *The Graduate* because I told him I could make it for a million dollars, which was much more then than it is now, but still cheap. I negotiated the deal with Joe myself. He assumed he would have an executive producer credit, as on all his films. Although today it's as commonplace as the sun rising each day, I felt it was intolerable. That's the precise word I used in my impassioned speech to Joe. I was rabid and intransigent in my conviction that if he had an executive producer credit it would devalue me. I can't believe I was ready to blow this last-stop-on-the-line deal over Joe's credit issue, but either I was or Joe thought I was. He finally acceded to my heated argument, after which he turned to his assistant and said, "I like this kid [I was nearly forty!]. I wish my salesmen were as passionate as this guy Turman." It was a nice compliment and, in that instance, surely earned.

I personally think one of the main reasons why Joe and his Embassy Pictures made a deal for *The Graduate* was that Mike innately has something Joe Levine lacked—class. Mike's friends were, and are, the best and the brightest, the most chic, and the most accomplished. Joe, who headquartered in New York, where Mike was making an ever-bigger splash, knew all that, and I think it greased the skids for our deal. Joe was crude and crass, but not dumb. With Mike (and I wasn't exactly chopped liver) and *The Graduate,* he indeed stepped up in class—so much so that the next year *The Lion in Winter,* another award-winner, came to him for financing.

The next question was, who would write *The Graduate* script? We settled on Calder Willingham, an important novelist who had done a screenplay adaptation of his own novel *End as a Man* for the renowned Sam Spiegel. I had a very pragmatic reason for wanting Calder: He lived in the east, and I figured his easy access to Mike, and Mike's to him, would ensure the best screenplay. But it was not to be. Mike got ever busier, with one Broadway success after another, so I ended up doing all the script work with Calder.

I'm not one to buy a book for a film because it has a couple of strong scenes, or a wonderful character, or even both. Rather, I'm a very literal guy, and unless I can see most of the movie right there in the book, I don't get involved. I thought the screenplay of *The Graduate* was nearly all right there in the novel, except for tone. In the novel, Benjamin Braddock is a whiny pain in the ass. I saw him more as a "doofus." I relentlessly imposed the structure of the book on Calder, but I couldn't get him to understand the tone I wanted. Calder's version was vulgar. He even added sexual innuendo to a story that was already sexually provocative for the 1960s. I told Mike my misgivings before showing him the script. After reading it, he, of course, agreed. I say "of course" because I don't think I've ever been as much in-synch with a director about story as I was with Mike on *The Graduate.* Mike then suggested that Buck Henry take a crack at the script. I did not know his work, but I trusted Mike's judgment.

Then, out of the blue, Ernie Lehman called me, saying that

Elizabeth Taylor and Richard Burton, who he had cast in *Who's Afraid of Virginia Woolf?*, were asking about Mike Nichols as a director. What could I tell Ernie about him? I told Ernie my genuine positive feelings about Mike, but I was even more encouraging than that. Secretly I figured, to myself, Let Mike get experience on his first picture elsewhere and, with that under his belt, come to me and make *The Graduate*. What I learned is talent is talent, and genuine talent is good the first time out, as Mike indeed showed on *Virginia Woolf* (just as Kazan had shown earlier with *A Tree Grows in Brooklyn*, and Alexander Payne showed later with *Citizen Ruth*). So when Mike got busy directing *Virginia Woolf*, I filled the gap by supervising some of the script work with Buck. My job with Buck, as with Calder, was very much about selection and emphasis—which scenes to keep from the book and which to eliminate, and still tell our story.

Just a month before we were to start shooting, rumors began flying that Levine couldn't raise the money (our budget by then was three million dollars). Discreetly (although there are no secrets in Hollywood), I immediately went back to every single studio that had turned me down a year earlier, but now with a shooting script and the cast of Dustin Hoffman, Anne Bancroft, and Katharine Ross, and a director with three Broadway successes under his belt. Did it make a difference to any of the major studios? Not a bit. They all turned me down yet again. Fortunately, Joe Levine scrambled up the money somehow, and *The Graduate* got made.

I already said how much I was in-synch with Mike, so it came as no surprise that we liked virtually all the same things from the novel. Most screenplays are 120 pages or so, but *The Graduate* screenplay came in at 176 pages. (Ernie Lehman's screenplay for *North by Northwest* was as long. There are no rules.) It included one scene of Dustin and Anne Bancroft in bed together, when she sternly warns him not to date her daughter. The scene was twenty-seven pages long, and I told Mike I was was concerned it wouldn't sustain. He said he liked the scene as it was. It was scheduled for three full days of shooting. The second day, while looking at the first day's work, Mike turned to me and said something like, "Damn you, Turman, you're right." I took no pleasure in that. What were we going to do now?

The very smart, imaginative thing Mike did was to use the lights being turned off and then back on, as written, to enable him, in editing, to place a click on the sound track, go to black, and eliminate that which he didn't like or which wasn't working. *Click,* the light goes on again, and the actors can be in a different position, at a different place in the scene. He ain't Mike Nichols for nothing, folks. And one reason for that is he's a worrier. In my experience, the best ones are worriers. It's the less-good ones who seem to look at their work with an uncritical eye. One of my favorite recollections—and Mike could have been kidding, although not 100 percent—was when he said to me, "Damn, what is it? I forgot what I was worrying about!" I smile as I write it, and have told the story many times.

An example of his creative worrying was about the ending of *The Graduate.* In the novel, Benjamin breaks into the church *before* the wedding ceremony is officially completed. Mike and I were on an airplane together when he offered the idea that Benjamin should grab the girl *after* the ceremony and she's officially married. I was totally unprepared and very surprised (remember, this was 1967), but I supported him. Some weeks later, Mike confided that he had become insecure about that idea. By then, though, I was totally on board and had to reassure Mike that we should stick with it, that he was right to make that bold change. And of course he was, and we were.

When it came time to determine the writing credits, Mike and I naturally listed Buck Henry as sole writer. We had never shown Calder's script to Buck, preferring that Buck work instead directly from the book and our thoughts. I felt it appropriate that I call Calder to tell him of our credit decision. I did, and was surprised (perhaps naïvely); Calder said he was going to ask the Writers Guild to arbitrate. "But Calder," I said, "Buck never even saw your script. The whole thing is his." That did not deter Calder, though, and guess what? The Writers Guild decided in his favor. They decreed that not only should Calder share the credit, his name should go first. In Hollywood, name order, who goes first, is very important. (As the old saw goes about why first position is important: "Ever heard of Barnum and Bailey? What do you know about Bailey?")

In working with Calder, I had imposed so many specific scenes from the book, the structure of the story, that were in fact the very same things that Mike wanted and got from Buck Henry. Since Calder was there first he shared the credit. The uninitiated didn't know it was all Buck's script, but the insiders did. Much like today, where many films have from four to fourteen credited producers, the insiders are the only ones who know who did the work in actually producing the movie. The whole town knew it was Buck's script— including his now famous "plastics" line. Buck got all the word-of-mouth credit in the industry, and it catapulted his writing career to more gigs for more money (including *Catch-22, What's Up, Doc?, The Owl and the Pussycat,* and *To Die For*).

We had a script we liked, and the financing was in place. All we had to do was cast the movie. All? After interviewing and reading dozens upon dozens upon dozens of boys for the lead, Mike turned to me one day and said, "Turman, you son of a bitch, you got me on a movie that can't be cast." But every movie can be cast if you look hard enough, have some judgment, and maybe a bit of luck. Mike, having worked successfully with Robert Redford on *Barefoot in the Park,* talked about him as a possibility. Redford was already on his way in Hollywood. I loved his acting, having known of him from his first twenty-minute film, the Academy Award–winning *A Time Out of War,* made by my friends, brothers Denis and Terry Sanders. We agreed to test him. (With, by the way, Candice Bergen, whose career was also on the move.) Not wanting the completed test to fall into the wrong hands, I kept it in my garage. Alas, some years later it got lost. I joke that if I hadn't lost it, I could auction it today at Sotheby's and buy a yacht with the proceeds.

Dustin Hoffman was one of a group of up-and-coming actors the *New York Times* had featured in a story. He piqued our interest. Fortuitously, our production manager, George Justin, had just completed work on *The Tiger Makes Out,* in which Dustin had a single, brief scene. George arranged for Mike and me to see it. Seeing Dustin on-screen for what was at most a minute made us want to have him read a scene for us. Two words came to mind then that I have used since to describe the qualities I instinctively thought made Dustin right for *The Graduate*: *sweetness* and *goofiness*. As I write this, I realize for the very first time, thirty-five years after the fact, that I probably unconsciously wanted those qualities to counteract what I described as the pain-in-the-ass, unsympathetic qualities the character had in the novel. I'm very big on casting against type, not that Dustin ultimately proved to be that.

Joanne Linley (then wife of director Mark Rydell) was the actress who read the Mrs. Robinson role opposite all the many young hopefuls. When she did the scene with Dustin, he made her cry, the only one to do so. We screen-tested Dustin, along with several other actors, including Charles Grodin (Mike loved his interview/reading) and Tony Bill, who later won an Academy Award for producing *The Sting.* To test the actors, Mike did something I'd not known of before, and have not seen much since: He had Buck write a brand-new scene for test purposes only. Mike felt that if he had to direct a test scene over and over from the film script, he'd be dead on it when the time came to really film it. Smart, huh? I thought so, and still do.

Dustin tested with Katharine Ross. Mike whispered to me while filming their test: "He's all over the place." Nonetheless, two days later, when we saw all the edited tests, Dustin seemed, together with Katharine, right for our picture. But no fireworks went off for us. We didn't jump up and down and say, "Wow, that's our guy." My recollection is that I turned to Mike and said, "I guess I'd be satisfied with those two, Dustin and Katharine." He didn't say anything. Then, walking back to our offices, Mike turned to me, "Yeah, me, too. Let's use them."

Redford's test, by the way, showed a talented, skilled actor doing everything intelligently right. But it was just too hard to believe him as an insecure bumbler, even—or especially—with the beautiful Candy Bergen. Incidentally, both Bob and Dustin were twenty-nine years old at the time, vying to play a twenty-one-year-old role. But hey, that's the magic of Hollywood. William Holden, Cary Grant, Gregory Peck, or Harrison Ford rarely ever play their true ages. And they always won the beautiful, much younger girl, didn't they?

Before we even screen-tested our actor candidates, I knew that Dustin would be the one. How? Easy. In those days, it was automatic and axiomatic that as part of the money deal for the actor's services if he got the part was an option for several future pictures at a relatively modest salary, in case the film proved to make a star of the actor. Of the six people we tested, Dustin was the only one who refused to grant those options. I'm not superstitious, but I thought to myself, "That means it'll probably turn out that he's the one we want." Prophetic.

I think everyone would agree that Anne Bancroft was ideal for

Mrs. Robinson. But she wasn't the first actress who came to mind. I pictured Doris Day; as I've said, I like casting against type. To me, Doris Day seemed so clean-cut, perky, and all-American that I felt she would be a wonderful dramatic contrast to Mrs. Robinson's sad, darker side. Although Doris Day was not considered at the top of the Hollywood acting ladder, her work in *Love Me or Leave Me*, opposite James Cagney, showed she had the chops. Early on I sent the book to her manager/husband, Marty Melcher, hoping to get at least an expression of interest. Melcher, however, wouldn't even pass the book along for her to read—he disliked it that much. Mike was considering Patricia Neal, a wonderful actress who would have possibly been an excellent Mrs. Robinson. Tragically, she had had a stroke and hadn't regained full physical powers. So Anne Bancroft was indeed our first choice, in terms of making the only firm offer we made for the role. The first read-through of the script with all the actors went fine, except, to my surprise, Anne said her lines in an uninflected, flat monotone, giving no indication whatsoever of the nuanced performance she ultimately delivered. Smart and lucky we were because no one could have played it better.

We had three unusual casting experiences on the film. The first was that the buxom blond woman sitting next to Katharine Ross on the Berkeley bus that Dustin Hoffman is running alongside in the film is Eddra Gale. Who? The very same woman who in a black wig was La Saraghina, dancing wildly on the beach in Fellini's classic *8½*. Mike and I were floored when she told us, and hired her that instant as much for good luck and homage as anything. In contrast to that on-the-spot decision, when we were auditioning for the dancer who twirled tassels on each breast simultaneously in opposite directions, the one and only girl available, Lainie Miller, finished showing us her wares and left the room. Mike turned to me, dead serious (remember he's an actor, too), and said, "Larry, this role is so important I think we should see everyone in town, as many actors as possible for this part." (Yes, amid all the hard work you can have a lot of fun making a movie.) Finally, the gas-station attendant who gives Dustin Hoffman directions to the church near the end of the film is not the actor Mike and I thought we had hired. Communication somehow went astray between us and our casting director, the estimable and experienced Lynn Stalmaster. He hired the wrong actor, Noam Pitlik, a different one than we had chosen. Pitlik worked out fine, though, and evidently the error didn't hurt our picture.

Mike and I did have one casting disagreement . . . about what kind of car Dustin would drive in the film. In those days, the big three Detroit car companies would give prominent producers and directors free use of one or even two brand-new cars for a year in the hope that those directors and producers would use their best efforts and show them on-screen. I had a deal with Chrysler, so I floated that idea to Mike. He didn't seem to jump at it, maybe because his deal was, I believe, with Ford. But he was also too much of an artist not to want what's right for the character and for the film. So Alfa Romeo it was. If I were a certain kind of producer, I would've negotiated some quid pro quo freebie for Mike and me with Alfa Romeo. But hey, how many cars can you drive? Only one at a time, anyway. Today, of course, that would fall under the rubric of payola, but at the time it was legal and commonplace.

Mike wanted—and we had—a three-week rehearsal on stage, with some sets lined out and our editor, Sam O'Steen, and occasionally the AD and cameraman Bob Surtees in attendance. During rehearsal, Mike became unhappy with Gene Hackman, who'd been cast as Katharine Ross's father, and wanted to replace him. To do so was a bit tricky psychologically, as Gene and Dustin had been roommates at Pasadena Playhouse and were buddies. But Mike did it, and substituted Murray Hamilton. As producer, I could see little difference in performance qualities between the two, but I supported my director. Many years later, when Mike chose Gene Hackman for *Postcards from the Edge,* his agent, Fred Specktor of CAA, told me Hackman muttered, "The son of a bitch will probably fire me again." Mike didn't, and Gene was wonderful in that film, as he is every time out. Indeed, Gene was the linchpin for my *Full Moon in Blue Water.* He read the script without a firm offer and agreed to do it, which enabled me to get financing. So, who you know, who you can get to . . . you can finish that sentence.

We may have used an ugly word, *fired,* for Gene Hackman, but it came right back at us; our cameraman, Haskell Wexler, fired us. That's right, he quit before shooting even began. I had facilitated Haskell Wexler's getting into the union by hiring him on *The Best Man.* Haskell is a passionate, caring artist, and he did a superb job on that film, as he has for the succeeding forty-five years of his brilliant DP career. Mike had also used him, on *Who's Afraid of Virginia Woolf?*, so Haskell was an easy, ideal choice for us for *The Graduate*. In preproduction, however, Haskell asked for a meeting with Mike and me wherein, to our surprise, he said he wasn't crazy about the script. We said we were and thus parted ways, but remained friends.

Even though Mike pretty much always knew who he wanted for his crew, I nonetheless suggested Robert Surtees as cameramen. People generally like to work with their contemporaries, and Mike and I were no exceptions; production designer Dick Sylbert and editor Sam O'Steen were our age. Surtees was a generation older, and crusty. But he was also an artist. Mike trusted me and what I said about Surtees, did his homework, and decided to use him. And surely he got the best out of Surtees; the look of *The Graduate* is damned good. But I credit others for that as well. Dick Sylbert was as good as they come; I had used him on my first film, as had Mike, another commonality we had. Editor Sam O'Steen was the best; there's a reason pictures in trouble would bring in Sam—he's helped or saved many. But the famous cut of Dustin pulling himself out of the pool and onto the rubber raft, only to land on Mrs. Robinson; or seeing Mrs. Robinson's face reflected in the black-topped table where Dustin is sitting, waiting for her; or watching Katharine Ross's face slowly come into focus as she realizes Dustin slept with her mother—all these are as much, if not more, Nichols than O'Steen, Sylbert, and Surtees.

Production designer Dick Sylbert found the perfect church for the wedding scene in *The Graduate*. Mike Nichols loved it, as did I, but we couldn't get permission to film there, so I said, "We're back to square one. Keep looking, Dick." Mike turned to me and said, "No, Larry. That's the one I want." It was just what I didn't want to hear, but I went to work. I found out the final authority lay with the church elders. I solicited a meeting with them to present our case. I truly believed what I told them: "Our script is sexually provocative, but deals with the very issues the church itself should be dealing with in today's world." I was genuinely passionate, and thus persuasive. They granted permission. But if Mike Nichols hadn't pushed, we never would have had that perfect location for the end of our film. That's the kind of director you want, even though I might not have felt that way at the time.

Mike is the best director I've worked with. This is an easy statement to make because Mike has proved himself over many pictures to be one of the very best. But I've also made many pictures and worked with a lot of enormously talented directors. Marty Ritt was fabulous with the actors; Curtis Hanson is terrific with storytelling, and is a strong master of the ship; Franklin Shaffner was unflappable, organized, and great with male actors; Irv Kershner is passionate and energetic; Glenn Jordan is meticulous and on top of every aspect. But Mike has it all. He knows what he wants, and he knows how to get it. He's amazing with actors. He's imaginative and stylish with the camera. He inspires above-and-beyond loyalty in his crew. And he's as good as any producer at dealing with the studio front office and business folks.

That said, working with Mike was great, but it wasn't perfect. He was so damn charming (and probably wanted to be liked) that when he and I would interview key personnel together, Mike would be encouraging in a way that made that person think he or she had the job. After the interviewee left, Mike would turn to me and say, "Naw, he/she is not for us." After a couple of those experiences, I learned to quickly jump in to make sure the applicant knew that we were going to interview others for the job.

My recollection of the shoot was that it was relatively trouble-free. During the filming, there were some focus problems with the Panavision lenses and with Surtees being the crusty guy he was, Mike would occasionally put me in the line of fire to deal with him. The University of California Berkeley was the school designated in the novel, so naturally I tried to obtain permission for us to shoot there, but no go. Whether it was their bureaucracy or our script (too risqué for 1967?) I never found out, but the answer was still "no." It was the same with UCLA, which is part of the Cal system. So we ended up shooting at USC. Teaching at USC these past fourteen years has given me great nostalgic pleasure every day as I walk the campus past locations where we filmed. It served us and our film well. We also filmed in the town of Berkeley and in the San Francisco Zoo, as per the novel and the script. While in Berkeley, we sneaked onto the Cal campus and stole one shot, just for the fun of it and having it in our film. Kids will be kids, no matter what age.

I was so brimming with excitement, I don't remember *The Gradu-ate*'s first day's rushes. The first cut Mike showed me, however, hit me like a sledgehammer. Mike had captured all the humor and added to it, but I was unprepared for the power of the darker moments; they added immeasurably to the film. Sam O'Steen's editing con-stantly improved the film. One day I wandered into the editing room to check how things were going and made a casual, almost inadver-tent, contribution. Mike and Sam were working on the swimming-pool scene with Dustin in his scuba suit. The scene ended with a brutally hard-to-get helicopter shot (I had to sweet-talk and negotiate with the city of Beverly Hills to be permitted to fly lower than the law allowed): close on Dustin underwater, then pulling up, up, and away, until the screen was filled with dozens of homes, each one dotted with a swimming pool. This imaginative shot was pointedly about materialism and conspicuous consumption (Mike is a New Yorker to his marrow), but I felt, and commented, that ending on Dustin, close-up, underwater, would have a claustrophobic, stronger emotional im-pact. Sam and Mike tried it then and there, liked it, and bought it.

The Graduate fortified my opinion that if a picture is "working," an audience will forgive or not even notice its flaws. For instance, Dustin, in his mad dash to Berkeley over the San Francisco bridge, is driving in the wrong direction. It was a second-unit shot, sweepingly gorgeous but hard to get. We couldn't redo it. Did anyone notice, let alone care, that Dustin was driving away from Berkeley rather than toward it? He got to Berkeley anyway, somehow, and our story kept going, and the audience kept going with it. Unfortunately, the re-verse is also true: If an audience doesn't go with your film, they are oblivious to any exceptional scenes that may be in it.

The Simon and Garfunkel music score is a story unto itself. Using them was Mike's suggestion. I leapt at it, as I had tried to get them to write the title song for my previous film, *The Flim-Flam Man*, but they'd turned it down. Sometimes you get saved from your own mistakes. *The Flim-Flam Man* was a rural story, and Simon and Garfunkel are poetically urban. But I lucked out anyway because I got the very special Linda Ronstadt, at the beginning of her super career, to do *The Flim-Flam Man* title song. For *The Graduate*, I con-tracted for Paul Simon to write, and Simon and Garfunkel to per-form, three new songs. This was long before we started filming.

They, however, became very busy touring and performing, so by the time we finished shooting and were editing, Paul hadn't yet delivered a single song. He had finished part of one called "Punky's Dilemma," which he had written for the intercut montage of Dustin swimming and shacking up with Anne Bancroft—the swimming, bedroom, swimming, bedroom sequence.

In editing, each sequence and the entire film itself is looked at and re-looked at ad nauseum. During that process, many directors, with their editor, lay in temporary music to get the emotional feeling of a scene and the rhythm of the cuts. Mike was no exception. He and Sam O'Steen temporarily put in the old Simon and Garfunkel songs "Scarborough Fair" and "Sound of Silence." Then one day Mike said to me, "We're going to be so accustomed to those old songs we won't like the new ones." I casually responded, "So, we'll use the old ones." Well, that's exactly what we did. Except it wasn't that casual.

As they tell stories in Hollywood: dissolve to when we showed the finished picture to Joe Levine in New York. Joe loved it, as well he should have, considering the junky films he was used to putting out. But even if he hadn't, his style would have been to rave about our film—you can take the boy out of the salesman, but you can't take the salesman out of the boy. At the end of all his effusive compliments, Joe said, "Once you get the new songs in, the picture will be fantastic!" Mike and I exchanged a look. "Joe, these are the songs we're using," we told him. Joe turned white. "You can't. Every kid in America knows these old songs. You'll be laughed off the screen." Anybody can be made insecure, and Mike and I sure were. But after sleeping on it, we said to each other, "The heck with it. Let's stick to our guns." We did, and the rest is music history. (It didn't hurt that the deal I negotiated with Joe Levine gave us artistic control.)

"Mrs. Robinson" is the one song Paul Simon wrote specifically for *The Graduate*. It was an instant hit and has become a standard. It was also a hit with the saleslady who took care of me at Saks Fifth Avenue: Her name was Mrs. Robinson; she said, with a sly smile, that "my" film changed her life. I didn't ask what she meant, but I knew. I cannot swear to the following, but my recollection is that "Mrs. Robinson" ran for only about a minute and a half of screen time, to cover the off-to-San Francisco driving scene. Since I wanted a new song to plug the picture, I asked Paul to please add to, and finish, it. Paul was reluctant, as he was so busy with his and Art's skyrocketing performing career. When the picture opened to ecstatic reviews and smash business, Paul quickly completed "Mrs. Robinson" and got it out there. Today they would call it synergy: The Simon and Garfunkel score helped the picture, and the picture helped sell the record. In the recent AFI 100 Years . . . 100 Songs list of the hundred most memorable songs associated with movies, "Mrs. Robinson"/*The Graduate* was voted number six.

For the underscoring, we showed the picture to composer John Williams. John and I were friendly, as we had kids in the same school. Already, in 1967, his talent was clearly manifest. His career as one of the great film composers has since led to his conductorship of the Boston Pops and other prestigious, serious musical venues, along with being Spielberg's go-to composer. After showing John the picture, we all went back to Mike's office to talk. The first words out of John's mouth were, "I see where you can use some help." I don't recall whether he used the exact words *need* or *could use,* but no matter—his meaning was clear, and I saw Mike's eyes glaze over. Even though we went on for a half-hour longer, I knew the meeting was finished then and there.

We next went to composer Dave Grusin, and we clicked with him. Dave is one of the great jazz pianists and a favorite composer of many top directors. Doing the score for our film was neither a conventional nor an easy task. It required writing satiric, sometimes almost gauche, music to reinforce the crass materialism and shallowness of the parent characters. It was not the most enviable job for a composer, although in this case, David could console himself all the way to the bank. I accidentally saw a royalty statement for the album; Grusin's share was six figures (in those days!), even though the album's sales lure was the Simon and Garfunkel songs.

The film also pushed the paperback sales of the novel into the stratosphere. In hardcover, *The Graduate* sold barely a couple thousand copies. In paperback, after the film's release, it sold millions. So, whoever said producer Larry Turman took advantage of poor, struggling novelist Charles Webb by paying him only $20,000 for the movie rights to his novel (which, as I've said, no other producer or studio wanted, anyway) is way off the mark. Not only did Chuck Webb make a ton of money from the huge paperback sales, he was also then in a commanding position to negotiate a rich publishing deal for his future books. Caveat emptor and seller's remorse are obverse sides of the same coin.

I sometimes wonder if any of us really understands another person's movie. Mike held a rough but close-to-finished-cut screening for a group of his friends. And when I say friends, I mean big-time folks, top creative pros. I threw in a handful of my friends as well. Everyone liked the picture and seemed quite genuine. But, along with their congratulations, many expressed—not even subtly— reservations about that funny-looking new kid, Dustin Hoffman.

Another time, Mike screened our totally finished, locked edit (lacking only the final sound mix) to a director friend of his—a successful, very experienced pro who, after his initial, genuine compliment, added, "Once you trim the fat, cut it down, it'll be great." I didn't see Mike's reaction because my own eyes had glazed over.

When I really wanted Mike to hear me, I'd tell him "Even geniuses need someone to talk to." Mike was nothing if not reflective. I often wish I were like that—more reflective, less impetuous. Sometimes I would make a suggestion to him, and his response would be something like, "Turman, that's the dumbest, worst idea I ever heard." But later that same evening, I'd get a phone call from Mike, who, without even a beginning "hello," would launch right in, saying, "I've been thinking about what you said today, and . . ." The point I'm making is not about Mike accepting a particular idea of mine, but about the fact that it was always gestating within him.

At the famous lunch round table of comics at Hillcrest Country Club, populated by Jack Benny, Groucho Marx, George Jessel, you name them, when anyone told a joke, none of the others would laugh. The most they'd say was, "That's good," or "Nice," or they'd just point a forefinger and nod. On the other hand, at our first paying public preview of *The Graduate* in Chicago, the laughter was uproarious. It rose, ebbed and flowed in perfect synchronized timing with our edit. Every laugh played like gangbusters, and would die down just in time to not obliterate the next line of dialogue. After the screening at a quiet but nonetheless celebratory dinner at the Pump

Room, Sam O'Steen arrived late, as he'd stayed behind to retrieve the cans of film. He shook my hand and quietly, presciently, said, "Congratulations—you've got a hit."

Our second preview, in New York, was at a much larger theater, the Loews on 72nd Street, and the audience tore the roof off. It was wild and wonderful. David Picker, the United Artists production head, attended that preview because his company had bought the film's foreign distribution rights. I had originally submitted *The Graduate* to David, since UA had financed my first four films. But he, like all the other companies, had turned me down. After the film was completed, when Joe Levine sold the foreign rights to United Artists, I immediately called David to thank him, to congratulate him, and to rub it in a little that he had originally turned it down. "I'm glad you now see why I thought the book was so funny." His reply? "It's a terrific picture and I think we'll do well with it, but it's not really that funny." I realized he'd seen it either alone or with a handful of other executives in a projection room. Comedies play best in a crowded theater—laughter is contagious. Basking in the glow of that riotously laugh-filled, successful second preview, I walked up to David and, being a bit petty and vengeful, said without even a hello, "Not funny, huh?"

However, at our invitation-only industry screening at the Directors Guild, when everybody who mattered was there, Mike and I, seated in the back, were frankly unhappy. The audible laughter was so muted compared to the wildly raucous audience response we'd had in Chicago and New York. At the second reel, Mike whispered, "Dammit, Turman, I told you we shouldn't have showed it to this crowd." He was right, but only partially. The insiders are always a tough crowd, half of them hoping, wishing for your failure. Afterward, one of the most sought-after writers in Hollywood tepidly offered his congratulations: "It's a nice little film." In an old Hollywood novel, Merle Miller's *Only You, Dick Daring!*, I first read the all-too-true maxim, "To succeed is not enough. Your best friend must also fail."

Despite the buzz on *The Graduate*, we couldn't get the movie booked in the most desirable section of L.A., Westwood, an area chockablock with movie theaters and kids from UCLA. We were frustrated and had to settle for an undesirable stand-alone theater in an inconvenient location. We got our revenge, though, because after opening to big-time business and hot word-of-mouth, the Westwood theaters came after us, begging, but we decided to stay happily in our second-rate theater, where we had lines around the block. And in those lines were some studio executives who had originally turned the picture down. Please indulge my gloating. There's a long-ago book title, *Living Well Is the Best Revenge.*

Joe Levine was a high-powered, kick-ass salesman, and he sure sold the hell out of *The Graduate.* Mike and I had given him a good visual campaign ad—the image of the cap-and-gowned graduate underneath a woman's naked leg. Creativity feeds on other creativity, and I'll bet the talented British ad designer would not have come up with that memorable image had Mike not staged a similar shot in the film itself that gave birth to the concept.

Even though Joe Levine spent a lot on advertising, he only had to buy relatively inexpensive newspaper ads, not the high-cost TV spots that are so prevalent today. That's because *The Graduate* initially played in only a handful of theaters—one each in L.A., New York, Chicago, and Toronto. The picture got great reviews and was an instant hit. A month or two into the run, the distributor, National General, told me they expected the film to do $20 million in film rental (film rental is roughly half of box-office dollars). At our negative cost of only $3.2 million, that was a pie-in-the-sky figure. I was over the moon. Everybody was. But the picture didn't do $20 million in film rentals; it did $55 million. And that's just in the United States. Adjusted for today, that's the equivalent of several hundred million dollars. Only six months after its release, I got a profit check, a big one, and they kept coming.

The final cost of *The Graduate* exceeded our approved budget by a tiny bit, mostly because of the unanticipated music costs of obtaining the old Simon and Garfunkel songs and the new song "Mrs. Robinson." Joe Levine, true to his nature, tried to use that to get out of paying me my rightful profit share. He was wrong, both morally and legally. Not to be churlish, but at the time I did think of George Bernard Shaw, describing someone as "having all the qualities of a dog except loyalty."

Francis Ford Coppola has said that *The Godfather* put him on the map and enabled him to make some of his smaller pet projects, like *The Conversation.* Well, *The Graduate* put me on the map. But, me as a producer versus Francis as a director, it wasn't quite the same thing. Indeed, the *New York Times* did a major interview with me, and the headline read, "But they still say 'Larry Who' "!

There was a time, pre-*Graduate*, when Francis and I both officed at Fox. He was writing the script for *Patton*. We became close enough that he cooked a very good Italian dinner for me, and subsequently invited me to a screening of his first directed film, *You're a Big Boy Now*. I brought Mike Nichols and Buck Henry along. The film told the story of a young boy, not unlike *The Graduate*, and the movie already showed Francis's prodigious talent. When the film ended and the lights went on, Mike and Buck were depressed. Very. They thought Francis's film had clearly and totally preempted *The Graduate*. I didn't see it, and I said so, but they were, for a while, inconsolable. You know the rest of the story. But it does demonstrate the emotional roller coaster you and your compatriots are on in the making of a movie.

The more successful I became, the more enveloped I was with advisers: lawyers, tax experts, financial advisers, investment gurus. Although I was brought up comfortably and lived a middle-class life, I'd never before had to deal with how to invest money because I never had any extra money to invest. Post-*Graduate*, I got a relatively swift education, the hard way. Because I was unsophisticated and had no investment experience, I relied on the so-called experts. My lawyers put me on to a guy who did investing for Herb Alpert and Jerry Moss, who were the A and M of A&M records—big-time money. My *Graduate* profits, huge to me, were small in comparison. So naturally I threw my lot and my money in with the recommended guy.

Pretty soon, I owned shopping centers in St. Louis and Kansas City, farmland in mid-California, and San Diego raw acreage that was supposedly suitable for development, all of them complicated, sophisticated investments made in the service of minimizing and/or delaying taxes. What I learned too late in the game was that had I simply paid all my taxes quickly—and easily affordable at the time—I would've had plenty of money left over for the rest of my life. Instead, I was land-rich. Wrong—I was land-poor. I owned a lot of property, but I owed a lot more money in ongoing mortgage payments. The U.S. tax laws then abruptly changed, putting an end to a favorite real estate tactic: prepaying interest as a tax deduction.

Under the new laws, I had to keep up the future payments on my vast holdings sans tax deductions—but I no longer had the income flow to do so. I began to lose my real-estate properties one by one. But what's a million here and a million there? Only peace of mind.

Here's how I learned my fate: A month after receiving a $1 million profit check (yes, that's $1 million) from *The Graduate,* I wanted to buy a John Marin watercolor for $10,000. My accountant informed me that I did not have the necessary $10,000! As Lil' Abner's balloon says, "Gulp. Sob. Choke." I didn't have the money?! That's right. The million dollars had all gone toward upkeep payments on my various real-estate properties—most of which I ultimately lost, anyway. (Didn't J.F.K., after the Bay of Pigs fiasco, say "Beware the experts"?) Now, I do my own investing. And you know what? I learned it's pretty much like producing movies: mostly common sense. And what you don't know, you do your detective work, your homework, and find out the necessary information to make a decision. I've done better for myself than any of those advisers ever did for me.

As my friend novelist Ed McBain (Evan Hunter) said to me, "Nobody cares as much about you, as you." I wish I could say I took those financial losses with equanimity, but I cannot. They affected me, and deeply. But who hasn't had some hard knocks in life? And, corny as it may sound, if you have your health and some love in your life, coupled with meaningful work—all of which I had—you're better than okay.

When we made *The Graduate,* it was not like today, where virtually every director just out of film school gets the "a film by" credit. My deal with Mike was that we would share a production credit, with my name first. At the time I made the deal, Mike had yet to direct a film, and I was a credentialed producer, having done four films, the last of which was the acclaimed *The Best Man.* But three years (note: repeat, three years) elapsed between the time I made the deal with him and when we filmed *The Graduate.* By then, Mike had been nominated for an Academy Award for *Who's Afraid of Virginia Woolf?,* and had directed yet another hit play, so we agreed to reverse the order; Mike's name to go first. Did it matter? Not to me. From today's perspective, where the makeup person's dog might be credited, was our work appropriately recognized, despite our relatively modest billing? You decide. Mike received an Academy Award—and had his pick of all the best new projects. I, as I've recounted, was solicited to produce the Academy Awards show, and two different studios offered me the head of production job.

The year before Mike was nominated for *The Graduate*, the most bizarre experience occurred at the annual Directors Guild Award dinner. He had been nominated that year for *Who's Afraid of Virginia Woolf?*, and I was his guest at the ceremony. The presenter, Walter Matthau, began by saying, "And now for best direction, feature film. . . . Mike Nichols for *Who's Afraid of Virginia Woolf?*" Mike was genuinely surprised. He seemed truly overwhelmed, and could not have been happier, nor I for him. He gave a beautiful, moving acceptance speech and, upon returning to our table, passed around the Best Direction medallion for all to see. When the clamor died down, Walter Matthau continued, "Winner, best direction for a motion picture, Fred Zinnemann for *A Man for All Seasons*." We were all nonplussed, thrown for a loop—especially Mike. Then, Walter Matthau had the presence of mind to say, "Oh, I see, each nominee gets a medallion inscribed 'Best Direction.' The list of names I am announcing are nominees." That clarified things, but too late for Mike to save face after his stultifying acceptance speech. Mike thought—we all thought—he was *the* winner of that year's award. He had just given a gushing, heartfelt acceptance speech. Now he felt like a fool. Who wouldn't? And we felt for him.

There is justice, however, and Mike deservedly did win the next year, 1967, for *The Graduate*. He chose, however, to stay in New York and not travel to L.A. for the gala award dinner. It was left to me to make his acceptance speech, and I had the ammo to make a damn good one: "Mike regrets that he is unable to attend the awards dinner this year, but it doesn't really matter because all of you already heard his acceptance speech last year." This drew a huge laugh of appreciation as I knew it would. Maybe there is a God.

A few years ago the Producers Guild voted me into their hall of fame. Dustin Hoffman was at the awards ceremony and in my acceptance speech, I recounted how he had thoughtfully given me an art book before we started production and inscribed it "I hope it's good for you." I looked lovingly at Dustin and said, "It was great for me, darling. How was it for you?" That, along with my speech on Mike's behalf, go in the pleased-with-myself department.

If the right people aren't acknowledged and thanked at an awards ceremony, bad blood ensues. In my acceptance speech when *The Graduate* won the Golden Globes' best-picture award, I acknowledged the support and marketing skills of Embassy Pictures, but I did not mention Joe Levine by name, and he was pissed. Was it conscious on my part, to omit Joe? You bet it was. So I guess he had a right to be annoyed. (After all, it was I who, in this book, said, "Hey, we all have an ego.") But Joe had slighted me many times, including our post-premiere party in New York where he arranged to be seated next to Mike at the star table, and had me at a table so far in left field that I may as well have been at a different party. I actually had to enlist Mike's help to get me at the same table as *The Graduate* team. Was my slighting Joe in my Golden Globes acceptance speech petty? You bet it was. And I regret it, truly. It's unworthy. But it was me at that point in time.

The Graduate was nominated for seven Academy Awards, including best picture, which, had it won, I as producer was the designated person to accept. Naturally, I wrote a speech in preparation—everyone does, even those who claim not to. Unbelievable as it is to me now, I felt I had to memorize that speech rather than read it or refer to notes (and I thought—think—I'm a sophisticated guy?!). At the awards ceremony, when the announcement came, naming *In the Heat of the Night* as the winner, I was so caught up in trying to remember my speech that the producer of *In the Heat of the Night* was halfway down the aisle before I realized *The Graduate* had not won. Brian Grazer tells a parallel story:

> I've wanted to win an Oscar so badly my entire life, and I came so close with *Apollo 13*. I mean, it really was so close. And I remember sitting in the audience, and odds-makers were all going, "*Apollo 13* is going to win." And Jim Lovell, who was the real astronaut on the *Apollo 13*, flew in, 'cause he kind of felt like we'd win, too. Everything—arrows were pointing in the right direction. He sat right next to me. And, as Sidney Poitier said *Braveheart*, Jim Lovell grabbed my wrist and said, "You know, I never made it to the moon, either." And it's so poignant, you know? I understand. When he said it—same thing, I thought, "He's saying Brian Grazer. He's not saying *Braveheart*." It was very powerful. And, you know, that night, not having won, I had to develop an infra-

structure for myself to get through it because I really hoped to win and I realized that some of my favorite movies of all time did not win Oscars. I thought they did—I was certain you won for *The Graduate.* I'm very happy I won with *A Beautiful Mind,* and I get near tears every time because it meant so much to me.

In the Heat of the Night, which won over *Bonnie and Clyde* and *The Graduate,* was an excellent picture, beautifully acted and executed, with a pertinent racial theme. But I nonetheless choose to think (and this is not sour grapes) that both *The Graduate* and *Bonnie and Clyde* were better films, but likely split the vote that year. That is not to take anything away from *In the Heat of the Night,* but the innovative freshness of both *Bonnie and Clyde* and *The Graduate* has given these films a longer, stronger afterlife than *In the Heat of the Night.* In my mind, *In the Heat of the Night* was one of two films (the other being 1980's *Ordinary People*) that caused the present proliferation of producer credits and thus accelerated the devaluation of producers. The producer accepting the best-picture award for *In the Heat of the Night* was Walter Mirisch, who was later to become president of the Academy. However, I'm confident that Norman Jewison, the director, felt he was in fact as much the producer of that film. Norman's a capable, take-charge guy, and a knowledgeable producer in his own right.

From that film on—and I choose to think because of it—Norman, as part of his directing deal, insisted upon and took a producing credit as well. Similarly, *Ordinary People,* which won best picture in 1981, was Robert Redford's baby, but the producer of record accepting the award was Ron Schwary, one of the very best production managers/line producers in the movie business. I'm reasonably confident that Redford felt that best picture Oscar statuette rightfully belonged to him as well. I believe that those two films were the linchpins for virtually every and any director who can command it to now take a producing credit, and nothing will convince me otherwise. That gives every director two bites of the apple in any awards contest, be it the Academy Awards, the Golden Globes, or a film festival in Oshkosh, Wisconsin.

The Graduate, oddly, is as well known in the legal world as in the movie world. I was forced to sue the distributor, Embassy, for their shoddy accounting of profits. Joe Levine, off the huge success of *The Graduate* and, subsequently, *The Lion in Winter,* was able to sell his Embassy Pictures to conglomerate Avco for roughly $40 million (again, forty-years-ago dollars—haircuts were a buck). The main ancillary revenue for a film, pre-video and DVD, came from television. *The Graduate* was licensed to CBS as part of a group of Embassy Films, all of which, with the exception of *The Graduate,* were dogs— poorly performing, barely known films. Although Embassy scrupulously covered its tracks by having an individual contract drawn up for each picture to mask the fact that the films were sold as a "package," it did not prevent Embassy from arbitrarily assigning a higher value than what was fair and appropriate to every single film with the exception of *The Graduate,* to which, of course, they assigned a much lower than fair market value. This was done to diminish profits that would be due Mike Nichols and me (we shared one-third of all profits of the film). As all the other films in the group were losers, any money received from CBS would go directly and solely to Embassy to recoup their investment. My lawyers and I complained to Embassy, and under our questioning pressure, they negotiated a settlement to pay me an additional $35,000.

When the contracts for that agreement arrived, however, they were drafted to so favor Embassy that there was no real guarantee that I would see the agreed-upon $35,000. That was the last straw. I sued them in federal court on antitrust charges. It was a first because historically, profit participants had complained and threatened legal action based upon allocation of television monies—i.e., their apportionment among the various licensed films. I, however, sued on the basis of restraint of trade, thus creating an antitrust suit. The case went to trial by jury in federal court. I saw my lawyer prepare the case the way I prepare a film—carefully and in great detail. He, too, commented, as I do in the chapter on preproduction, that preparation is eighty percent of success—if you have a good case . . . (read script). Even though I was sure of the facts and confident about my just and good case, I was very nervous on the witness stand. I thought, If my heart's beating this rapidly in a civil case, what must it be like for someone on the witness stand in a criminal case?

The trial lasted an entire week. I watched two jurors actually fall asleep periodically. There were so many arcane facts and figures being thrown about, I was worried about the jury's ability to understand the issues and what was at stake—even those who were wide awake and paying careful attention. I was frustrated and discouraged. Leaving the courtroom one afternoon, I ran into the judge, an esteemed and tough-minded woman named Marianna Phaelzer. I shared with her my fears and complaints about the jurors. "Trust the jury system," she replied. She proved to be right, and not just because I won the case. The facts were overwhelmingly on my side, but the size of the judgment awarded was less than my lawyer had sued for. It was, though, the fair and appropriate amount. I may have hoped for, even wanted, the full amount we sued for, but, more important, the experience did reaffirm my faith in the American justice system. I was awarded a lot of money, anyway, because triple damages are the penalty in antitrust cases—and I deserved it all.

When the American Film Institute polled movie buffs throughout America to determine the hundred best films of all time, there was consuming interest within the movie industry and, I'm sure, outside of it as well. The rankings were announced on a special television broadcast (bringing beaucoup dollars to the AFI). As in a Miss America contest, the suspense was built by naming the winner last. I was eager to see the show, as I was hopeful—borderline confident— that *The Graduate* would be on that list. A personal family matter prevented me from seeing the show from the beginning. When I finally tuned in, they had just announced number twenty-five; I was crestfallen, thinking that I had missed hearing what ranking *The Graduate* had. I nonetheless stayed with the broadcast. To my happy surprise, *The Graduate* was then announced. It had been voted the seventh-best film of all time! I nearly fell off my chair, I was so elated. My elation, however, does not prevent me from noting that, as good as *The Graduate* is, as good as I think it is, I don't think it's the seventh-best film of all time. I suspect many of those who voted were not old enough to remember or to have seen landmark films like Chaplin's *City Lights,* Renoir's *Grand Illusion,* and other memorable, truly great movies. But I'm not complaining; I'll take number seven anytime, and forever. The plaque commemorating that number seven is on my wall—but at home, in my clothes closet.

The afterlife of any achievement is quite lovely, whether it's Joe

DiMaggio's fifty-six-game hitting streak, Einstein's discovery of $E = mc^2$, or something as mundane as producing *The Graduate*. It lives after you until, finally, it's the lead item in your obituary. But until that time, it is continually referenced and, I must confess, continually pleasing. You have a dream, and although it's not as important as Martin Luther King's, it's your dream, and when you achieve it, there's no better feeling.

The afterlife of *The Graduate* continues. I just received an invitation from the Academy of Motion Picture Arts and Sciences to a special screening of a newly restored print of the film and, as a treat, printed in boldface is that Mike Nichols himself will be a special guest. No mention of me whatsoever. If you've read this far, you know I think the world of Mike, but *The Graduate* exists as a film only because of me.

So you want to be a producer?

The big surprise and bonus I got in writing this book was the discovery of myself. In examining my career, I reexamined my life, and I've learned things about myself along the way. I appear to be outgoing, gregarious, and confident. What I've been awakened to and am now confronting is that I'm an insecure loner. The six films I produced solely by myself, not in partnership, are each about someone who is isolated from society. Do you think that's an accident? I do not. *The Flim-Flam Man* was the first. It's about a kid on the run, AWOL from the army, who, through his love and respect for an older man, finds his core. (At seventeen, I enlisted in the navy for two years, though I never went AWOL.) Next was *The Graduate*, which enough of you readers have likely seen, and therefore recognize that boy as an outsider, estranged even from his own family. Next I produced *The Great White Hope*, about a person forced to be an outsider, an expatriot. *Pretty Poison* followed; again, this film is about a young boy, this one mentally unstable and living in a fantasy world. He reclaims his manhood, much as in *The Great White Hope*, through self-abnegation.

Next I directed, as well as produced, *The Marriage of a Young Stockbroker*. If you guessed it's about a young man, you guessed right. He is literally on the outside looking in, a voyeur. Although married to a beautiful girl, he covets other women from afar. His genuine love for his wife, and hers for him, saves him. The last film, *Walk Proud,* is about a young Latino who is alienated from his gang culture. He finds the power to break with the gang through his love for an Anglo girl. I'm six for six—all outsiders, one black, one Latino, one crazy, one feckless, one AWOL, and one sexually hungry and insecure. All guys. All me. Each discovers who he is and takes positive action to change his life through the power of love. In writing this book, I got therapy without having to pay for it.

I'm afraid I have to say that there is no "How-To" guide for producing, any more than there is to being president or a rock star.

What I've set down between these covers, what I've given you, is *my* "How-To." That doesn't mean it will work for you. You are unique. You must be authentic to yourself, and remain so. Only say and do those things that are truly you. Your essence can get you where you want to go, on your terms—if you want it badly enough. Good luck.

Let me end with my very favorite show-business story. Once I had successfully launched my career as a producer, my mother asked me, "Is it true Joan Crawford is having an affair with so-and-so [I forget the actor's name]?" "How would I know?" I said. "Well, that's your business, isn't it?" she replied.

It was, and it is.

APPENDIX 1: *BUTCH CASSIDY AND THE SUNDANCE KID* CORRESPONDENCE

September 18, 1964

Mr. William Goldman
510 East 86th Street
New York City, New York

Dear Bill:

I had a dream last night about the Sun Dance Kid. No kidding—he was near the train station and I couldn't determine if he was about to pull a heist or was just promenading like the Cock o' the Walk. So it shouldn't be a total loss, ask your doctor and if you get a good answer send me a bill.

Best,
Lawrence Turman

22 sept 64

larry

before i get into the meat of this, let me ask you: did you give david picker that sheet of paper outlining my western or do you still have it. i am suddenly in fear that some fink is going to steal it. but that's my problem.

now to your problem:

i did not discuss your dream with my shrinker (i have enough trouble discussing my dreams with my shrinker) but i have given it a good deal of thought and the following is my lay analysis interpretation of it.

i am not kidding.

you are (this is obvious) the sundance kid. whether it's because of being the fastest gun or because of california weather or what, i'm not sure. the train is usually a freudian symbol (i don't much believe in them) for the subconcious. now for the rest, you are torn between robbery and acting like a stud. (cock of the walk has to be a play on words.)

unfortunately, i can't make a coherent whole out of the above. but i wish you would ask your shrinker if any of this is possible.

do not send me a bill.

Bill

September 24, 1964

Mr. William Goldman
510 East 86th Street
New York City, New York

Dear Bill:

Your dream interpretation must be right—I am torn between
robbing you of your Western and acting like a stud with your wife,
who I really dig.

To make amends for that bad joke I am herewith returning to you
your outline. What kind of a guy do you think I am, anyway, that
you would even suggest I would leave it with David Picker. I have
merely had a dozen copies mimeoed and am now awaiting bids
from Ernie Lehman, Dalton Trumbo et al (et al is Latin for "ganiff").

I expect to be back in New York in two to three weeks and this time
I will bring my wife, who looks forward to meeting you. She thinks
I'm the original article and that no-one else could possibly have
similar neurotic patterns.

> Best,
> *The Kid*

encl

P.S. Since I wasn't kidding when I said you are like me, I thought
I'd better add here that I <u>was</u> joking about having copies made of
your outline. I just re-read the outline and I am convinced you have
the makings of a wonderful western. I am also convinced that even
though it is historical it must be bold and bigger than life. I don't
mean that it should be taken in the direction of farce or, indeed,
even satire, but the whole western film of itself is of epic
proportions and I was struck that in your outline even you tend
towards fun and games. Don't lose this quality in the screenplay.

The fact that it is anchored in historical fact will keep it anchored to the kind of reality and characterization you are striving for.

At any rate, be sure to show it to me first when you're finished with it so if I decide I don't like it you'll have real, instead of imaginary, cause for your feelings of anticipated rejection (from one who knows).

510 East 86th Street
New York City, New York

december 21, 1964

Mr. Lawrence Turman
Lawrence Turman Inc.
1041 North Formosa Avenue
Hollywood, California 90046

Dear Larry:

My New Year's resolution:

I, William Goldman, hereby resolve to sit down and write THE
SUNDANCE KID and upon finishing same will send to Lawrence
Turman who, even though he leches after my wife, would be fun to
do the film with.

William Goldman

March 4, 1965

AIR MAIL
SPECIAL DELIVERY

Mr. William Goldman
150 Cleveland Lane
Princeton, New Jersey

Dear Bill:

In case you're still stymied in front of your typewriter and don't want to start the Western, I have an original idea that I think can make a very topical, pertinent film and, possibly, a novel.

Let me list and remind you of the series of relatively recent news events, all concerning college:

1. The students' revolt at Cal for political rights (embodied in civil rights); this is also echoed in the Brooklyn riots.

2. The cheating scandal at the Air Force Academy.

3. The Seattle basketball players shaving points for gamblers.

4. The hub-bub about drug taking at Cornell and Harvard.

5. The several Stanford teachers that quit over a rhubarb about eroticism both in teaching and between teachers and students.

6. The general attention by the slick magazines (e.g., Life Magazine story on the pressure today's college student faces).

7. Even your stomping grounds, Princeton, has had a recent rhubarb with pressure being put on for co-eds.

In short, there is as big and dramatic a topic as there is today, and I personally believe the operative word is "today" because it seems to be dynamically different than when "cockers" like you and I were at school. At the worst (and one may be forced to talk a studio into it this way), one could make "THE INTERNS" or "PEYTON PLACE" (ugh to both of them, but they cleaned up)— at the best, one could make a trenchant, penetrating film of real comment.

Now, who understands young people very well and writes marvelous novels about them? And who is living in a college town where he can research it at first hand? And who can mirror all my neuroses so that working together would be a pleasure? Think on the idea, and then please call me collect either at home or in the office.

Best,
Lawrence Turman

LT:ps

9 Mar 65

Larry:

You said in your letter to me that i should call you (collect, naturally) but i thought that since your letter was serious, that i should answer you seriously, and since i tend to bullshit on the phone, therefore this note. (note the stylistic effect of that last: compression the poets call it)

of course we must work together and live forever and both get rich and of course the events you outline are interesting and disturbing to me, but there are problems. first of all, i have just spent several unpleasant years putting down in boys and girls etc what i thought was bugging the people i knew. granted they are older than the people in college today, still i have spent a good deal of time on this general overal problem. then again, i'm not the person who wrote the temple of gold. (my god that was ten years ago. i weep for lycidas, he is dead) still, never one to underrate myself, i suppose my brilliant style would exhume that person and i would be able to come up with the young persons (sigh) point of view. so probably, i'm saying, i could write the goddam thing.

BUT WHAT IS IT? I DONT KNOW.

i mean, i have spent hours boring ilene and others to death on this subject: what is fucking up our young? (I think that's what the picture you have in mind would be about, isn't it?) it's not that i give such a shit about the young, it's just that i'd like to know. because they are <u>different</u>. and if there's one thing today that pisses me off it's the goddam sociologists and their ilk who say that there is nothing essentially different. "After all, when we were young we did the blackbottom." i hate that.

but here's the thing. i don't want to do a picture in which all that is said is: look: you better understand us 'cause we're here and we're gonna take over in fifteen years. because i don't think that's enough.

there was a moment in the blackboard jungle where vic morrow was harrassing glenn ford and ford asked something about why are you doing this and morrow said, if i get a prison record of a few months so what, i won't be drafted.

now granted that the reason is superficial; granted that it was true in only a teeny weeny minority of cases. still, it was some kind of an answer and i in my seat stopped munching popcorn and thought, and i have not forgotten it to this day.

but i don't even have anything as superficial as that to hang this notion on. what is it with these kids? is it the bomb? is it just an overdue generational explosion? (whatever that means) and why are the kids so fucked up over sex? the beetles are fucking women run by a faggot and the rolling stones make the beetles look like rock hudson (i think there is a joke in there somewhere) and the goddam girls on the streets are all wearing fucking boots and boots have been perversion fare for lo these many years so there is a gigantic confusion of roles going on, but what's the <u>CONCLUSION</u>?

aside from the above, there is a problem with making a picture in which the main characters are collegians. and that is that i as the author have trouble taking them seriously. so big deal they're confused. so big deal they can't take the pressures of college life— it's a hell of a lot better than working. now i grant the above is a fairly limited attitude on my part and one i'm sure i could overcome, but still it is something to bear in mind. (and if you're going to do a college picture you can't do the standard hollywood cheat and put paul newman at princeton. my god i'm always stunned they don't explain what an old man is doing as an undergraduate. if you don't cast old i suppose there's always annette, but that's worse than the chinese water torture. i am touching on the obvious problem of casting, but again, it's something to bear in mind.)

i suppose to start to close, larry old stick, that until i know or at least think i know what it is with these children, i can't give you an answer as to whether i would want to do this kind of thing. (after all, i might find an answer if there is one and discover the whole thing bored me—so might you by the way—it could be that the interest lies in the fact that we thought we understood what was going on and now we're old old old and don't anymore.)

how do you make the collegians interesting, real and understandable?

you tell me.

non-picture-making-wise, i am fine, my wife is terribly pregnant (early april hopefully) my daughter is getting remarkably good about going on the toilet and our st bernard named renfroo is in all ways, admirable.

over and out.

Bill

March 11, 1965

Mr. William Goldman
150 Cleveland Lane
Princeton, New Jersey

Dear Bill:

First of all, my secretary must think you are a dirty writer.

Secondly, for a writer with as much talent, taste and intelligence as you, in your sentence "the beetles are fucking women run by a faggot . . .", you left out a comma between fucking and women—because I, myself, personally know of a girl who was sleeping with at least one, and probably two, or them.

Thirdly, when you ask, "why are the kids so fucked up over sex?", you reveal how really much over the hill you are! Most of them are getting more, earlier and better, than you or I ever did.

So, we'll stick with the Sundance Kid, okay? I am happy with that.

Seriously, though, folks, I agree with much of what you say in your letter although I don't necessarily buy your conclusions. Must we always know and show the reason behind people and their actions? That question is a big switch for me. I am usually a one-foot-in-front-of-the-other type of fellow and always do ask why, and yet, some of the films I've seen that have affected me the most profoundly (European films mainly) merely show and allow the audience to draw their own collective or, and I think this is a vital point, individual conclusions. And, Antonioni is no bum. He may be a bore, although I don't even think that anymore, but not a bum. And there is Fellini and Truffaut, who never even bore.

The important thing, I am beginning to feel, in any film is to make the people real and interesting. Understanding? Hell, one seldom really understands even one's friends. But, since it's virtually impossible to get studio "front money" to develop an original idea, there is little point in pursuing this anyway, expecially given your attitude. And, anyway, part of my motivation was money, not art.

"THE BEST MAN" got festival awards, and, in the main, wonderful reviews, but was about "old men in a dry season" (the New York Times says half the population of America in now under 25) and the box office reflected it, while the producers of "BIKINI BEACH PARTY" and "RETURN OF THE NEW INTERNS" laughed all the way to the bank. My problem is: I have the kind of an ego that wants to do true quality films while at the same time supporting my hedonistic Veblen tastes. (Are they incompatible?)

My writing style sounds to me a bit convoluted and prolix—I can see why you get paid for it and I don't.

Lifewise, my eldest boy, after 5½ years of good health, had, within a three-week span, a concussion, the chicken pox, and a double hernia discovered; but, happily, it's all behind us now save the operation, which, I have been assured, is relatively minor. Our younger son has now just started the chicken pox (you have that to look forward to), but all else is well.

Best,
Lawrence Turman

LT:ps

16 mar 65

larry

it is very important to me to sustain my position as an honest gossip, so let me start by saying that when i said the beatles were 'fucking women' i did not mean to besmirch ringo's virility; they are all four straight and you can quote me; what i meant was that they are, as performers, basically women. they have long hair and they are all teeny weeny and it all goes into the confusion of roles business i went into later: so many of the male performers that appeal to the kids (ugh) today are teeny weeny and cute and overly hairy and like that.

the newest thing in my life is virna lisi (spelling?) (the broad in the lemmon picture) do you know anybody who is screwing her? why aren't we?

the reason i am writing this is because i haven't got anything else to do.

meathead, when you say 'do we always have to know and show the reason behind people and their actions?' of course the answer is no. what i meant was this: we don't have to state the answers for all to see in big bold here's the mssage folks print, but i think it would be nice for us to know what they were so we can at least ask the right questions. after reading your feeble missive (nobody criticizes my writing style and gets away with it) i got to thinking of a story about a kid in college who kept getting excited and then eventually bored with various things, whether they be causes, girls, ideas, etc, going from fad to fad ending up lost and i thought that it wasn't a bad idea, but i still find myself saying 'who cares?' i think the best way maybe of dealing with your basic idea (and i know that we're not dealing with it anymore but i thought this might be nice to get out in case somebody came up with a notion in the future) is like the idea i had about the guy who wanted me to do a script about the problem of kids getting into college? in case you don't remember, I'll be brief—his point was that parents were getting involved and kids were killing themselves and I said that I thought the problem was how to isolate the phenomenon because, i said, kids who kill themselves because harvard said no would likely kill themselves anyway and the harvard rejection is only a catalyst and what you need was to isolate and then i came up with the notion of a script about trying to get a child into a spiffy nursury school in manhattan and you play it straight as if you are shooting for bryn mawr but it's really brearley nursury school all the tummeling is about. (it's still a goddam funny idea and steal it and i'll sue you) that way, i said, you could make a genuine comment, satiric and sound, about the pressures parents are under and put themselves under and like that. and i think maybe your idea of the college kids today needs a similar kind of approach, but god knows what it is. a different avenue to the core of the material. a surprise.

one more note on what the creators have to know: antonioni (who is drecky) and fellini (who isn't) and their ilk (any writer who uses the work ilk correctly can't be all bad) are very particular about what limited views of reality they show. they want the audience to draw conclusions but they want the audience to draw their (fellini's, not the audience's) conclusions. i think if you said that to fellini that dolce vita was even sexier than irma la douce he might not be pleased. he is using sex a certain way, just as he is using the values of the day in a certain way. and he is saying, in that film, i think (and among other things): here is a valuable man (mastroianni) who through contact with society loses his value; how funny it is, how sad.

i also want to talk about money vs art, since it's inevitable that we're going to do something someday and also inivitable that when we do, this problem is going to come up. we both want, as does ever-buddy as my daughter would say, <u>LOVE</u> . . . #&#_" %¸!!! we want love from the intellectuals and also from the hoi polloi. the last persons to get this orgiastic reception are stanley kubrick, edward albee and saul bellow. three people in five years.

larry, the odds are against us.

however

i think that the best man, even though you fucked up and made a good picture, probably will in the long run do you more good that three bikini pictures. for example it got you me. i would imagine it has and will influence most of the decent craftsmen with who you will work in the next years.

i don't know the answer to the sellout question and that i suppose is why i am putting this down. for example, i have high hopes for the western being a major western, like shane. in my mind i would guess i would write it for lemmon and newman. now; assuming i write it and sinatra and martin are looking for something, what do you do? obviously nothing with sinatra and martin can be worth more than shit. so any artistic pretense goes out the window. so i guess the answer to this specific is that if you can make a LOT of money with sinatra and martin, then you do it with them. is that right do you think?

what if either lemmon or newman said yes, the other no. do you take peppard for the other? he killed breakfast at tiffany's, he could kill this easy. my answer to this specific would be you don't take him because he can't make you enough money. if he can, then you do.

i suppose the conclusion i'm drawing is that you should only go for money if by money, you mean MONEY!!! and don't go for art if one of the main roles is going to be played by kim novak.

i am sorry this is all so incoherent but as a budding movie writer i am confused by the problem which i know is a crucial one in films. i know that as a novelist i have no such confusion. the ending to the book of soldier in the rain, for example was complained of as being downbeat. i replied to the publishers that i would be delighted to change it and make it happy if they on their part could guarantee that the book would sell. (i wouldn't have changed it, but i was safe in making the offer because no one can guarantee that a book will sell. not even herman wouk sells all the time) in

the movies though, there are guarantees. certain stars. so the
problem is different here. moss hart once told jerry chodorov that
'you can't be a whore six months a year,' (i just made a freudian—i
typed 'six moneys a year'—but i guess that's obvious.)

larry, this is a dull, relatively stupid letter and i didn't mean for it to
be. i think i'm tired. goodbye forever

                                        S. Katzman

March 22, 1965

Mr. William Goldman
150 Cleveland Lane
Princeton, New Jersey

Dear Bill:

All right, all right; so you were right and I was wrong. Jack Smight, who you will be meeting shortly, is a friend of mine and told me about the deal for Paul Newman to do your script. But, how was I to know that even you could make those repetitive Lew Archer interrogation scenes into a bright, action-packed screenplay (which I have not read as Hal Landers has failed to fulfill my request to see the screenplay)!

Which leads me to reaffirm that, while my interest in THE SUNDANCE KID remains undiminished (one has to phrase very carefully for neurotic artists), I would <u>also</u> love to work on something contemporary with you—our generation, our milieu.

Meathead indeed—you had a Freudian reading slip. . . . I criticized <u>my</u> writing style, not yours. The only thing I can say about your writing style is that you should show your letters to your head doctor because they must be every bit as good as your dreams. What I mean is, you write real good.

But, let's not do a college story together, even though your nursery school idea would make a great skit, if not movie. (You needn't worry about my stealing it—I am compulsively honest but have not yet discovered the reason why . . . until this very minute, by thinking of your letter; I am compulsively honest because I want LOVE! Eureka!)

Now, about money vs. art. If I understand your letter correctly, you'll sleep with someone for a lot of money but you're not a two-buck whore. Right? Welcome to the human race. You do make one mistake however: <u>no</u> star is a guarantee, although, presumably, they help a good film. . . . Audrey Hepburn and Burt Lancaster bombed in "THE UNFORGIVEN," Marilyn Monroe and Clark Gable failed in "THE MISFITS," Marlon Brando went down the drain in "THE UGLY AMERICAN" and "ORPHEUS DESCENDING," Shirley Maclaine with Bob Mitchum died in "TWO FOR THE SEESAW," "THE OUTRAGE" didn't gross Paul Newman's salary, etc., etc., etc. There are, actually, only two surefire stars: Elvis Presley and Jerry Lewis!

Only one of Stanley Kubrick's films made money, and only one of Edward Albee's plays made money—the odds may, indeed, be against us; that's why it's so important to work with someone compatible because the excitement and the fun is in the doing. (I forgot if I either read that somewhere or some non-neurotic person told it to me.) So, "THE BEST MAN" got me Mike Nichols, a fat multiple picture deal with U.A., and you—what's it done for me lately?

Your letter started out with a bang and ended with whimpering contrite despair—be different, despair is too common today to be worthy of the likes of you and me. I like you. Onward and Upward.

Boris (not Joe) Pasternak

LT:ps

P.S. Some day you can go to Parke-Bernet and buy back your letters to me at auction. Allavei.

PRINCETON UNIVERSITY
PRINCETON, NEW JERSEY
Department of English
McCosh 22

larry

in the desk in the room they gave me to use for the year was this
stationery. i am using it in this note to you as a kind of joke. i don't
want, under any conditions, for it to inhibit you. i mean, the fact
that when you disagree with me you are disagreeing with a
FUCKING PROFESSOR OF ENGLISH should in no way make you
feel humble, insecure, or in any way inferior to me intellectually.
remember that. and <u>don't</u> <u>you</u> <u>ever</u> <u>forget</u> <u>it</u>! after all, even though
you are nothing but a lowly hollywood producer, the butt of jokes
around the world, the cliché of clichés, you still have as much right
as the next to disagree with a GODDAM EDUCATOR like me as the
next guy.

my brother in law, allen case, is playing frank james in the jesse
james series. as a consequence, i bought all the papers yesterday
from philly as well as new york, which is why i am writing you
now. the reviews were bad, which is neither here nor there. it is the
nature of their badness that prompts this note.

the thing is this: most of the critics panned the show on moral
grounds. how dare they whitewash outlaws? how could abc try to
make a hero out of such a legendary badman etc.

i assume you now see what disturbs me and also that it is nothing
new. i am bugged by how to get rid of the moral problem with our
western. i think what i want is for the moral problem never to enter
anyones mind. how do you do that? it would be, i think, the easiest
way in the world to sabotage our project if the moral problem
comes up. i think actors might object to playing because of it and i
certainly think that banks might object to bankrolling it. and so i
am perturbed.

one way i guess to beat the moral problem is to never have the characters discuss it. no 'gee what a lousy break' shit. perhaps what i mean is just have them go about their business of getting through life as well and painlessly as possible, just like the rest of us. you think?

i'm not really sure and i have no answers but i though i ought to state the question again, just so that it stays with us.

my situation is formless at present. i'm about a hundred pages into a novel and I'm good for about maybe 50 more but then i may be hung. if so, i will likely try sundance. all this depends on the teaching which starts sometime next week. i assume it will not affect the amount of time and energy i can give to my own work and only hope my assumption is correct.

anyway, i am alive and fine as is my family and i wish the same to you and yours.

Bill

September 21, 1965

Dear Bill:

I saw the second episode of the JESSE JAMES series last night and, my friend, I think you are tilting at windmills. The aim of a television series is to go on and on and on, which means that there can never be <u>the</u> climactic character resolution—no real third act. And that's where movies have always gotten by, and that's how we'll get by. Butch and the kid <u>do</u> get killed, and in a godforsaken place bereft of friends or family. And that's why, historically, many films of outlaws and gangsters have been both commercially successful, and satisfying to critics as well. The practical problem we may face is that a studio front office will want either or both to live for a more upbeat (and less moral) ending.

Even a fucking professor of English should be able to see the clarity of my argument. <u>Even</u> an intellectually inferior fucking professor of English! And after I ride in on your coattails (see, I don't mind learning things even from Elliot Kastner!) I won't be a lowly hollywood producer—I'll have klass.

We're awaiting the new baby in a couple of weeks, and Suzanne joins me in sending best to you and Ilene.

Best,
Lawrence Turman

P.S. One day I will write you using all capital letters for a real putdown and then where will you be?

Mr. William Goldman
150 Cleveland Lane
Princeton, New Jersey

WU TLX LAS +

TWECENTFOX LSA

WUB248 SSD328 L BHA333 (P PSA328)

PD

PRINCETON NJER 12 551P EST

LAWRENCE TURMAN, 20TH CENTURY FOX FILM CORP

BEVERLY HILLS CALIF

PART ONE FINISHED TODAY 86 PAGES GOD BLESS US EVERYONE

BILL GOLDMAN

555P PST JAN 12 66

+

TWECENTFOX LSA

January 24, 1966

Dear Paul:

Bill Goldman told me he's already spoken to you about THE
SUNDANCE KID AND BUTCH CASSIDY, so here it is. This first
draft, like all of Bill's work, has marvelous dialogue and colorful
dramatic scenes. I look forward to talking with you after you've
read it. Bill will be anxious for your reaction and, of course, is
available to come out to meet with you too. I hope you like it—he
wrote it for you.

        Best,
        Lawrence Turman

Mr. Paul Newman
Universal Studio
Universal City

LT:kp
enc: THE SUNDANCE KID AND BUTCH CASSIDY

LAWRENCE TURMAN INC.
c/o 20TH CENTURY–FOX

Rich:

As discussed here is Bill Goldman's original western. Part II is where it really goes off the track—in fact only a few of those scnes will remain—but even this rough draft I think shows the slam-bang, colorful, and very castable picture this can be.

I'll be anxious for your reaction. Have a good New Year's.

Larry

Since this is my only copy, please be sure I get it back. Thanks.

19 January 67
Lawrence Turman

Richard Zanuck

Rich:

As you requested I'm herewith returning to you the William
Goldman original, THE SUNDANCE KID AND BUTCH CASSIDY.
Part I of this rough draft is the kind of picture it will be—slam-bang,
colorful and castable. The entire New York sequence will be
eliminated and only a few of the scenes in South America (like the
bank robbery) will remain. And of course it will not be in two
parts . . . although it's big and commercial, it's not a road show.
This is my only copy of this script so please make sure it doesn't go
astray. Thanks.

As I told you, Paul Newman is familiar with and interested in this
material.

January 27, 1966

Dear Dick:

Here is Bill Goldman's script for which he has expressly written the role of Butch Cassidy for Jack Lemmon (the co-starring role was written for Paul Newman, who just filmed HARPER, Bill's last screenplay).

I think the story offers wonderful potential for an unsual, colorful film, and the quality of Bill's writing speaks for itself. As I told you, Bill will be in Los Angeles this coming Monday through Wednesday and it would be ideal if Jack Lemmon could read it by then, and hopefully meet with us about it. We'll both be very anxious for his reaction.

Best,
Lawrence Turman

Mr. Dick Carter
11368 Burnham Street
Brentwood Glen, California

LT:kp
enc: THE SUNDANCE KID AND BUTCH CASSIDY

February 1, 1966

Dear Bob:

Bill Goldman is delighted, as am I, that you can make the time to read his screenplay THE SUNDANCE KID AND BUTCH CASSIDY so swiftly. We feel the second part is less formed than the first at present, and are looking forward to talking to you about it. We also will have met with Paul Newman before seeing you.

Best,
Lawrence Turman

Mr. Robert Mulligan
236 Tigertail Road
Los Angeles 49, California

LT:kp
enc: THE SUNDANCE KID AND BUTCH CASSIDY

1 Sept '83

Larry—

—yours was a lovely letter. God, how life etches on us. (From the philophical works or Geoge Lucas.)

I would have replied sooner but we have been in London all summer and just returned. In preparation for our children fleeing— we take them both to Oberlin tomorrow where Jenny is a senior, Susanna a freshman—we have taken a small flat in London.

It was a glorious summer. I hid in Knightsbridge and watched British television. I was exhausted having just finished a long and I suppose painful book. It will come out in Spring with a title as yet undecided.

I plan to start another book this fall. (As you may detect, there is less than glee in my re-entering the picture business.)

The Mass Appeal cast sounds wonderful. I did not know Mr. Kroc, having fucked up his baseball franchise was into chasing starlets, but good for you that he is.

We don't see L.A. in our future (it may be been two years since I was there) but surely New York must be in yours and we must talk and eat and rekindle.

Good bless,
Bill

APPENDIX 2: CONTRIBUTOR CREDITS

DAVID BROWN

Academy Award Nominee
  Chocolat (2000) Best Picture
  A Few Good Men (1992) Best Picture
  The Verdict (1982) Best Picture
  Jaws (1975) Best Picture

Irving G. Thalberg Memorial Award—1990 (with Dick Zanuck)

Producer—filmography
  Framed (2002) (TV) (executive producer)
  Along Came a Spider (2001) (producer)
  Chocolat (2000) (producer)
  Angela's Ashes (1999) (producer)
  Deep Impact (1998) (producer)
  Kiss the Girls (1997) (producer)
  The Saint (1997) (producer)
  Season in Purgatory, A (1996) (TV) (executive producer)
  Canadian Bacon (1995) (producer)
  Watch It (1993) (executive producer)
  Rich in Love (1993) (co-producer)
  The Cemetery Club (1993) (producer)
  A Few Good Men (1992) (producer)
  The Player (1992) (producer)

Women & Men 2: In Love There Are No Rules (1991) (TV) (producer)
Driving Miss Daisy (1989) (executive producer)
Cocoon: The Return (1988) (producer)
Target (1985) (producer)
Cocoon (1985) (producer)
The Verdict (1982) (producer)
Neighbors (1981) (producer)
The Island (1980) (producer)
Jaws 2 (1978) (producer)
Jaws (1975) (producer)
The Eiger Sanction (1975) (executive producer)
The Girl from Petrovka (1974) (producer)
Willie Dynamite (1974) (producer)
The Black Windmill (1974) (executive producer)
The Sugarland Express (1974) (producer)
SSSSSSS (1973) (executive producer)
The Sting (1973) (A Richard D. Zanuck/David Brown Presentation)

WILLIAM GOLDMAN

Academy Award Winner
All the President's Men (1976) Best Adapted Screenplay
Butch Cassidy and the Sundance Kid (1969) Best Original
   Screenplay

Writer—filmography
Dreamcatcher (2003) (screenplay)
Hearts in Atlantis (2001) (screenplay)
The General's Daughter (1999) (screenplay)
Absolute Power (1997) (screenplay)
Fierce Creatures (1997) (uncredited)
The Ghost and the Darkness (1996) (written by)
The Chamber (1996) (screenplay)
Maverick (1994) (written by)
Chaplin (1992) (screenplay)
Year of the Comet (1992) (written by)
Memoirs of an Invisible Man (1992) (screenplay)
Misery (1990) (screenplay)
The Princess Bride (1987) (book) (screenplay)
Heat (1987) (also novel)
Mr. Horn (1979) (TV)

Magic (1978) (also novel)
A Bridge Too Far (1977)
Marathon Man (1976) (novel)
All the President's Men (1976) (screenplay)
The Great Waldo Pepper (1975)
The Stepford Wives (1975) (screenplay)
The Hot Rock (1972)
Butch Cassidy and the Sundance Kid (1969) (written by)
No Way to Treat a Lady (1968) (novel)
Harper (1966) (screenplay)
Masquerade (1965)
Soldier in the Rain (1963) (novel)

BRIAN GRAZER

Academy Award Winner
  A Beautiful Mind (2001) Best Picture

Academy Award Nominee
  Apollo 13 (1995) Best Picture
  Splash (1984) Best Writing

Producer—filmography
  Friday Night Lights (2004) (producer)
  The Missing (2003) (producer)
  The Cat in the Hat (2003) (producer)
  Arrested Development (2003) TV Series (executive producer)
  Miss Match (2003) TV Series (executive producer)
  Intolerable Cruelty (2003) (producer)
  BS* (2002) (TV) (executive producer)
  8 Mile (2002) (producer)
  Blue Crush (2002) (producer)
  Undercover Brother (2002) (producer)
  A Beautiful Mind (2001) (producer)
  24 (2001) TV Series (executive producer)
  The Beast (2001) TV Series (executive producer)
  How the Grinch Stole Christmas (2000) (producer)
  Nutty Professor II: The Klumps (2000) (producer)
  Wonderland (2000) TV Series (executive producer)
  Student Affairs (1999) (TV) (producer)
  Beyond the Mat (1999) (producer)

Bowfinger (1999) (producer)
Life (1999) (producer)
Edtv (1999) (producer)
The PJs (1999) TV Series (executive producer)
Psycho (1998) (producer)
Felicity (1998) TV Series (executive producer)
Sports Night (1998) TV Series (executive producer)
From the Earth to the Moon (1998) (mini) TV Series (producer)
Mercury Rising (1998) (producer)
The Big House (1998) TV Series (executive producer) (2003)
Hiller and Diller (1997) TV Series (executive producer)
Inventing the Abbotts (1997) (producer)
Liar Liar (1997) (producer)
Ransom (1996) (producer)
The Nutty Professor (1996) (producer)
Fear (1996) (producer)
Sgt. Bilko (1996) (producer)
The Chamber (1996) (producer)
Apollo 13 (1995) (producer)
The Cowboy Way (1994) (producer)
The Paper (1994) (producer)
Greedy (1994) (producer)
My Girl 2 (1994) (producer)
For Love or Money (1993) (producer)
CB4 (1993) (executive producer)
Boomerang (1992) (producer)
HouseSitter (1992) (producer)
Far and Away (1992) (producer)
My Girl (1991) (producer)
Backdraft (1991) (executive producer)
Closet Land (1991) (executive producer)
The Doors (1991) (executive producer)
Kindergarten Cop (1990) (producer)
Cry-Baby (1990) (executive producer)
Parenthood (1989) (producer)
Like Father Like Son (1987) (producer)
Armed and Dangerous (1986) (producer)
Spies Like Us (1985) (producer)
Shadow Chasers (1985) TV Series (executive producer)
Real Genius (1985) (producer)
Splash (1984) (producer)

Night Shift (1982) (producer)
Thou Shalt Not Commit Adultery (1978) (TV) (producer)
Zuma Beach (1978) (TV) (producer)

Writer—*filmography*
House Sitter (1992) (story)
Armed and Dangerous (1986) (story)
Shadow Chasers (1985) TV Series (creator)
Splash (1984) (story)

CURTIS HANSON

Academy Award Winner
L.A. Confidential (1997) Best Adapted Screenplay

Academy Award Nominee
L.A. Confidential (1997) Best Picture, Best Director

Director—*filmography*
In Her Shoes (2005)
8 Mile (2002)
Wonder Boys (2000)
L.A. Confidential (1997)
The River Wild (1994)
The Hand That Rocks the Cradle (1992)
Bad Influence (1990)
The Bedroom Window (1987)
The Children of Times Square (1986) (TV)
Losin' It (1983)
The Little Dragons (1980)
Sweet Kill (1973)

Producer—*filmography*
In Her Shoes (2005) (producer)
8 Mile (2002) (producer)
Wonder Boys (2000) (producer)
L.A. Confidential (1997) (producer)
The Little Dragons (1980) (executive producer)
The Silent Partner (1978) (associate producer)
Sweet Kill (1973) (producer)

Writer—filmography
   L.A. Confidential (1997)
   The Bedroom Window (1987)
   The Children of Times Square (1986) (TV)
   White Dog (1982)
   The Silent Partner (1978)
   Sweet Kill (1973)
   The Dunwich Horror (1970) (as Curtis Lee Hanson)

KATHLEEN KENNEDY

Academy Award Nominee
   Seabiscuit (2003) Best Picture
   The Sixth Sense (1999) Best Picture
   The Color Purple (1985) Best Picture
   E.T. the Extra-Terrestrial (1982) Best Picture

Producer—filmography
   War of the Worlds (2005) (producer)
   Seabiscuit (2003) (producer)
   Signs (2002) (executive producer)
   Jurassic Park III (2001) (producer)
   AI: Artificial Intelligence (2001) (producer)
   A Map of the World (1999) (producer)
   The Sixth Sense (1999) (producer)
   Snow Falling on Cedars (1999) (producer)
   The Lost World (1997) (executive producer)
   Twister (1996) (producer)
   The Indian in the Cupboard (1995) (producer)
   Congo (1995) (producer)
   The Bridges of Madison County (1995) (producer)
   Milk Money (1994) (producer)
   The Flintstones (1994) (executive producer)
   Schindler's List (1993) (executive producer)
   A Dangerous Woman (1993) (executive producer)
   We're Back! A Dinosaur's Story (1993) (executive producer)
   Jurassic Park (1993) (producer)
   A Far Off Place (1993) (executive producer)
   Alive (1993) (producer)
   Noises Off (1992) (executive producer)
   Hook (1991) (producer)

An American Tail: Fievel Goes West (1991) (executive producer)
Cape Fear (1991) (executive producer)
Arachnophobia (1990) (producer)
Gremlins 2: The New Batch (1990) (executive producer)
Back to the Future Part III (1990) (executive producer)
Joe Versus the Volcano (1990) (executive producer)
Always (1989) (producer)
Dad (1989) (executive producer)
Back to the Future Part II (1989) (executive producer)
Indiana Jones and the Last Crusade (1989) (executive producer)
The Land Before Time (1988) (co-executive producer)
Who Framed Roger Rabbit (1988) (executive producer)
*batteries not included (1987) (executive producer)
Empire of the Sun (1987) (producer)
Innerspace (1987) (co-executive producer)
An American Tail (1986) (producer)
The Money Pit (1986) (producer)
The Color Purple (1985) (producer)
Young Sherlock Holmes (1985) (executive producer)
Back to the Future (1985) (executive producer)
The Goonies (1985) (executive producer)
Fandango (1985) (executive producer)
Gremlins (1984) (executive producer)
Indiana Jones and the Temple of Doom (1984) (associate producer)
E.T. the Extra-Terrestrial (1982) (producer)
Poltergeist (1982) (associate producer)

FRANK PIERSON

Academy Award Winner
  Dog Day Afternoon (1975) Best Original Screenplay

Academy Award Nominee
  Cool Hand Luke (1967) Best Adapted Screenplay
  Cat Ballou (1965) Best Adapted Screenplay

Director—filmography
  Paradise (2004)
  Soldier's Girl (2003) (TV)
  Conspiracy (2001) (TV)
  Dirty Pictures (2000) (TV)

Truman (1995) (TV)
Lakota Woman: Siege at Wounded Knee (1994) (TV)
Citizen Cohn (1992) (TV)
Somebody Has to Shoot the Picture (1990) (TV)
Alfred Hitchcock Presents (1985) TV Series
King of the Gypsies (1978)
A Star Is Born (1976)
Nichols (1971) TV Series
The Neon Ceiling (1971) (TV)
The Looking Glass War (1969)
The Bold Ones: The New Doctors (1969) TV Series
Route 66 (1960) TV Series (episode "Build Your Houses with Their Backs to the Sea") (as Frank R. Pierson)

Writer—filmography

Presumed Innocent (1990) (screenplay)
In Country (1989) (screenplay)
Haywire (1980) (TV)
King of the Gypsies (1978)
A Star Is Born (1976)
Dog Day Afternoon (1975) (screenplay)
Nichols (1971) TV Series (creator) (writer)
The Anderson Tapes (1971) (as Frank R. Pierson)
The 42nd Annual Academy Awards (1970) (TV)
The Looking Glass War (1969)
Cool Hand Luke (1967) (screenplay) (as Frank R. Pierson)
The Happening (1967)
Cat Ballou (1965) (as Frank R. Pierson)
Route 66 (1960) TV Series (writer) (episode "Build Your Houses with Their Backs to the Sea") (as Frank R. Pierson)
Naked City (1958) TV Series (writer) (episode "A Case Study of Two Savages")

Producer—filmography

Conspiracy (2001) (TV) (executive producer)
Nichols (1971) TV Series (producer) (as Frank R. Pierson)
Have Gun—Will Travel (1957) TV Series (producer) (as Frank R. Pierson)

CHRISTINE VACHON

Producer—filmography

Mrs. Harris (2005) (executive producer)
The Notorious Betty Page (2005) (producer)
A Dirty Shame (2004) (producer)
A Home at the End of the World (2004) (producer)
The Company (2003) (producer)
Camp (2003) (producer)
Party Monster (2003) (producer)
Far from Heaven (2002) (producer)
One Hour Photo (2002) (producer)
Fine and Mellow (2001) (producer)
Chelsea Walls (2001) (producer)
The Grey Zone (2001) (producer)
Storytelling (2001) (producer)
The Safety of Objects (2001) (producer)
Women in Film (2001) (producer)
Series 7: The Contenders (2001) (producer)
Hedwig and the Angry Inch (2001) (producer)
Crime and Punishment in Suburbia (2000) (producer)
Boys Don't Cry (1999) (producer)
I'm Losing You (1998) (producer)
Velvet Goldmine (1998) (producer)
Happiness (1998) (producer)
Office Killer (1997) (producer)
Kiss Me, Guido (1997) (producer)
Plain Pleasures (1996) (producer)
I Shot Andy Warhol (1996) (producer)
Stonewall (1995) (producer)
Safe (1995) (producer)
Kids (1995) (co-producer)
Postcards from America (1994) (producer)
Go Fish (1994) (executive producer)
Dottie Gets Spanked (1993) (TV) (producer)
Swoon (1992) (producer)
Poison (1991) (producer)
Oreos with Attitude (1990) (producer)
He Was Once (1989) (producer)
La Divina (1989) (producer)
Tommy's (1985) (producer)

DOUGLAS WICK

Academy Award Winner
  Gladiator (2000) Best Picture

Academy Award Nominee
  Working Girl (1988) Best Picture

Producer—filmography
  Bewitched (2005) (producer)
  Jarhead (2005) (producer)
  Memoirs of a Geisha (2005) (producer)
  Win a Date with Tad Hamilton! (2004) (producer)
  Peter Pan (2003) (producer)
  Stuart Little (2003) TV Series (executive producer)
  Stuart Little 2 (2002) (producer)
  Spy Game (2001) (producer)
  Hollow Man (2000) (producer)
  Gladiator (2000) (producer)
  Girl, Interrupted (1999) (producer)
  Stuart Little (1999) (producer)
  Hush (1998) (producer)
  The Craft (1996) (producer)
  Wolf (1994) (producer)
  Working Girl (1988) (producer)
  Starting Over (1979) (associate producer)

Writer—filmography
  Stuart Little 2 (2002) (story)

DAVID WOLPER

Academy Award
  Jean Hersholt Humanitarian Award 1985

Academy Award Nominee
  The Race for Space (Best Documentary Feature) 1959

Emmy Award Winner
  Roots: The Next Generations (Outstanding Limited Series) 1979
  Roots (Outstanding Limited Series) 1977

Emmy Award Nominee
   Queen (Outstanding Miniseries) 1993
   Murder in Mississippi (Outstanding Drama Special) 1990
   Hollywood: The Gift of Laughter (Outstanding Informational
     Special) 1982
   The Scarlett O'Hara War (Outstanding Limited Series) 1980

Producer—filmography
   Roots: Celebrating 25 Years (2002) (TV) (executive producer)
   The Mists of Avalon (2001) (mini) TV Series (executive producer)
   Celebrate the Century (1999) (mini) TV Series (producer)
   To Serve and Protect (1999) (mini) TV Series (executive producer)
   Warner Bros. 75th Anniversary: No Guts, No Glory (1998) (TV)
     (executive producer)
   A Will of Their Own (1998) (mini) TV Series (executive producer)
   Terror in the Mall (1998) (TV) (executive producer)
   L.A. Confidential (1997) (executive producer)
   Surviving Picasso (1996) (producer)
   The Thorn Birds: The Missing Years (1996) (TV) (executive
     producer)
   Murder in the First (1995) (executive producer)
   Without Warning (1994) (TV) (executive producer)
   Fatal Deception: Mrs. Lee Harvey Oswald (1993) (TV) (producer)
   The Flood: Who Will Save Our Children? (1993) (TV) (executive
     producer)
   Bed of Lies (1992) (TV) (executive producer)
   Dillinger (1991) (TV) (executive producer)
   Murder in Mississippi (1990) (TV) (executive producer)
   The Plot to Kill Hitler (1990) (TV) (executive producer)
   Imagine: John Lennon (1988) (producer)
   Napoleon and Josephine: A Love Story (1987) (mini) TV Series
     (executive producer)
   The Betty Ford Story (1987) (TV) (executive producer)
   Liberty Weekend (1986) (TV) (producer)
   North and South II (1986) (mini) TV Series (executive producer)
   North and South (1985) (mini) TV Series (executive producer)
   The Mystic Warrior (1984) (TV) (executive producer)
   The Thorn Birds (1983) (mini) TV Series (executive producer)
   Hollywood: The Gift of Laughter (1982) (TV) (executive producer)
   Murder Is Easy (1982) (TV) (executive producer)
   This Is Elvis (1981) (executive producer)

The Silent Lovers (1980) (TV) (executive producer)
The Scarlett O'Hara War (1980) (TV) (executive producer)
This Year's Blonde (1980) (TV) (executive producer)
Roots: The Next Generation (1979) (mini) TV Series (executive producer)
Roots: One Year Later (1978) (TV) (executive producer)
Roots (1977) (mini) TV Series (executive producer)
Collision Course: Truman vs. MacArthur (1976) (TV) (executive producer)
Victory at Entebbe (1976) (TV) (executive producer)
Lincoln (1975) (mini) TV Series (executive producer)
I Will Fight No More Forever (1975) (TV) (executive producer)
Up from the Ape (1974) (executive producer)
Get Christie Love (1974) TV Series (executive producer)
Visions of Eight (1973) (producer)
Wattstax (1973) (executive producer)
The 500 Pound Jerk (1973) (TV) (executive producer)
King, Queen, Knave (1972) (producer)
Make Mine Red, White and Blue (1972) (TV) (producer)
One Is a Lonely Number (1972) (executive producer)
Willy Wonka & the Chocolate Factory (1971) (producer)
The Hellstrom Chronicle (1971) (executive producer)
I Love My Wife (1970) (executive producer)
The Unfinished Journey of Robert Kennedy (1970) (TV) (producer)
Hemingway's Spain: A Love Affair (1969) (TV) (producer)
Making of the President 1968 (1969) (TV) (executive producer)
The Bridge at Remagen (1969) (producer)
If It's Tuesday, This Must Be Belgium (1969) (executive producer)
Sophia: A Self-Portrait (1968) (TV) (executive producer)
The Devil's Brigade (1968) (producer)
A Laurel and Hardy Cartoon (1966) TV Series (producer)
The Legend of Marilyn Monroe (1964) (producer)
National Geographic Specials (1964) TV Series (executive producer)
Hollywood and the Stars (1963) TV Series (producer)
D-Day (1962) (TV) (producer)
Biography (1961) TV Series (producer)
Hollywood: The Golden Years (1961) (TV) (executive producer) (producer)
The Race for Space (1959) (TV) (executive producer)

Director—filmography
  Hollywood: The Golden Years (1961) (TV)
  Race for Space, The (1959) (TV)

SAUL ZAENTZ

Academy Award Winner
  The English Patient (1996) Best Picture
  Amadeus (1984) Best Picture
  One Flew Over the Cuckoo's Nest (1975) Best Picture

Irving G. Thalberg Memorial Award—1996

Producer—filmography
  The English Patient (1996) (producer)
  At Play in the Fields of the Lord (1991) (producer)
  The Unbearable Lightness of Being (1988) (producer)
  The Mosquito Coast (1986) (executive producer)
  Amadeus (1984) (producer)
  The Lord of the Rings (1978) (producer)
  Three Warriors (1978) (producer)
  One Flew Over the Cuckoo's Nest (1975) (producer with Michael
    Douglas)

DICK ZANUCK

Academy Award Winner
  Driving Miss Daisy (1989) Best Picture

Academy Award Nominee
  The Verdict (1982) Best Picture
  Jaws (1975) Best Picture

*Irving G. Thalberg Memorial Award—1990 (with David
Brown)*

Producer—filmography
  Charlie and the Chocolate Factory (2005) (producer)
  Dead Lawyers (2004) (TV) (executive producer)
  Big Fish (2003) (producer)
  Road to Perdition (2002) (producer)
  Reign of Fire (2002) (producer)

Planet of the Apes (2001) (producer)
Rules of Engagement (2000) (producer)
The 72nd Annual Academy Awards (2000) (TV) (producer)
True Crime (1999) (producer)
Deep Impact (1998) (producer)
Chain Reaction (1996) (executive producer)
Mulholland Falls (1996) (producer)
Wild Bill (1995) (producer)
Clean Slate (1994) (producer)
Rich in Love (1993) (producer)
Rush (1991) (producer)
Driving Miss Daisy (1989) (producer)
Cocoon: The Return (1988) (producer)
Target (1985) (producer)
Cocoon (1985) (producer)
The Verdict (1982) (producer)
Neighbors (1981) (producer)
The Island (1980) (producer)
Jaws 2 (1978) (producer)
Jaws (1975) (producer)
The Eiger Sanction (1975) (executive producer)
The Girl from Petrovka (1974) (producer)
Willie Dynamite (1974) (producer)
The Black Windmill (1974) (executive producer)
The Sugarland Express (1974) (producer)
SSSSSSS (1973) (executive producer)
The Sting (1973) (A Richard D. Zanuck/David Brown
  Presentation)
The Chapman Report (1962) (producer)
Sanctuary (1961) (producer)
Compulsion (1959) (producer)

LAWRENCE TURMAN

Academy Award Nominee
  The Graduate (1967) Best Picture

Producers Guild of America Hall of Fame

Producer—filmography
  What's the Worst That Could Happen? (2001) (producer)
  Kingdom Come (2001) (executive producer)

Miracle on the Mountain: The Kincaid Family Story (2000) (TV)
  (executive producer)
American History X (1998) (executive producer)
The Long Way Home (1998) (TV) (executive producer)
Booty Call (1997) (executive producer)
Pretty Poison (1996) (TV) (executive producer)
The River Wild (1994) (producer)
The Getaway (1994) (producer)
Gleaming the Cube (1989) (producer)
Full Moon in Blue Water (1988) (producer)
Short Circuit 2 (1988) (producer)
News at Eleven (1986) (TV) (executive producer)
Running Scared (1986) (producer)
Short Circuit (1986) (producer)
Surrogate Mother (1986) (TV) (executive producer)
The Mean Season (1985) (producer)
Mass Appeal (1984) (producer)
Second Thoughts (1983) (producer)
The Thing (1982) (producer)
Between Two Brothers (1982) (TV) (executive producer)
The Gift of Life (1982) (TV) (executive producer)
Caveman (1981) (producer)
Tribute (1980) (producer)
The Legacy (1979) (producer)
Walk Proud (1979) (producer)
Heroes (1977) (producer)
First Love (1977) (producer)
The Drowning Pool (1975) (producer)
The Nickel Ride (1974) (executive producer)
The Morning After (1974) (TV) (executive producer)
Get Christie Love (1974) (TV) (executive producer)
Unwed Father (1974) (TV) (executive producer)
She Lives! (1973) (TV) (executive producer)
The Marriage of a Young Stockbroker (1971) (producer)
The Great White Hope (1970) (producer)
Pretty Poison (1968) (executive producer)
The Graduate (1967) (producer)
The Flim-Flam Man (1967) (producer)
The Best Man (1964) (producer)
Stolen Hours (1963) (executive producer)
I Could Go On Singing (1963) (producer)
The Young Doctors (1961) (producer)

Director—filmography
Second Thoughts (1983)
The Marriage of a Young Stockbroker (1971)

INDEX

ABC, 44, 49, 64, 111, 163, 164
Academy Awards, 2, 8, 68, 81, 175, 213–215. *See also specific person or film*
Academy of Motion Picture Arts and Sciences, 43, 56
acclaim, 172–77
actors: as big name stars, 109–13; casting, 109–17; communication with, 122–24; crew for care of, 108; and editing, 128; and financing, 91, 93; and functions of producers, 3; insurance on, 120; perspective of, 128; and then vs. now in Hollywood, 178. *See also* stars
Actors Studio, 106
ageism, 185–86
agents, 77, 110, 188. *See also specific person or agency*
Alexander, Jane, 106, 115, 181
Allen, Woody, 18, 101, 104, 113, 114, 122, 152, 173
Almodóvar, Pedro, 142
Altman, Robert, 44, 161
Amadeus, 18, 75
American Film Institute, 54, 217

American History X, 4, 116–18, 133–35, 137–38
Apollo 13, 214
Apted, Michael, 72
Arlen, Harold, 122, 124
art: and commerce, 140, 142, 183, 184
Ashby, Hal, 189
Ashley, Ted, 30
audience, 67–68, 85–86, 126, 136–42
authors. *See* writers/novelists
Avco, 216
Avedon, Richard, 194

Badham, John, 24, 68, 121
Bancroft, Anne, 107, 180, 197, 200–1, 206
A Beautiful Mind, 3, 63, 215
Begelman, David, 75, 123
Bergen, Candice, 199, 200
The Best Man, 3, 5, 38, 40, 64, 65, 69, 84, 99, 128–29, 155, 181–83, 202, 212
Between Two Brothers, 64
Bickford, Charles, 171
Bill, Tony, 49, 200
Bonnie and Clyde, 98, 106, 146, 215
Bookman, Bob, 143
Braveheart, 79, 214

Brodkey, Harold, 55
Brokaw, Tom, 176
Brooks, Mel, 45, 61, 101, 195
Brooks, Richard, 163–64
Brown, David, 14, 51, 61, 74, 120, 141, 153, 186
Bruck, Connie, 28
Bruckheimer, Jerry, 15, 23, 41, 55, 126, 154, 173, 184
budget, 103, 113, 117–20, 129, 130, 136
Burnt Offerings, 161–62
Butch Cassidy and the Sundance Kid, 23, 30, 46, 79, 83, 112, 159–60, 161

camera crew, 102, 104, 105, 106, 107
Cameron, James, 96, 117
Cannes Film Festival, 38, 129, 145, 173–174, 182
Capra, Frank, 174
Carson, Johnny, 63
casting, 52, 109–17
casting directors, 113–14
Caveman, 2, 63, 114
CBS, 25, 44, 64, 98, 111, 112, 194, 216
CBS Films, 162
Chaplin, Charlie, 85, 217
character, 17, 40, 187, 190

Chayefsky, Paddy, 42, 172
Citizen Kane, 119
Citizen Ruth, 57, 197
City Lights, 85, 217
clarity, 80, 86, 87, 100, 128, 171, 188
Clark, Dick, 33, 35, 36, 164, 185–86
Clayton, Dick, 30, 48
clients: signing or stealing, 27
Cocteau, Jean, 95
Cohen, Harry, 109, 179
collaboration, 169–70
Columbia Pictures, 23, 42, 163. *See also specific person or film*
commerce: and art, 140, 142, 183, 184
commitment: importance of, 6
communication: modes of, 190–92; with team, 105, 108–09, 121–24, 149
compromises, 69
control, 70–76, 95, 118–19, 170–72
The Conversation, 117, 210–11
Coppola, Francis Ford, 15, 97, 117, 210–11
Coppola, Sofia, 15
Corman, Roger, 13–14, 117
costume designers, 107
Countdown, 44, 161
Creative Artists Agency (CAA), 11–12, 24, 183, 202
creativity, 5, 17, 79, 165, 210
credits, 183, 217
crew: communicating with, 121–24; selection of, 103–4. *See also type of crew or specific film*
crisis-management, 20, 120, 124, 125
critics, 140

dailies, 53, 121, 122, 134
Darling, Joan, 55–56

Day, Doris, 201
De Luca, Mike, 116, 134
Death of a Salesman, 81, 153
DeCuir, John, 102, 106
DeLaurentiis, Dino, 186
DeMille, Cecil B., 126, 173
Demme, Jonathan, 117
design crew, 102
Destiny Turns on the Radio, 163
development process, 52, 72, 77–89
Dick Clark Productions, 36
Diller, Barry, 42, 44, 49, 56, 65–66, 176
director(s): acclaim for, 172–73, 174; assistant, 103; bill of rights for, 172; and budgets, 117, 119; and casting, 110, 113–14, 116–17; characteristics of, 92–93, 147; communication with actors by, 122; communication with, 121; control by, 118; decision-making by, 119; and editing, 128, 129–30; everybody wants to be a, 113; and financing, 91, 92–93; functions of, 96, 103–7, 108; and functions of producers, 52, 54, 128, 129–30, 137; importance of, 103; insurance on, 120; and making a game plan, 100–1; and marketing/distribution, 137; perspective of, 128; producer's relationship with, 3, 188; professional secret of, 112; selection of, 3, 52, 95–99; and studios, 116, 118; style of, 122; vision of, 96–97, 108.

See also specific person
Directors Guild of America, 172, 209, 213
directors of photography (DP), 29, 103–4, 107–8, 121
discretionary development fund, 40
Disney Studios, 41, 43, 96, 99
Donen, Stanley, 168
Doniger, Walter, 26
Doran, D. A., 24, 25, 82
Doran, Lindsay, 16, 82
Dowling, Bob, 96
Drabinsky, Garth, 145
dramatic irony, 85
DreamWorks SKG, 44
Drexel production company, 36
Driving Miss Daisy, 66, 165–66
The Drowning Pool, 39–40
dubbing process, 131–32
Durning, Charles, 12

e-mail, 191
editing, 36, 54, 97, 99, 123, 124, 127–31, 133–34, 137, 150, 160
editors (ED), 103–4, 106, 121
8-1/2, 81, 201
Eisner, Michael, 44, 56, 99
Embassy Pictures, 195–96, 214, 215–17
emergencies, 118, 120
EMI, 64
Emmanuel, Ari, 150
The English Patient, 18, 61
ethics/morals, 10–12, 17, 67
Executive Suite, 30, 83

Famous Artists Agency, 30–31
Far from Heaven, 5, 94
faxes, 190–91
Feldman, Charles, 30–31
Fellini, Federico, 15, 60, 103, 201

film business:
musical–chairs aspect
of, 43–45
financing: and
budgeting, 117; and
casting, 109–10, 111;
and discretionary
development fund,
40; and functions of
producers, 3, 51, 52,
57; of independent
films, 94, 141; and
location, 101–2, 126;
and private funding,
94; where to get,
90–94
First Artists, 39
first assistant director
(AD), 103–4
First Blood, 163–64
First Love, 43, 44,
55–56, 113–14
Flight from Ashiya,
32–33
The Flim–Flam Man:
cast for, 50, 115–16;
Kershner as director
of, 98; music for,
205; production
activities for, 121;
reviews of, 98, 178;
script development
for, 80, 84; source of
idea for, 2–3, 61, 62;
and then vs. now in
Hollywood, 178;
why Turman was
attracted to, 66, 67,
69, 218
Focus Films, 94
Ford, John, 33, 48
Forman, Milos, 75
Fosse, Bob, 161–62
Foster, David, 28, 39
The 400 Blows, 79, 81
Fox Searchlight, 141
Frankenheimer, John,
44, 98–99
Frankovich, Mike, 195
Freeman, David, 55
Friendly Persuasion, 30,
36, 45
Frings, Ketti, 43, 45
Frings, Kurt, 22–23,
26–32, 43, 45, 48,
110, 168

*Full Moon on Blue
Water*, 3, 202
Fuller, Sam, 174

Gabler, Neal, 144
gaffer, 107
Gale, Eddra, 201
game plans, making,
100–1
Gangs of New York, 102
Garland, Judy, 37, 54,
75, 97, 115, 122–24,
147–48
Geffen, David, 44
Gershwin, Jerry, 33
Gibson, Mel, 76, 109,
140–41
Gilroy, Frank, 49
Gilroy, Tony, 49
Gladiator, 4, 62
globalization, 138–41,
178–79
The Godfather, 210–11
Goetz, William, 173, 176
Gold Circle Films, 60
Goldberg, William,
72–73
Golden Globes, 214, 215
Goldman, William
"Bill": and access, 46;
and audience, 68;
and *Best Man*, 38;
*Boys and Girls
Together* by, 62,
157–58; and *Butch
Cassidy*, 46, 159–60;
and costs of making
movies, 184; and
Drowning Pool, 39;
and *Graduate*, 159;
and *Harper*, 33, 39,
158, 159; and
mistakes in
judgment, 157–60,
161; and production
activities, 96; and
script development,
77, 78, 79–80, 83; as
source for ideas,
61–62, 157–58, 159;
Turman's relationship
with, 39, 157–58,
159–60; views about
Hollywood of, 165,
184; and Ziegler, 30,
54

Goldwyn, Samuel,
78–79, 101, 160, 184,
189
Goldwyn, Samuel Jr.,
189
Goldwyn Studios, 119
Goleman, Daniel, 147
Gordy, Berry, Jr., 49
The Graduate: acclaim
for, 175, 176; awards
and honors for,
212–15, 217; as case
study, 193–219;
casting for, 114, 115,
199–222; control of,
74, 171; cost of, 210;
costume design in,
107; credits for,
195–96, 198, 212–13;
editing of, 198, 203,
205, 206; effects on
Turman's career of, 7,
49, 127, 129, 131,
148, 157, 161, 175,
176, 193, 211–12,
217–18; ending of,
198; as financial
success, 7, 193,
207–8, 210; financing
for, 91, 195–96, 197;
flaws in, 205; hiring
crew for, 202–3;
lawsuit concerning,
215–17; locations for,
102, 203, 204;
marketing/
distribution for, 138,
209–10; and mistakes
in judgment, 159;
music/scoring of,
205–7, 210; Nichols
selected as director
for, 99, 194–95,
196–97; paperback
sales for, 207–8;
previews of, 208–9;
production activities
for, 101, 107, 114, 115;
rating system for,
180; re–release of,
180; rejections for,
195; reviews of, 98,
173, 178, 208–10;
rights to, 194, 207–8;
screenplay for, 195,
197; script

The Graduate: (cont.)
development for, 79,
80, 83–84, 88–89,
196, 197; shooting of,
204–5; source of idea
for, 2, 61, 62, 193–94;
as success, 58, 166,
207–8, 210; and
tenacity of Turman,
58, 166; and then vs.
now in Hollywood,
180; Turman's
passion for, 69; why
Turman was attracted
to, 40, 66–67, 218;
writers considered
for, 159, 194
Grazer, Brian: and
Academy Awards,
214–15; and casting,
110; and controlling
stories, 72, 74; and
difficulties of
producing, 154, 169;
and doing homework,
45; and game plans,
100; and joys of being
a producer, 3; and
marketing/
distribution, 136–37;
organization of, 41;
and post–production
activities, 129–30;
style of, 126; and
what producing really
takes, 143
The Great White Hope:
casting of, 115; and
controlling stories,
75; director for, 185;
financing for, 106;
and joys of being a
producer, 4; location
for, 102; marketing/
distribution of, 138;
post–production
activities for, 132;
ratings for, 180–81;
Ritt selected as
director for, 106;
selection of crew for,
106; source of idea
for, 3, 63, 64; and
Turman's character,
40; why Turman was
attracted to, 66, 218

Grodin, Charles, 200
Grusin, Dave, 207
Guare, John, 145
Guber, Peter, 176
*Guess Who's Coming to
Dinner,* 84, 121, 178
Guffey, Burnett, 106

Hackman, Gene, 146,
202
hairdressers, 108
Halmi, Robert, 43
Hanley, William, 194
Hanson, Curtis, 2, 13,
59–60, 118, 119, 120,
130, 137, 146, 147,
204
Harper, 33, 39, 158, 159
Harriman, Pamela, 187
Hayes, Joseph, 84
Hays Office, 80
HBO, 43, 111, 142
Heard, John, 113–14
Hecht, Harold, 32
Hellman, Jerry, 29–30,
116, 146
Henry, Buck, 84, 196,
197, 198–99, 200, 211
Hepburn, Audrey, 26,
43, 171
Higgins, Colin, 12
Hill, George Roy, 44,
112, 135, 161, 162
Hitchcock, Alfred, 31,
81, 85, 103, 126, 154,
168
Hoffman, Dustin: and
acclaim, 175; in *The
Graduate,* 107, 197,
199–200, 201, 202,
203, 205, 206, 208;
and *Little Big Man,*
38, 201; in *Midnight
Cowboy,* 115, 181;
options for, 201; and
The Tiger Makes Out,
199; and Turman's
induction into
producers hall of
fame, 213
Hollywood:
celebrity–homes in,
175–76; corporate
mentality in, 179;
creative accounting
practices in, 154–55;

Golden Age of,
177–79; Goldman's
views about, 165;
institutionalization
of, 139–40, 179;
"old", 142, 195;
social life in, 176–77;
then vs. now in,
177–84
homework, doing, 29,
46, 76, 77, 104, 180
Houseman, John, 30
Howard, Ron, 97
Howe, James Wong,
106
Hunter, Evan, 112, 212
Hunter, Ross, 143
Hupfeld, Herman, 9
Hyams, Nessa, 55

I Could Go On Singing,
37, 44, 97, 115,
122–24, 147–48
In the Heat of the Night,
214, 215
"in" places, 46
independent films, 9,
23, 92, 94, 106, 108,
119, 120, 133, 134,
141–42, 155
instincts: trusting, 60,
67, 71, 104, 114–17,
124
insurance, 119–20
integrity, 11–12, 47, 69,
190
International Creative
Management, 164
*It's a Mad Mad Mad
Mad World,* 84, 121,
178
Iverson, Allen, 116

Jackman, Hugh, 81
Jacobs, Arthur, 23
Jaffe, Sam, 25, 26, 113,
167
Jaws, 66, 138, 141
Jewison, Norman, 98,
160, 215
Joad, C.E.M., 140, 187
Johnson, Jack, 4, 66,
106, 180
Jones, James Earl, 66,
106, 115, 138, 181
Jordan, Glenn, 204

Josephson, Marvin, 164
Josephson, Michael, 11
Josephy, Bill, 26, 27
judgment: mistakes in, 157–65
Justin, George, 199

Kael, Pauline, 150
Kahn, Herman, 15
Karlovy Vary International Film Festival, 38
Karlson, Phil, 35
Karp, Jack, 195
Kassar, Mario, 164
Kastner, Elliott, 33, 34–35
Katzenberg, Jeffrey, 44, 56, 96
Kaye, Tony, 116–17, 133–34
Kazan, Elia, 111–12, 185, 197
Kennedy, Kathleen: and collaboration, 169; and deal making, 183; and financing, 90; and globalization, 139; and importance of communication, 108–9; and lack of formula for success, 150; motivation of, 58; organization of, 41; and selecting the crew, 104; style of, 125; and then vs. now in Hollywood, 183; and vision, 104, 108–9, 139
Kershner, Irvin, 98, 121, 204
Keston, Steve, 148–49
King, Henry, 178
Kissinger, Henry, 3, 169
Korchek, Jeff, 118, 119
Kraft, Gilman, 16
Krim, Arthur, 34
Kroc, Joan, 12
Kubrick, Stanley, 15, 103, 159, 191

Ladd, Alan, Jr., 180
Lansbury, Edgar, 49–50
Lantz, Robby, 99, 150, 173, 194

Lawrence of Arabia, 63, 95–96, 165, 187
Lazar, Swifty, 163
Lean, David, 95, 122
Lear, Norman, 55
LeBorg, Reginald, 25–26
Lee, Ang, 16
Lee, Harper, 62
Lehman, Ernest, 31, 38, 82, 83, 101, 168, 186, 196–97
Lemmon, Jack, 11, 12, 43, 65, 66, 108, 112, 145, 155, 159–60
Lester Horton Company, 25
Lethal Weapon series, 61, 139, 140
letter: self-serving quasi-legal, 32
Levine, Joseph E., 195–96, 197, 206, 209, 210, 214, 216
Lewis, David, 25
Linley, Joanne, 200
The Lion in Winter, 196, 216
Lithgow, John, 63
LL Cool J, 91
location, 101–3, 108, 125–26
The Long Way Home, 43, 112
The Longest Day, 161
The Lord of the Rings series, 61, 139, 184
Los Angeles County Museum of Art, 173
Lost in Translation, 81, 140
Lovell, Jim, 214
Lucas, George, 98, 117, 130
luck, 47–50, 146, 165, 168
Lumet, Sidney, 13, 33, 44

Macdonald, Ross, 39, 158
makeup, 108
A Man for All Seasons, 48, 82, 213
managers: of stars, 111, 188
Mancuso, Frank, 56

Mandel, Loring, 44, 161
Mankiewicz, Joseph, 80, 133
manners, 188
Manulis, Martin, 44
Marasco, Robert, 162
March, Fredric, 35, 84, 185
marketing/distribution, 3, 53, 94, 110, 111, 130, 136–42, 180
The Marriage of a Young Stockbroker, 21, 218
Marshall, Frank, 41, 125
Mass Appeal, 3, 11–12, 39, 64, 65, 66, 67, 108
The Matrix Revolution series, 61, 140
Matthau, Walter, 213
May, Elaine, 194
Mayer, Louis B., 179
MCA, 26, 33, 168. *See also specific person*
McBain, Ed, 212
McElwaine, Guy, 23
McGurk, Chris, 182–84
McHale, Kevin, 158
McQueen, Steve, 39, 160, 161
Medavoy, Mike, 176
meetings: face-to-face, 191–92
Melcher, Martin, 201
Mengers, Sue, 176
Merchant, Ismail, 61
Mercury Theatre, 30
MGM, 22, 25, 27, 28, 29, 30, 48. *See also specific person or film*
Midnight Cowboy, 61, 79, 115–16, 146, 181
Millar, Stuart, 13, 31, 33–38, 99, 134, 164, 193
Miller, Arthur, 81, 153
Miller, Lainie, 201
Miller, Merle, 209
Mindlin, Mike, 194
Miramax, 102
Mirisch, Walter, 215
Mirisch Company, 37, 119
"momentum," philosophy of, 37

Monash, Paul, 30
Monroe, Marilyn, 110–11
Morrell, David, 163
Morrissey, John, 134
Moss, Jerry, 211
motivation, 16
Mulligan, Bob, 44
Murphy, A.D., 7
music, 3, 52. *See also* sound design; *specific film*
My Big Fat Greek Wedding, 60, 141, 184
Myers, Mike, 91
Mystic River, 140

Napoleon Dynamite, 141
narrative drive, 81–83
National General, 210
NBC, 111
Neame, Ronald, 54, 115, 122, 124
negotiating, 70, 71, 73–74, 76, 110, 111, 113, 147, 183
Nelson, Peter, 194
New American Library, 74
New Line, 116–17, 133–34
New York Critics Circle Award, 101
New York Film Critics Society, 80, 150
Newman, Paul, 39, 159, 160, 161, 164
News at Eleven, 50
Nichols, Mike: and acclaim, 173; awards and honors for, 212–13, 214; control of, 171; and Coppola's film, 211; creative worrying of, 198; and *The Graduate*, 66–67, 88, 99, 114, 115, 127, 129, 138, 171, 173, 194–95, 196, 197–98, 199, 200, 201–7, 208, 209, 211, 212, 214, 216; and importance of clarity, 100; and instincts, 114, 115; and Levine, 196; and marketing/

distribution, 138; Turman's relationship with, 54, 99, 171, 194–95, 196, 197, 204, 212, 218; and *Who's Afraid of Virginia Woolf?*, 197, 203, 212, 213
Nicholson, Jack, 91, 117, 176, 178
Nicita, Rick, 112
nonstudio films. *See* independent films
North by Northwest, 31, 82, 168, 197
Norton, Edward, 111, 116–18, 133–34, 135, 137

on-the-job training, 13, 26
On the Waterfront, 23, 111, 148, 165
One Flew Over the Cuckoo's Nest, 18, 79
Oppenheimer, Jess, 22, 23–24
options, 70–73, 75–76, 201
Ordinary People, 215
organizational skills, 144–47, 150, 187–88
O'Steen, Sam, 127, 202, 203, 205, 206, 209
Ostrow, Stuart, 59
O'Toole, Peter, 95–96, 171, 187
overhead deals, 39, 41
Ovitz, Mike, 11–12, 78

Pakula, Alan, 23, 24, 26, 32, 45, 62, 92–93
Paramount Studios, 24, 29, 43, 44. *See also specific person or film*
passion, 68–69, 73, 75
The Passion of the Christ, 140–41
Patton, 63, 99, 129, 211
Payne, Alexander, 57, 104, 197
Peace Corps, 37–38
Penn, Arthur, 37, 38, 44, 98
people skills, 30, 147, 170–71, 189–90

Perkins, Anthony, 45, 66, 148
Perry, Frank, 194
personality: and teaching producing, 16, 17
Peter Stark Producing Program: and art and commerce, 142; benefits for Turman from, 47; credo for, 9; founding and funding of, 30; graduates of, 141; how Turman teaches, 9–11, 23, 59; internships for students in, 44; students in, 22; Turman invited to head, 7, 39, 42; Turman's changes to, 8; and Turman's movie work, 42; and what can't be taught, 14–16; and what producing really takes, 144
Phaelzer, Marianna, 217
Phillips, Michael, 49
Picker, David, 43, 55, 69, 195, 209
Pierson, Frank, 43, 48–49, 56, 112, 121, 144, 179
Pitlik, Noam, 201–2
A Place in the Sun, 61, 127, 185
Planet of the Apes, 23, 129
Playhouse 90 (CBS), 31, 44, 98, 194
playing the percentages, 22
Poitier, Sidney, 39, 164–65, 214
Poledouris, Basil, 54
Pollack, Sydney, 67, 189
Preminger, Otto, 79
Pretty Poison, 16, 40, 45, 61, 62, 66, 67, 80, 101, 127, 132, 218
problem-solvers: producers as, 147–50
producer(s): benefits for, 3, 172, 175, 186;

characteristics of good, 20, 53–58, 92–93, 143–50, 186–92; definition of, 52; devaluation of, 41, 126, 215; functions of, 2–3, 51–58, 103–4, 105–6, 120, 121, 167; how Turman became a, 21–50; ideal, 120, 137; levels and categories of, 1–2; proliferation of credits for, 41, 126, 215; qualities of good, 143–51; reasons for being a, 1–6; and rejection, 155–57; salaries/income of, 76, 154–55; taste of, 137, 143–44, 150, 151, 165, 166; tenacity of, 139, 143, 144–46, 150, 165; tricks of the trade for, 187; Turman's decision to be a, 23–24; you already are a, 18–20. *See also specific person*
Producers Guild of America, 52–53, 58, 159, 213
producing: and finding directors, 95–96; how hard is, 152–92; and how you actually produce the movie, 95–135; lessons Turman has learned about, 97–99; and looking for a similar vision, 96–97; as misunderstood profession, 173–74; as responsibility, 8; teaching, 7–17; and what does it really take, 143–51
production: actual, 120–26; and budgeting and scheduling, 117–20; and casting, 109–14; and communication

with team, 105, 108–9, 121–24; and functions of producers, 3, 52–53; and instincts, 114–17; and location, 101–3, 125–27; and making a game plan, 100–1; and marketing/ distribution, 137; micromanaging, 97; and post-production activities, 127–35; and preproduction activities, 100–20; and selection of crew, 103–4
production designer (PD), 103–4, 105, 106, 107–9
production manager, 103–4, 105
professional volleyball league, 49
prop person, 105, 107, 108

ratings, 180–81
Ray, Bingham, 181–83
Redford, Robert, 93, 173, 199, 200, 215
rejection, 22, 144, 155–56, 165, 173, 180
reliability, 188–89
reputation, 167, 188, 190
reshootings, 130, 132
Richardson, Tony, 97
rights, 73–74, 93–94, 207–8, 209
Riley, Pat, 51
Riskin, Robert, 174
Ritt, Martin, 106, 115, 132, 161, 164, 204
The River Wild, 2, 28, 107, 112, 118–19, 131
RKO Studios, 22
Roach, Jay, 14
Robinson, Bill, 26–27, 31
Rogers, Henry, 22, 23
Ronstadt, Linda, 205
Rose, William, 68, 80, 82, 121, 178
Rosenberg, Marion, 158
Rosenberg, Stu, 39

Ross, Hal, 29–30
Ross, Herb, 165
Ross, Katharine, 197, 200, 201, 202, 205
Rossen, Robert, 83
Rudin, Scott, 73, 129–31, 154, 184
Running Scared, 3, 4, 39
Russo, Tom, 156
Rydell, Mark, 46, 162, 176, 200
Rysher Entertainment, 163

Sackler, Howard, 115
Sagansky, Jeff, 154–55
Sanders, Denis and Terry, 199
Sarrazin, Michael, 66, 115–16
Saturday Night Fever, 24, 68
Schaffner, Franklin, 44, 99, 128–29
Schary, Dore, 175–76
scheduling, 117–20
Schlesinger, John, 120
schooling: school of life versus formal, 12–14
Schulberg, Budd, 24
Schulman, Max, 71
Schwary, Ron, 215
Schwarzenegger, Arnold, 138, 150
Scorsese, Martin, 15, 102, 130
screenings, 128, 130, 132–35, 176
screenwriters, 3, 29, 37, 52, 54, 77–89, 97
script supervisor, 106–7
scripts: adaptation of, 83–84; and art versus commerce, 142; and casting, 110, 111, 112; clarity of, 80, 86, 87, 128; conflict in, 87; developing, 77–89; and editing film, 127; and engaging the audience, 85–86; manipulation of, 89; and narrative drive, 81–83; point of view in, 88–89; and

272 | *Index*

scripts: *(cont.)*
  screenwriters, 77–81;
  sorting through,
  65–66; story and plot
  of, 87–88
Second Thoughts, 3, 64
selling, 139, 150,
  166–69
Selznick, David O.,
  12–13, 56, 176
Semple, Lorenzo Jr., 21,
  80, 148, 150
set dressers, 105, 107–8
Shaffner, Franklin, 204
Shakespeare, William,
  60, 68, 69, 86, 90
Shaw, George Bernard,
  184, 210
She Let Him Continue,
  62, 129, 148–50
Sheinberg, Sid, 131, 139
Short Circuit, 24, 68,
  121, 154–55
Shpetner, Stan, 32, 33
Silver, Casey, 118–19,
  131
Silver, Joel, 61, 184
Simon and Garfunkel,
  131, 205–7, 210
Simon, Mayo, 44
Simon, Neil, 86, 165
Simpson, Don, 55, 56
Slade, Bernard, 145
Some Like It Hot, 110–11
*Somebody Up There
  Likes Me,* 83
Sondheim, Stephen, 194
Sony-Columbia, 80–81
sound design (mixing),
  105, 107, 127, 130–32
The Sound of Music, 29,
  83
Specktor, Fred, 202
Spiegel, Sam, 12–13,
  165, 169, 196
Spielberg, Steven, 44,
  56, 104, 130, 136,
  175, 207
Stage Struck, 13, 33
Stallone, Sylvester, 74,
  164
Stalmaster, Lynn, 201–2
Star Wars series, 58, 98,
  139
Stark, Ray, 30, 173
stars: big name, 91,

109–13, 160; casting,
  116; crew for care of,
  109; managers of, 111,
  188
Steelyard Blues, 49
Steers, Burr, 182
Stevens, George, 31, 36,
  54, 61, 127, 185
Stewart, James, 48
The Sting, 49, 112, 162,
  200
Stone, Peter, 164–65
stories: being
  passionate about,
  68–69; controlling,
  70–76; finding,
  57–58, 59–69;
  negotiating for, 76;
  overpaying for,
  72–73; selecting, 52;
  and story vs plot of
  scripts, 87–88; what
  attracts Turman to,
  66–67
*A Streetcar Named
  Desire,* 66
studio executives, 54,
  142, 179. *See also
  specific person*
studios: and casting,
  110; and directors, 96,
  116, 118; and editing,
  130; and financing/
  budgets, 92–93, 117,
  119; and globalization
  of audience, 139, 140;
  as source of
  screenwriters, 77; and
  then vs. now in
  Hollywood, 178. *See
  also specific studio or
  executive*
Stulberg, Gordon, 162
style, 15, 27, 77, 85–86,
  125, 167, 187
success: as happening,
  165–67; non-,
  157–65; recipe for,
  150–51; as revenge,
  213
Sundance Film Festival,
  141
Surtees, Robert, 202,
  203, 204
Susskind, David, 163
Swanholme, Ruth J., 61

Swink, Robert, 36
Sylbert, Richard, 55,
  203

talent, 146, 158, 197
Tanen, Ned, 112
Tarantino, Quentin, 163
taste, 137, 143–44, 150,
  151, 165, 166
Taylor, Juliet, 113–14
teaching: and what
  can't be taught,
  14–17. *See also* Peter
  Stark Producing
  Program
technical help, 104–9
television business, 8,
  43–44
tenacity, 139, 143,
  144–46, 150, 165
TF1, 94
Thalberg, Irving, 13, 22
Thalberg Award, 160,
  166, 186
Tharp, Twyla, 68
Thaw, Benny, 27–28
Thompson, Hunter S.,
  155
Todd, Jennifer, 14
Todd, Suzanne, 14
Toronto Film Festival,
  134, 183
Travolta, John, 11–12,
  24, 111, 116
Tribute, 3, 39, 64, 145
TriStar, 154–55
True Grit, 164
Turman, Jack (father),
  21–22, 166, 174
Turman, Larry: as
  agent, 22–23, 26–34,
  76, 110, 168, 171,
  177–79; career path
  of, 21–52, 168, 174,
  175; financial affairs
  of, 211–12; first film
  produced by, 33–38;
  regrets of, 7–8
Twentieth Century Fox,
  42, 69, 75, 145,
  160–61. *See also
  specific person or film*
Twins, 138

United Artists: and
  Millar-Turman

partnership, 34–38; overhead deals at, 42; and Peace Corps project, 38; producers' relationship with, 13; and *Some Like It Hot*, 110–11; Turman's deals with, 39, 65, 69, 112, 209; and *The Young Doctors*, 13, 34–36, 55. *See also specific person or film*

Universal Studios, 24, 26, 28, 42, 112

University of California—Berkeley, 102, 204

University of California—Los Angeles (UCLA), 21, 204, 210

University of Southern California (USC), 8, 14, 43, 102, 204. *See also* Peter Stark Producing Program

Unruh, Jesse, 90

Vachon, Christine, 5, 20, 94, 101, 144, 173–74

Vajna, Andy, 164

Valenti, Jack, 175

values, 10–12, 63, 64

vanity projects, 140

Verhoeven, Paul, 158

Vidal, Gore, 5, 40, 128, 129, 181–82

Villon, François, 183

visibility: importance of, 42–47, 94

vision, 96–97, 104, 108, 139

von Braun, Wernher, 3, 46

Wald, Jerry, 24–25

Walk Proud, 218

Wallis, Hal, 173

Ward, David, 48–49

wardrobe, 108

Warner, Jack, 179

Warner Bros., 30, 93

Wasserman, Lew, 28–29, 169

Wayans, Shawn and Marlon, 138–39

Webb, Charles, 193, 194, 207–8

Weintraub, Jerry, 176

Welles, Orson, 1, 30

Wells, Frank, 99

West, Jessamyn, 30, 37

West Side Story, 83, 119

Wexler, Haskell, 202–3

White Chicks, 138–39

White, Larry, 25

"who you know," 30, 42–47, 94, 176

Who's Afraid of Virginia Woolf?, 197, 203, 212, 213

Wick, Doug, 4, 16, 47, 67, 78, 81, 96, 126, 128, 149, 169

Wilder, Billy, 68, 86, 96, 110–111, 154, 185

William Morris Agency, 30

Williams, John, 207

Williams, Richard, 138

Williams, Tennessee, 66

Willingham, Calder, 84, 196, 197, 198–99

Willis, Gordy, 39

Winant, Ethel, 44

Wise, Robert "Bobby," 119

Wizan, Joe, 153

Wolf, Dick, 164

Wolfe, Tom, 44

Wolper, David, 14, 44, 49, 53, 127, 132, 148, 167

work ethic, 16–17, 44

Writers Guild, 74, 161, 198

writers/novelists: and casting, 110; and characteristics of good producers, 188; and financing, 91, 93; obtaining rights from, 74–75; screenwriters compared with, 84; as screenwriters of own works, 84. *See also* screenwriters; *specific person*

written agreements, 160

Wyler, William, 13, 30, 33–34, 36, 36–37, 45, 84, 122, 171, 193, 208

The Young Doctors, 13, 28, 33–36, 43, 48, 55, 84, 148, 164, 174–75, 185

Zaentz, Saul, 13, 18, 23, 75, 90, 105, 121, 125, 170, 190

Zanuck, Darryl, 12–13, 48, 66, 133, 161, 178, 179

Zanuck, Richard: and art versus commerce, 142; and *Butch Cassidy*, 159, 160; and difficulties of producing, 153; and *Driving Miss Daisy*, 165–66; firing of, 48; and *The Graduate*, 166; and importance of story, 66; and *Jaws*, 138, 141; and Kershner–Turman disagreements, 98; and marketing/distribution, 138, 141; mistakes in judgment of, 166; and problem-solving/people skills, 147; and production of movies, 100; and rejection, 165–66; style of, 125; and then vs. now in Hollywood, 178, 179; Turman's first meeting with, 178; and what producing really takes, 147

Zemeckis, Bob, 59, 97

Ziegler, Evart, 29–30, 54

Zinnemann, Fred, 48, 179–80, 213

ABOUT THE AUTHOR

For someone who claims, or disclaims, there is no "how to" about producing, Larry Turman has lectured about producing around the world from Femis in Paris to the Polytechnic in Singapore, all the while presiding over the prestigious Peter Stark Producing Program at the University of Southern California. Along the way, he has produced over forty films (including, solely, *The Graduate*) but lists as his proudest achievement his close, large, extended family, each and all of whom he acknowledges at the beginning of this book.